EVENT MANAGEMENT IN SPORT, RECREATION AND TOURISM

Now in a fully revised and updated third edition, *Event Management in Sport, Recreation and Tourism* provides a comprehensive theoretical and practical framework for planning and managing events. Focusing on the role of event managers and their diverse responsibilities through each phase of the event planning process, this is still the only textbook to define the concept of knowledge in the context of event management, placing it at the centre of professional practice.

Designed to encourage critical thinking on the part of the student, this book helps them develop the skills that they will need to become effective and reflective practitioners in the events industry. Containing a rich array of international real-world case studies, data and practical examples from sport, recreation and tourism contexts, this third edition is also enhanced by two completely new chapters on contemporary management issues and ethics in event management.

Event Management in Sport, Recreation and Tourism is essential reading for any student or practitioner working in event management, sport management, leisure management, outdoor recreation or tourism.

Cheryl Mallen is Associate Professor in the Department of Sport Management at Brock University, Canada. Her research involves knowledge, event management and environmental sustainability. She is well published, with articles in the *Journal of Sport Management*, *Sport Management Review* and *European Sport Management Quarterly* as well as other journal outlets.

Lorne J. Adams is Associate Professor (Retired) in the Department of Kinesiology at Brock University, Canada. He is the recipient of four teaching awards, including the prestigious 3M Teaching Fellowship. He has been a coach and served as Athletic Director for 10 years.

EVENT MANAGEMENT IN SPORT, RECREATION AND TOURISM

THEORETICAL AND PRACTICAL DIMENSIONS

THIRD EDITION

EDITED BY CHERYL MALLEN AND LORNE J. ADAMS

Routledge
Taylor & Francis Group

LONDON AND NEW YORK

First published 2017
by Routledge
2 Park Square, Milton Park, Abingdon, Oxon OX14 4RN

and by Routledge
711 Third Avenue, New York, NY 10017

Routledge is an imprint of the Taylor & Francis Group, an informa business

British Library Cataloguing in Publication Data
A catalogue record for this book is available from the British Library.

Library of Congress Cataloging in Publication Data
Names: Mallen, Cheryl, editor. | Adams, Lorne James, editor.
Title: Event management in sport, recreation and tourism : theoretical and practical dimensions / edited by Cheryl Mallen and Lorne J. Adams.
Description: [Third edition] | New York : Routledge, 2017. | Previous edition: 2013. | Includes bibliographical references and index.
Identifiers: LCCN 2016033710 | ISBN 9781138234758 (Hardback) | ISBN 9781138234765 (Paperback) | ISBN 9781315306155 (eBook)
Subjects: LCSH: Special events—Management. | Sports administration. |
Recreation—Management. | Tourism—Management.
Classification: LCC GT3405 .E9 2017 | DDC 394.2—dc23
LC record available at https://lccn.loc.gov/2016033710

ISBN: 978-1-138-23475-8 (hbk)
ISBN: 978-1-138-23476-5 (pbk)
ISBN: 978-1-315-30615-5 (ebk)

Typeset in Melior
by Keystroke, Neville Lodge, Tettenhall, Wolverhampton
Printed and bound in Great Britain by
CPI Group (UK) Ltd, Croydon, CR0 4YY

CONTENTS

1 TRADITIONAL AND NICHE EVENTS IN SPORT, RECREATION AND TOURISM   1

CHERYL MALLEN AND LORNE J. ADAMS

CHERYL MALLEN

vi

3 THE ROLE OF THE EVENT MANAGER: TO BE A FACILITATOR   28

AMY CUNNINGHAM AND JOANNE MACLEAN

4 THE EVENT PLANNING MODEL: THE DEVELOPMENT PHASE   47

MAUREEN CONNOLLY, LORNE J. ADAMS AND CHERI BRADISH

vii

5 THE EVENT PLANNING MODEL: THE EVENT OPERATIONAL PLANNING PHASE   67

CHERYL MALLEN

6 THE EVENT PLANNING MODEL: THE EVENT IMPLEMENTATION, MONITORING AND MANAGEMENT PHASE   87

LORNE J. ADAMS

viii

7 EVENT OPERATIONAL PLANNING ISSUES AND STRATEGIES 105

NICOLE GRECO AND CHERYL MALLEN

8 THE EVENT PLANNING MODEL: THE EVENT EVALUATION AND RENEWAL PHASE 116

SCOTT FORRESTER AND LORNE J. ADAMS

9 SAFEGUARDING THE NATURAL ENVIRONMENT IN EVENT MANAGEMENT 132

CHRIS CHARD, MATT DOLF AND GREG DINGLE

X

xi

12 POLITICS IN EVENT BIDDING AND HOSTING   181

TRISH CHANT-SEHL

13 ETHICAL DECISION MAKING IN EVENT MANAGEMENT   195

CHERYL MALLEN

xii

14   CONCLUSIONS   204

LORNE J. ADAMS

CONTRIBUTORS

Lorne J. Adams: Associate Professor (Retired), Department of Kinesiology, Brock University, St. Catharines, Ontario, Canada.

Cheri Bradish: Associate Professor, Marketing Management, Ted Rogers School of Business Management, Ryerson University, Toronto, Ontario, Canada.

Trish Chant-Sehl: Director, University Advancement, McMaster University, Hamilton, Ontario, Canada.

Chris Chard: Associate Professor, Department of Sport Management, Brock University, St. Catharines, Ontario, Canada.

Maureen Connolly: Professor, Department of Kinesiology, Brock University, St. Catharines, Ontario, Canada.

Amy Cunningham: Musician and recording artist at Independent, Vancouver, British Columbia, Canada.

Greg Dingle: Lecturer, Sport Management, Centre for Sport and Social Impact, Department of Management and Marketing, La Trobe Business School, La Trobe University, Bundoora, Australia.

Matt Dolf: Manager, Centre for Sport and Sustainability, Vancouver, British Columbia, Canada.

Scott Forrester: Associate Professor, Department of Recreation and Leisure Studies, Brock University, St. Catharines, Ontario, Canada.

Nicole Greco: Graduate of the MA Program in the Department of Sport Management, Brock University, St. Catharines, Ontario, Canada.

Craig Hyatt: Associate Professor, Department of Sport Management, Brock University, St. Catharines, Ontario, Canada.

Joanne MacLean: Dean, Faculty of Health Sciences, University of the Fraser Valley, Abbotsford, British Columbia, Canada.

Scott McRoberts: Athletic Director, University of Guelph, Guelph, Ontario, Canada.

Cheryl Mallen: Associate Professor, Department of Sport Management, Brock University, St. Catharines, Ontario, Canada.

PREFACE TO THE THIRD EDITION

OBJECTIVES

- To focus on a readership that includes second- and third-year higher education students in the fields of sport, recreation, sport tourism and/or program management.
- To provide a combination of the theoretical foundations, practical principles and examples that specifically relate to event operational planning and management.
- To encourage students and practitioners to act as critical interpreters of the requirements for event environmental management. The text will avoid providing a series of checklists as this does not reflect the fluidity of environmental management or foster critical thinking.
- To provide theoretical information and show how theory integrates with the practical elements of the subject in a manner that assists students to be event managers.
- To present an operational planning model for event environmental management, including: the bidding phase; the development phase; the logistical phase; the implementation, monitoring and management phase; and the evaluation and renewal phase.
- To avoid the general approach of other textbooks in the field of event management which tend to have a formulaic application and to concentrate only on the operational planning aspects.

AN OVERVIEW OF THE FOCUS OF THIS TEXT

This text focuses on sport, recreation and tourism event management and emphasizes the complex role of an event manager as a facilitator throughout the event planning phases.

Other textbooks provide one chapter on each of the multiple areas of events (including one chapter on marketing, one on selling sponsorship, one on law and liability, etc.) or they have offered a "to do list" for creating an event. There are a multitude of courses and textbooks on event and facility management in the areas of marketing, law and human resource management. However, none of these textbooks in the marketplace concentrate specifically on the theoretical foundations and practical principles of event operational planning, or provide examples. The contemporary sport, recreation and tourism manager needs a text that concentrates on the application of theory to practice, specifically in event management.

EVENT ELEMENTS OUTSIDE THE FRAMEWORK OF THIS TEXT

An event manager has a complex role in the staging of an event that necessitates managing a multitude of activities within a changing event environment. In performing this role, both depth and breadth of knowledge are necessary for multiple areas of focus. These areas of focus include the four phases of the planning model:

1   the development phase;
2   the logistical phase;
3   the implementation, monitoring and management phase;
4   the evaluation and renewal phase.

Additionally, knowledge is needed in areas such as bidding, environmental sustainability, ethics, the management of the politics associated with events, along with staff and volunteer management. Furthermore, an event manager's training needs to be diverse and extend beyond the focus of this text. Examples of additional areas within the realm of event management are financial management, marketing, sponsorship, facility management and law. Each of these areas of expertise can be applied to the organizing and production of an event and each is sufficiently important to warrant a full text on their topics. There are multiple texts on the market that focus on the additional areas in event management – but not on the role of the event manager as a facilitator during operational planning. Therefore, this text aims to concentrate on that gap in the literature.

ACKNOWLEDGEMENTS

Cheryl Mallen would like to acknowledge her wonderful family for a lifetime of support and encouragement. Love to you all!

Lorne J. Adams would like to acknowledge Liana for her support and patience with this project. Thanks also to my co-editor, Cheryl, who has redefined the meaning of deadlines and turnaround time. I am dedicating this edition to Bruce Wormald, a dear friend who always believed in me and supported me even when I doubted myself.

CHAPTER 1

TRADITIONAL AND NICHE EVENTS IN SPORT, RECREATION AND TOURISM

CHERYL MALLEN AND LORNE J. ADAMS

This chapter examines the unique characteristics that differentiate *traditional events* from *niche events* (or hybrid events) in the sport, recreation and tourism industries. An explanation is offered for the emerging proliferation of niche events. The discussion leads to a conclusion concerning the demand for skilled traditional and niche managers in the burgeoning field of event management.

TRADITIONAL EVENTS

For the ease of this discussion, each traditional event is considered to be a sport event which is staged for recreational or competition purposes and/or acts as a driver for tourism. Traditional events exhibit two key characteristics. The first characteristic is a governing body. The second characteristic is that the activity is a recognizable and time-honoured event.

Traditional event characteristic: a governing body

Traditional events have a governing body that sanctions events and establishes and enforces standardized rules and regulations to be followed during the production of the event. This governing body can be structured as an organization, association or federation that governs the event. Their rules and regulations specify elements such as the competition area, the number of participants, their dress and acceptable actions for participation.

The governing body can operate in a range of markets and on small to large-scale events. Examples include governing bodies for traditional events held in particular countries, such as netball in Australia, box lacrosse in Canada, high kick and leg wrestling competitions in the Arctic Inuit Games, hurling and Gaelic football in Ireland, rodeo and jai alai in the United States and sumo wrestling in Japan. Additional examples include governing bodies for traditional events that engage multiple countries and tourism markets, such as the Olympic Games, the Youth Olympic Games and Paralympic Games, the Arctic Games, the Asian Games, the Commonwealth Games, the International Children's Games, the Highland Games and the Mediterranean Games.

Traditional event characteristic: a recognizable and time-honoured activity

The second characteristic of a traditional event involves the utilization of an activity that is recognizable and time-honoured. Adaptations can be made to the activity, including the format for a conference, convention or rules and regulations in a traditional sport event based upon a range of pressures, such as a particular culture or country, the need to adapt for the age of the participant population or due to the impact of new technologies. A traditional event may undergo adaptations or transformations over time; however, the transformations do not give rise to an entirely new event. Change is limited. There is universality in the implementation that is repeated and traditional. From generation to generation, the event is conducted in the same manner. The event follows the rules and regulations, including the traditions, customs and routines for a consistent, mature, respected and recognizable event. The general rules for a traditional event are followed even as the focus changes from a recreational activity to a high level of competition and/or a tourism event.

An example of a traditional event is what is called football in a large part of the world and soccer in North America. This sport event can be played at a range of levels from a large elite competition to a local recreational activity that uses a homemade ball and makeshift fields whereby the players emulate the characteristics of the traditional event. The consistent use of rules and regulations at any level makes the event a time-honoured and recognizable game of football/soccer. If played as a single game, or in a league or circuit format, the rules and regulations for the football/soccer events are standardized by the bodies that govern such elements as the

2

size of the playing field, the number of players, their dress and the conduct of each player. Multiple bodies govern football/soccer at the regional, provincial or state, national and international levels throughout the world. Some bodies adapt the rules for their particular purposes, such as age level; however, the event itself resembles the football/soccer that is played worldwide.

Another traditional event can involve a convention whereby the hosting body provides the typical opportunities for patrons to gather to hear speakers, to learn about the latest research in the industry, and to partake in standard tourism opportunities within the region. This event can be held at convention centres around the world and will be hosted in a similar fashion regardless of the hosting site.

Overall, a traditional event is regulated by a governing body and involves a recognizable and time-honoured activity. Each traditional event, whether it is small or large, can benefit from an event manager. The demand for event managers, however, does not end there as the world of event management extends beyond the traditional events to include niche events.

NICHE EVENTS

In contrast to a traditional event, anyone can design and host niche events by setting new directions and offering creative event opportunities. Each niche event is forged through innovations that either alter or renew an event or generate a completely new event. Many niche events are progressive hybrid events that generally stem from the roots of a traditional event. This means that niche events can be founded within the base of a traditional event and then it is altered to produce the "next generation" of the event. A niche event has no requirement for the number of traditional components that could be utilized or the form in which they can be combined. Yet a niche event can exhibit elements that are recognizable as those of a traditional sport event.

There are three key characteristics of niche events. The first is that the event is created and adapted for a particular sport, recreation or tourism audience. The second is that there does not have to be a traditional governing body that has established time-honoured rules and regulations, although an organizing body may exist that can provide rules and regulations. The third characteristic is that the event may exhibit recognizable traditional event components or may be unconventional in its form.

Niche event characteristic: event is created or adapted for a particular audience

A niche event can be continuously adapted for a particular audience. The event can be adapted at any time to meet innovative designs or the changing needs of the participants and tourists or spectators. Adaptations can be made to any individual element of the event, or the entire event can be adapted at any given time. Niche events involve the freedom to design an event with the use of conventional or unconventional components or activities. This type of event thus can be adapted to another generation of the event at any time for a particular audience. Whatever the focus – an individual event, a circuit of events or a league at the local, regional, national or international level – the possibility remains for full-scale changes to the niche event at any time based on the needs of the audience.

Niche event characteristic: no traditional governing body

One of the reasons a niche event can adapt to a particular audience quickly is that it does not have a traditional governing body establishing rules and regulations that have been devised over time. The rules and regulations established are not expected to be traditional or passed down from generation to generation or from event to event – they can be brand new! There is always the potential for adapting the rules and regulations due to the influences of culture, new technology, a particular age group or ability or the creative desire of the event managers.

Niche event characteristic: an unconventional form

Niche events are springing up throughout the world in unconventional forms. Examples include:

- *Utilizing a unique conference/festival/media event/activity venue.* Events held in niche venues, such as European castles or on a ship that is anchored or floating past.
- *Generating niche events at tourism destinations.* Scandinavian iceberg and northern lights sightseeing; ghost tour at Niagara-on-the-Lake, Canada; Nik Wallenda's high-wire tightrope walk between skyscrapers in Puerto Rico; a wildlife festival.

4

- *Adapting the sport or recreational activity playing surface.* Basketball played on a series of trampolines instead of a traditional basketball court in the United States; snowmobile racing moved to the summer months by competing on grass instead of snow in Canada; skiing and snowboarding conducted around the world on hills of sand instead of the traditional mountains of snow; European football/ North American soccer events staged in a three-on-three format played on sand instead of grass.
- *Changing the sport or recreational activity rules.* A World Outdoor Hockey Championship in Canada utilizes adapted rules to award a goal for each penalty to avoid having a participant sit out in the cold when serving the penalty; soccer played in "bubble" suits; and cricket played with adapted rules in the West Indies, England, New Zealand and South Africa.
- *Extending and/or combining sport or recreational activities.* An adapted rhythmic gymnastics team event for men that combines dance and tumbling routines; an Asian-developed adapted version of volleyball that involves a lowered net, three players per side, no hands allowed, where players kick and head the ball back and forth over the net and can leap, twist and flip using kung-fu and gymnastics moves that aid them in returning the ball back over the net; the "Tough Mudder" event whereby individual participants or teams complete obstacle courses; and the Australian adaptation of a triathlon called Adventurethon in which participants paddle kayaks, do mountain biking and off-road or trail running.
- *Focusing on the skill component.* The golf long ball drive as well as putting and hole-in-one contests; baseball home run derbies; ice hockey shooting and skating skills competitions; and football skills competitions.

Niche events exist in multiple forms, as the use of innovative designs and formats are generating new sport, recreational and/or tourism events. Interestingly, companies can create niche events to promote a product. For instance, Red Bull (an energy drink company) has created niche events to promote their products. Two examples are their "crashed ice" series of events whereby competitors wear ice hockey equipment, including skates, and race down a man-made ice course that includes jumps and fast turns: this involves beating others on the course as well as being a timed event. There is also the Red Bull Stratos, a free-fall space dive.

Niche events can evolve into traditional events

Niche events can evolve into traditional events. The triathlon is an example of a niche sport that has become a traditional event. This tri-activity sport event combines swimming, cycling and running. The combination of traditional sports established a niche event that grew from a local to an international phenomenon. The Ironman World Championship triathlon, held in Hawaii, USA, is also an example of a triathlon that is a successful tourism event. Over the course of time, the triathlon developed rules and regulations that were practised in a consistent manner. The event was eventually accepted into the group of sports to be staged at the Olympic Summer Games. This acceptance meant that participants were selected from a series of events conducted with standardized rules and regulations. In addition, there was recognition of the event as a triathlon at every level from local to internationally staged events. At this point, the triathlon entered the realm of a traditional event.

Even as some triathlons evolve into traditional events, the triathlon continues to develop as a niche event. The niche triathlon event has been spurred on by continuing to adapt the multi-activity event elements. This includes adapting to use two sport activities, such as walking and cycling, or adjusting to allow a team of three members to compete, each completing one of the sport activities. This continual use of adaptations to the triathlon keeps the event in the niche event realm; however, it is possible for an event to be produced in both the traditional and the niche event realms simultaneously.

Other examples of events that were born as niche events and evolved to traditional event status can be found in the sport of skiing or snowboarding. Niche events began as moguls competitions, the half-pipe, ski cross and ski dancing – and then these events transformed into traditional events. Volleyball is a further example of a traditional event that generated a niche element in beach volleyball which has now moved to a traditional event. Today, all of these events with niche roots have been included in major traditional events such as the Olympic Games and have standardized traditional rules and regulations.

DESIGN A NICHE EVENT

Niche events continue to emerge and they may or may not move to the realm of traditional events in the future. Regardless, they are expanding

6

the array of sport, recreation and tourism events being produced annually. Event managers are needed to stage each of these small and large niche events around the world.

Examine the niche events that are springing up in your area. Next, consider adaptations or innovations that could be made within a local traditional event to give rise to a niche event. This niche event does not have to be a wholesale innovation to generate a new event. It can involve basic, simple adaptations. Remember, someone designed each niche event and had the courage to host such an event. Many event managers have developed their own careers through this avenue. Can you design a niche event that could potentially be implemented in the future? If so, what would you do to generate an innovation for a traditional sport in your hometown? Read the next section to develop your understanding as to why niche events will continue to expand the event industry into the future.

WHY ARE CONTEMPORARY NICHE EVENTS ARISING?

This text proposes that niche events stem from an outgrowth of our need to learn about, and to practise for, change. According to Gallagher (2012), we are mentally seeking change as it is just the way humans are "wired." We need change or novelty to develop the skills necessary to improve our chances of survival during evolutionary change. Jensen (1999) stated that survival is contingent on the individual or group that "is most adaptable to change" (p. 16). We thus adapt elements in our lives as part of a cycle to acquire opportunities to practise for change (Gallagher, 2012).

Our current period of contemporary change has been described as a post-industrial era (Bell, 1973; Zuboff, 1988). The impact of postindustrial change on contemporary society has produced an environment of complexity and unpredictability (Choo & Bontis, 2002). According to Homer-Dixon (2001), contemporary change impacts all aspects of contemporary society. This impact demands a process of active and continuous learning in order to accommodate change (Hirschhorn, 1984; Sproull & Kiesler, 1991). Adapting to this challenge of change necessitates a mindset for adapting and innovating.

In the process of learning to accommodate change, a new concept has surfaced that Limerick, Cunnington and Crowther (1998) call "collaborative individualism" (p. 103). This concept involves a group or a collective of responsible individuals being "held together by common cultures, shared

7

world meanings and values" (Limerick et al., p. 128). This new form of collective encourages a mindset that one must "embrace individualism, collaboration, and innovation" (Limerick et al., p. 22). Each of these elements must be embraced simultaneously, and all members within the collective have a voice. As these individuals retain and develop their personal voice, they are encouraged to collaborate in order to develop innovations for managing in our contemporary environment.

Applying the concept of collaborative individualism to niche events requires a change-based mindset, an individual voice and a push for individuals to collaborate and to be innovative. At the grassroots level, collaborative individualism is occurring as groups are using innovative design to create niche events. Bound together by common threads from an event's culture, meaning and value, groups are capable of creating, sharing and nurturing adapted meanings and values to create niche events. These niche events can be described as design experiments.

Cobb, Confrey, diSess, Lehrer and Schauble (2003) describe design experiments as "test-beds for innovations" (p. 10). Cobb and his group of researchers indicate that design experiments offer the opportunity to complete a series of cycles of development and allow for regular revisions to an event. A test-bed implies that not all innovations will succeed. However, the test-bed concept for events suggests that opportunities to design niche events abound. Niche event experiments can explore and reflect designs and activities that offer new understandings and innovations which create niche events. In sport, recreation and tourism event management, design experimenters are producing a growing body of dynamic and creative niche events.

A NEED FOR SKILLED TRADITIONAL AND NICHE EVENT MANAGERS

The sport, recreation and tourism industries have undergone phenomenal growth since the 1960s. The combination of increased traditional and niche events is changing the sport, recreation and tourism event landscape, in that each event often utilizes one or more event managers.

Consider the potential number of event managers that could be needed in the world on an annual basis. Event managers are necessary for local recreational and competitive events that extend to regional, provincial or state, national and international events, including leagues, circuits or

8

tours for a variety of age groups and abilities. In addition, these traditional events can include a wide variety of sports ranging from archery to yachting. The number of niche events is growing annually in the form of tourism-focused festivals, banquets and shows. Add to this the number of sport and recreational events that are being altered or renewed to produce the next generation of events and the number of event managers required increases concomitantly.

The exact number of events held annually is an unknown. Calculations are difficult due to the complex conditions of the sport, recreation and tourism industry. However, a general estimation is that millions of traditional and niche events are staged annually around the world. Well-informed, prepared and knowledgeable managers are in high demand – hence the need for this text.

CONCLUSION

A growing body of traditional and niche sport, recreation and tourism events drives the demand for experts who are knowledgeable and experienced in the field of event management. Today's event managers need skills to advance beyond using pre-established lists that dictate the replication of actions used to stage previous events. *Contemporary event managers must be able to think through and self-determine the requirements of staging traditional or niche events. This requirement demands knowledge of, coupled with experience in, event management.*

We now head to Chapter 2, where the concept of knowledge and a knowledge transfer race is discussed. Also, a uniquely formed definition of knowledge for sport, recreation and tourism event managers will be presented. Chapter 2 aims to guide event managers in their pursuit of knowledge for use in the event industry.

CHAPTER QUESTIONS

1 State the two key characteristics of traditional events.
2 List three traditional events and justify why they are traditional events.
3 State the characteristics of a niche event.

4 Describe three niche events that are being hosted in your area and explain the characteristics that make them niche events and not traditional events.
5 Can an event move from being traditional to becoming a niche event? If not, why? If so, what changes are necessary to make the transition?
6 Why are niche events growing in our contemporary times?
7 What does the dual growth of traditional and niche events mean for the field of event management?

CHAPTER 2

THE CONCEPT OF KNOWLEDGE IN EVENT MANAGEMENT

CHERYL MALLEN

This chapter discusses the concept of knowledge and, in particular, the elements that make up *common and advancement knowledge* within the event management industry. In addition, a unique definition of knowledge designed for event management is provided and suggestions are offered concerning how to acquire event knowledge. Further, this chapter indicates that we are all in a *"knowledge transfer race"* (English & Baker, 2006) and the relevance of this race is discussed based on the event industry. The underlying theme within this chapter is that if you cannot articulate your definition of knowledge, then how can you obtain the necessary knowledge to be a valuable member of the event management field? Or, how can you know what types of knowledge you will need to be accomplished in event management in the fields of sport, recreation and tourism? Complete the assignment at the end of the chapter and design a knowledge transfer plan to facilitate your growth and development in the event management industry.

It is important to note at the beginning of this chapter that the terms knowledge, information and data have been used interchangeably in some contexts. However, in this text, the opinion of Boisot (2002) is followed whereby you "Think of data as being located in the world and of knowledge as being located in agents [within your mind], with information taking on a mediating role between them" (p. 67). In this view, knowledge, information and data are considered to be three separate entities.

THE CONCEPT OF KNOWLEDGE

As far back as 1973, Bell noted that knowledge was situated as a "central" feature within our advancing society. Over the past several decades, the value of knowledge has continued to escalate. One reason for the meteoric rise in the value of knowledge is the recognition that knowledge is a resource that aids productivity (Grant, 1996). Thus, productivity, and ultimately, success in event management is in part contingent upon the knowledge that you acquire, create, share and apply.

DEFINING KNOWLEDGE

How do you currently define knowledge? Think about your currently held definition of knowledge and record your answer. Review your definition of knowledge and be sure that you have listed the key dimensions, features or characteristics of knowledge and consider how these dimensions apply to event management in sport, recreation and tourism.

This is a difficult exercise. Researchers have been trying to define knowledge for decades. A single definition of knowledge for one to adopt does not exist in the literature – it has been elusive. The difficulty in arriving at a consensus on a definition of knowledge stems from the intangible nature of knowledge and one definition for all purposes is simply not available (Edvinsson & Malone, 1997). Although researchers cannot agree on the definition of knowledge, there is no reason for not articulating contextual understandings of knowledge. This is because researchers offer tangible components that mark one's knowledge and can be applied to event management in sport, recreation and tourism. I will now review a number of these definitions as they relate to two categories of knowledge that I am calling *common knowledge* and *advancement knowledge*.

---

1 Record how you currently define knowledge.
2 List at least three key dimensions, features or characteristics of knowledge in your definition.
3 Apply your definition of knowledge to either the field of sport, recreation or tourism event management.
4 Review your definition and consider the question: If you have knowledge in the field of event management, this means you have knowledge in what?

Figure 2.1 Defining knowledge in event management

12

COMMON KNOWLEDGE

Common knowledge involves *general understandings* that are gained as it "grows – emerges – out of . . . interactions" (Spender, 2002, p. 160). This means that the development of your common knowledge is dependent upon the interactions that you obtain concerning event management. *This type of knowledge is gained through interactions – including interactions such as taking event management classes, reading research, participating in short experiential activities in the field and having conversations with individuals in event management.* Instructors in the classroom and those individuals in the industry can describe, teach and guide the acquisition and development of your common knowledge. Each interaction helps you to contextualize, interpret and conceive options concerning event management knowledge.

Common knowledge is explicit and provides a foundation that is necessary for your participation, including the judgments that you make. This is because common knowledge is "the platform for everything else. It lies deep and brings together, in contextualized thought and action, all the other types of knowledge that are judged relevant – for it is the source of such judgments" (Spender, 2002, pp. 157–158). The more varied your common knowledge, the greater the foundational base of event management knowledge you develop. This base of knowledge is used to judge the value of new knowledge and facilitates integration of one's currently held knowledge with new knowledge.

Common knowledge is defined in a number of ways. I will now examine definitions of common knowledge in order to delineate the multiple dimensions within common knowledge that are applicable to event management.

Common knowledge means acquiring *systemic knowledge* in event management

One dimension of common knowledge is systemic knowledge. This type of knowledge involves having a general understanding of the overall organization and its methodological systems, technological systems and general processes. This type of knowledge extends to include understandings of the general procedures, schemes, techniques and the contents of manuals and information packages (Nonaka, Toyama & Konno, 2000).

Each dimension described within systemic knowledge is applicable to the knowledge one would require in the production of sport, recreation and tourism events. Understanding one organization does not mean that one has a full understanding of all event organizations. The systemic knowledge could be different for a variety of event organizations and thus, systemic knowledge can involve acquiring knowledge of multiple organizations within the broad base of the event industry.

Common knowledge means understanding of *what one does* in event management

Blackler (1995) defines common knowledge as what one does. This implies that a dimension of common knowledge includes an overall understanding of the human resource structures and the multiple roles that are played by people in event management. These roles include the event manager and the managers of the multiple event components, such as the accommodation manager, accreditation manager, the ceremonies manager (including opening, closing and awards ceremonies), the drug testing or doping manager, the food and beverage manager, along with the managers of protocols, public relations, transportation, venue and warehousing. Further, many of these management roles are supported by staff and/or volunteers and common knowledge extends to understandings concerning what one does within each of these supporting roles. This knowledge also encompasses understandings of the facilitation role to ensure that what one is supposed to do within each of these roles gets completed. For example, one may facilitate event operational planning or volunteer program development. Knowledge of what one does, therefore, encompasses a multitude of roles in event management.

Common knowledge means "*know how*," including knowing theories and their application to practice, processes and procedures in event management

Common knowledge is described by English and Baker (2006) as the basic "know how" or theoretical knowledge and the understanding of how to apply the theory to event practices, processes and procedures. This type of knowledge implies that one needs to understand key characteristics of contemporary theories. Examples of these theories include agency theory,

14

complexity theory, contingency theory and systems theory. Beyond knowing the characteristics that make up each theory, knowledge includes having the general capability to apply the characteristics of each theory in professional event practice.

Common knowledge involves *understanding the basics of culture, politics and personalities* in event management

Gupta and MacDaniel (2002) describe common knowledge as possessing basic understandings of culture, politics and personalities. This type of knowledge requires one to be able to participate in the event management environment, including the ability to conduct oneself in the social culture(s) that have been established. Additionally, there is a need to be able to recognize, understand and apply one's knowledge to political situations and to assess the impact of such political maneuvers. Consequently, this type of knowledge requires a talent for understanding and deciding how to manage differing personalities in event management, including any cultural associations.

Common knowledge includes *basic conceptual understandings* in event management

Nonaka, Toyama and Konno (2000) indicate that common knowledge can be conceptual (ideas are conceived and understood mentally) and that this type of knowledge is obtained based on abstract capabilities. Conceptual knowledge includes ideas that are expressed or visualized. An example includes generating the initial designs for the entertainment elements in event opening and closing ceremonies.

Common knowledge means having *common sense* for the event management industry

Common knowledge has been described as common sense for a particular context or field (Spender, 1996). This means gaining general knowledge on the language, including common terms used within the event field. It also means having a basic awareness and understanding of the subtleties of the feelings and meaning within the language that is shared (Grant, 1996).

Further, there is a sense of knowing how to apply the common knowledge at the appropriate time.

ADVANCEMENT KNOWLEDGE

In contrast to common knowledge, advancement knowledge is in-depth experiential knowledge which can only be acquired from long-term experiences that include high levels of responsibility in the industry. These experiences generate perspectives and understandings that provide a competitive advantage and offer value with a high level of knowledge sophistication. Advancement knowledge provides quick insights, understandings and intuition and is used for decision making (Leonard & Sensiper, 2002). This type of knowledge, however, is difficult to obtain as it is tacit in nature or not-describable (Nonaka & Takeuchi, 1995). This means that it is constructed during the process of interactions and, thus, you must find experiential opportunities and take the risk of sharing knowledge with others in the industry to gain this level of knowledge (Crane & Bontis, 2014).

Tacit knowledge is what an individual holds in their mind about perspectives, beliefs and models (Nonaka & Takeuchi, 1995). This mental capacity can take decades to develop through personal experience (Winter, 1987). Time is necessary, as this type of knowledge is difficult to articulate and discuss. Due to this difficulty, advancement knowledge has been described as a type of "iceberg" (Schorr, 1997, p. 29). This means that much of advancement knowledge is buried in one's memory, but cannot be easily explained. Therefore, because of its hidden nature, acquiring advancement knowledge from someone else can be challenging as the knowledge holder has generally never expressed the knowledge either verbally or in writing (Spender, 1996). A solution to fully alleviate this issue and find ways to mine this type of knowledge has not been found. A person can have advancement knowledge, which is considered to be deep, intimate and personal, but they may not realize that they possess the knowledge. Therefore, the process of exchanging the knowledge with someone else continues to be elusive.

Overall, advancement knowledge has multiple definitions. We will now examine a number of these definitions in order to delineate the multiple dimensions within event management.

16

Advancement knowledge involves an *in-depth understanding of event management routines* gained through practice

According to Nonaka et al. (2000), advancement knowledge is an in-depth awareness and intellect regarding routines in the event processes and procedures, including the best sequential order of events. This "know-how" concerns insights into daily activities that are acquired through years of hands-on participation and use of practices or long-term experiential opportunities (Nonaka et al., 2000). Advancement knowledge of routines means knowing the subtle details of how to be efficient, effective and successful, and this is learned with practice. This definition is supported by Nelson and Winter's (1982) seminal work which indicates that gaining intimate understandings of daily routines and practices comes from analyzing situations and making decisions. This type of knowledge can lead to the pioneering of ideas for efficiencies and effectiveness in routines to make progress and ultimately achieve success in event management.

Advancement knowledge includes *"enbrained" knowledge* gained through practice in event management

Enbrained knowledge comprises high-level conceptual understandings and encompasses cognitive abilities that are produced with practice (Collins, 1993). According to von Krogh and Grand (2002), this "knowing means holding certain beliefs about the world, this knowledge being justified in experience and current observations as well as conceptual reasoning and thinking" (p. 172). Enbrained knowledge thus requires the development of a keen awareness, the ability to think through requirements that underscore actions and the sensing of needs. This definition of advancement knowledge implies that beliefs of what constitutes knowledge are affected by experiences, observations and abilities to conceptually reason and to think.

Advancement knowledge involves *"encultured" knowledge* gained through practice in event management

Encultured knowledge also encompasses cognitive abilities, but in this case, these abilities consist of intimate understandings of the subtleties required for full participation in a particular culture (Collins, 1993). Encultured knowledge is derived from being immersed within a specific culture – even if it is just for a period of time. For example, one can live in an area – such as in Asia, Europe, or the Middle East – and be immersed in the culture. This type of knowledge requires deep understandings of the thought processes, practices and social norms of the particular culture.

Advancement knowledge is foundational for the generation of your new knowledge

For years, we have understood that creating new knowledge does not occur in a way that is disconnected from our current abilities and understandings (Kogut & Zander, 1992). Rather, new knowledge in the form of innovations "are products of a firm's *combinative capabilities* to generate new application from existing knowledge" (p. 390). This implies that, generally, to create new knowledge, it is the combination of what you already know, along with the application of this knowledge to a new situation, which produces new knowledge. Overall, the process of creating new knowledge requires individuals to synthesize their current knowledge for different applications or situations.

THE VALUE OF BEING ABLE TO DEFINE KNOWLEDGE IS THAT IT CAN GUIDE YOU IN SEEKING AND ACQUIRING THE KNOWLEDGE YOU NEED FOR SUCCESSFUL EVENT MANAGEMENT

Overall, obtaining common knowledge in event management is important in order to manage the multiple aspects of an event; however, it is advancement knowledge that can provide the difference when dealing with emerging issues or when event situations do not have well-defined parameters. This means that advancement knowledge is the foundation for judgments or decisions.

Earlier in this chapter you were asked to record a definition of knowledge. Now . . . go back and review your initial definition of knowledge and the dimensions or features of knowledge that you were able to describe, and compare them to the definitions and features of common and advancement knowledge described above. Rework your definition.

18

A UNIQUE DEFINITION OF KNOWLEDGE TO GUIDE YOU IN THE CONTEXT OF EVENT MANAGEMENT

To further develop your understandings, a definition specifically for knowledge in event management is provided. This definition was constructed by applying the multiple definitions and descriptions of common and advancement knowledge offered above. The ensuing definition of knowledge is outlined in Figure 2.2.

The author of this chapter provides a definition of knowledge for the context of sport, recreation and tourism event management as:

Event management knowledge = The synergy of common knowledge and advancement knowledge in the sport, recreation and tourism event industry that leads to perspicacity (quick insights and understandings) for competence (in actions and ability).

Figure 2.2 An umbrella definition of sport, recreation and tourism event management knowledge

Based on the definition of knowledge outlined in Figure 2.2, a synergy, or the confluence of common and advancement knowledge involves more than just adding up your knowledge to create a total sum of knowledge. This synergy gives rise to a personalized combination of types of knowledge that can be achieved through interactions for use in practice. The aim is, therefore, to acquire personalized knowledge.

THE ADVANTAGE OF YOUR *"FLEXIBILITY EFFECT"* OR PERSONALIZED KNOWLEDGE

A knowledge advantage can be derived from what Conner and Prahalad (2002) call the *flexibility effect*. This effect includes knowledge that is personalized by intertwining one's personal perspectives, opinions, approaches, experiences, ideas and options. In addition, personalization includes the impact of one's skill, personality, motivations, abilities, perceptions and interpretations on those elements. This impact creates differentiation, or one's flexibility effect. According to Zack (1999), a flexibility effect includes differentiated ideas, interpretations and responses that provide a competitive advantage. This advantage is produced through

Your flexibility effect includes the use of personal perspectives, opinions, approaches, experiences, ideas and options to create knowledge differentiation, or one's "flexibility effect[s]." Differentiated ideas, interpretations and responses provide a potential competitive advantage in the contemporary change-based environment (Zack, 1999).

In other words . . . it is important to be yourself!

Figure 2.3 Flexibility effect

the personalization process that leads to insights, understandings and the development of new knowledge.

The personalization of knowledge facilitates the production of ideas and new knowledge. This is because differentiation ensures that ideas are varied and not limited to one particular person's viewpoint (Carney, 2001). Accepting and nurturing the personalization of your knowledge encourages the development of options, varied interpretations and solutions. When sharing or exchanging knowledge, it is important that one develops their flexibility effect for potential advantage.

YOU NEED TO CONTINUOUSLY DEVELOP KNOWLEDGE

An emphasis on knowledge in society has generated the need for a continuous search for new knowledge together with a thorough, detailed, relevant and contemporary knowledge development process and sharing process. The sharing process is crucial, as there is what English and Baker (2006) call "the knowledge transfer race." This means that a key component in the continuous development of knowledge involves a race to transfer or share knowledge in order to facilitate the creation of more knowledge.

The value of knowledge transfer, or a sharing process, was highlighted by George Bernard Shaw (1930) when he expressed the following in his play *The Apple Cart:*

> If you have an apple and I have an apple and we exchange these apples then you and I will still each have one apple. But if you have an idea and I have an idea and we exchange these ideas, then each of us will have two ideas.
>
> (Shaw, 1930)

20

An application of Shaw's exchange concept to knowledge implies that transference aids the development of all parties in the knowledge-sharing process. This sharing concept was expressed by Shaw decades ago, but it has become a requirement for participants in today's knowledge-based environment.

Knowledge has been described by Boisot (2002) as being personal in nature; yet there is a critical dependence between the knowledge holder and the development of more knowledge with the use of a sharing process (Hall, 2001). Individual effort simply does not provide enough knowledge to fully develop knowledge transfer. A connection to others is needed to further one's knowledge development.

For years, transferring knowledge has been seen as a top priority because "the fast and effective transfer of knowledge is the only truly sustainable competitive advantage" (Drucker, 1994, p. 10). However, English and Baker (2006) posit that only those who acquire the appropriate knowledge to share can participate and gain additional knowledge through the transferring process. This is because you need to have knowledge to share with others so that they will, in return, share their knowledge with you.

An application of this transference process indicates that those in sport, recreation and tourism event management must share knowledge in order to advance their own personally held knowledge. The development of knowledge within a process of sharing can develop even more knowledge for the staging of events, including the development of innovations for the event industry and the solving of contemporary event problems.

To be competitive in event management, it seems logical that a strategy is needed for knowledge transfer. In this chapter, the strategy proposed is a self-directed plan to develop the ability to become efficient and effective in the process of acquiring and transferring different types of knowledge for event management.

At the core of this strategy is the definition of knowledge as it applies specifically to sport, recreation and tourism event management. Once knowledge is defined, a strategy for participating in the knowledge transfer process can be developed. However, defining knowledge is not a clearly articulated process. Difficulties arise as one attempts to establish a definition of knowledge and the key characteristics that it entails.

YOU NEED A KNOWLEDGE DEVELOPMENT AND A KNOWLEDGE TRANSFER STRATEGY: A PLAN TO GUIDE YOU TO ACQUIRE THE COMMON AND ADVANCEMENT KNOWLEDGE FOR A SUCCESSFUL CAREER IN EVENT MANAGEMENT

A knowledge development and transfer strategy is a self-directed plan to assist you to become efficient and effective in the process of acquiring and transferring knowledge in event management. This strategy articulates a deliberate means to guide you to develop your capacity for knowledge for competitive use. In event management, a knowledge transfer strategy aims to increase your common knowledge, to acquire advancement knowledge, to advance your perspicacity (quick advancement insights and understandings) and to advance your competence (actions and ability) for use in the event management field.

A knowledge transfer strategy is a deliberate means to act to develop your capacity for knowledge for use in the fields of sport, recreation and tourism event management. This strategy involves developing a thorough, relevant and contemporary personal knowledge transfer plan.

Figure 2.4 Defining a knowledge transfer strategy

To effectively participate in a knowledge-sharing process, you need to establish an overview of the types of knowledge you are looking to acquire. Complete Figure 2.5 to create a path whereby you can acquire common and advancement knowledge for the event industry. This ongoing assignment should be revisited over time to update the knowledge you specifically require for your particular involvement in event management, and to establish the path for obtaining this knowledge. Implementing your knowledge transfer strategy and pursuing the knowledge will make you a valuable and successful member of the event management industry.

SOCIAL NETWORKS SUPPORT THE KNOWLEDGE TRANSFER STRATEGY

A description from Castells (2000, p. 697) indicates that "*Networks are dynamic, self-evolving structures, which, powered by information technology and communicating with the same digital language, can grow, and include all social expressions, compatible with each network's goals. Networks increase their value exponentially as they add nodes.*"

22

Features of "common knowledge"	Guiding questions are provided below to assist you to determine the common knowledge you require for the event management industry
1 Systemic knowledge: understandings about the overall organization	1a List a minimum of two local/regional event organizations and two national or international event organizations that you would like to investigate.
	1b Next, determine what can be read to gain basic knowledge about these organizations.
	1c List whom you could talk to and what questions you could ask to advance your common knowledge about these event management organizations (generate a minimum of five questions).
2 Systemic knowledge: understandings of organizational systems	2a What are the methodological systems used to aid the event management organizations you listed above? For instance, what procedures, schemes, techniques, manuals and/or information packages are utilized?
	2b How can you obtain common knowledge about these systems? Consider listing upcoming events by the organizations you provided above, and find out how you could gain volunteer or work experience on some of these events.
3 Understanding what one does in event management	3a Fully describe what a person does if they are an event manager. Consider the managers of event accommodation, accreditation, ceremonies (including opening, closing and awards ceremonies), drug testing, food and beverage, media management, protocols, public relations, results, transportation, venue and warehousing.
	3b Where can you obtain written job descriptions and/or whom can you talk to about the role played by each of these event managers to advance your common knowledge?
	3c Each manager needs to facilitate event activities: (i) what is involved in this role, (ii) whom can you watch to learn about this role, and (iii) how can you obtain experience in facilitation?

Features of "common knowledge"	Guiding questions are provided below to assist you to determine the common knowledge you require for the event management industry
4 Understandings of theories	4a Record the dimensions or characteristics of a minimum of three theories that relate to event management (such as agency, complexity, contingency, legitimacy and systems theory).
	4b Record how each theory can guide an event manager to do their job.
5 Understandings of the basics of culture, politics and personalities	5a Determine the cultures potentially involved in the event organizations that you listed above. Next, state at least three methods that you can use to advance your understandings about the beliefs and practices within each of these cultures.
	5b Determine whom you could talk to about political issues that can arise in event management and how they can be handled . . . and what this individual has learned in hindsight.
	5c Also, determine whom you could talk to about difficult personalities that they have encountered in event management and their strategies for handling these situations to ensure excellent coordination and cooperation between workers.
6 Conceptual understandings	Create a list of the types of conceptual understandings found in event management. Consider your conceived understandings regarding planning events and working with a number of people.
7 Common sense	Record three common sense decisions that you may encounter in event management. Determine whom you can share your information with to gain more knowledge.
8 In-depth understandings of routines	8a Outline a potential career path to pursue over the next 10 years in event management. This path should contain two or three career changes and consider traditional and niche events.
	8b Next, record the types of routines that are pertinent to each career option and indicate a long-term strategy for learning these routines.

Features of "common knowledge"	Guiding questions are provided below to assist you to determine the common knowledge you require for the event management industry
9 "Enbrained" knowledge or an awareness and ability to think through the requirements to complete tasks	Develop a strategy for participating in the hosting of events and practise thinking through the task requirements and implementing plans.
10 "Encultured" knowledge or deep understandings of a particular culture	Develop a strategy for gaining intimate knowledge of cultures. Who can you share your cultural stories with in order to gain theirs? Consider both the "stay home" option and the travel option.
11 New knowledge	Continuously seek to advance new knowledge with the application of what is already known that can be applied to new situations.

Figure 2.5 Ongoing assignment: develop a strategy for development and sharing to advance your knowledge in event management

The combination of individual member relationships creates the structure of a network. The social nature of networks has communication as their key characteristic. Communication is a constant requirement for the formation and maintenance of the network. The key role of every member in the network is communication.

Each member within the network needs to develop the competence to be a valuable communicator. Harris, Coles and Dickson (2000) indicate that network competence includes the ability to:

> Share their understanding of issues and devise ways to relate to each other in carrying out the work necessary to bring about a shared vision of the future. This vision provides the context that orients all network activity. Retaining this orientation is critical to developing and maintaining networks.
>
> (Harris et al., 2000, p. 6)

The sharing within the network provides opportunities for ideas to be generated and knowledge to be created (von Krogh & Grand, 2002).

> Network activism is a conscious effort to (a) expand the number of nodes (people or groups) within your personal network, (b) encourage contacts between the nodes, and (c) advance the quality of the network relationships.

Figure 2.6 Network activism

To form an event management knowledge transfer network, other knowledgeable individuals are necessary to encourage the relationships for a knowledge-sharing process. Preferably, these individuals possess different types of knowledge to contribute in the sharing process. This requires an investment of the time, attention and competence to develop and maintain the network relationships. A key component in a knowledge transfer strategy is *network activism*. This involves a conscious effort to expand your personal network, to encourage contacts between the members in the network, and to advance the quality of the network relationships for exchanging knowledge.

You should seriously consider creating your own network for knowledge sharing. To develop a network, consider the following questions:

- Whom would you contact to begin a personal network in order to pursue event management knowledge?
- What do you expect from each network member in terms of the transfer of knowledge, and what are you providing in return?
- How will you encourage a greater number of contacts between you and others in your network?
- How will you advance the quality of the network relationships to gain more knowledge?

CONCLUSION

Those in event management cannot expect to be exempt from the knowledge requirements inherent in contemporary society. To begin to gain the required knowledge, you need to develop your personal definition of knowledge and create a knowledge transfer strategy to guide you in the acquisition of the multiple dimensions of knowledge needed for the event management industry. The implementation of your knowledge transfer strategy includes the search for knowledge with the expansion of your relations in event management, advancing the contact and the quality of

26

the network relationships. Your participation in a network that encourages collaboration and sharing of knowledge facilitates the effort to obtain more knowledge.

To support the concept of a knowledge transfer strategy, this text *does not* provide a list of elements that you can follow to produce a sport, recreation or tourism event. A list of elements is not conducive to the traditional and niche events being hosted. This is because all events are not alike, and the contemporary environment of change means that you will be working on events in the future that have not yet been conceived. It is important, therefore, to be able to "think through" the particular requirements for the context and the event to which it will be applied. It is perspicacity that you are seeking – or the constant advance of your quick insights and understandings that will position you well for a future in event management.

CHAPTER QUESTIONS

1 Describe the characteristics of common knowledge in event management.
2 Describe the characteristics of advancement knowledge in event management.
3 Describe why advancement knowledge is more difficult to obtain than common knowledge.
4 What is knowledge transfer and how and why do you need to participate in it?

CHAPTER 3

THE ROLE OF THE EVENT MANAGER

TO BE A FACILITATOR

AMY CUNNINGHAM AND JOANNE MACLEAN

This chapter presents the key role of an event manager as a facilitator through-out the four phases of the event planning model outlined in Figure 3.1. A definition of facilitation is provided, along with the theory of facilitation. The facilitation role is outlined as guiding the development of the event structures for governance. Theories, including systems theory, contingency theory and complexity theory are applied to the facilitator's role.

FACILITATION

(by Amy Cunningham)

One of the most exciting aspects of event management is the creation and delivery of a team effort. The event needs a facilitator to guide the process of *sharing of knowledge* between members. In addition, the event manager is responsible for *facilitating* event processes. These are the processes that are found within the collaborative effort of planning and imple-menting an event, where all members of the group need to feel they are an equal part of the team effort.

The role of the event manager as a facilitator is established in the develop-ment phase of the planning model. This facilitation role will be discussed in more depth below, but first let us take a step back and investigate the meaning of facilitation itself. The concept of facilitation is crucial to the role an event manager must play and will provide the theoretical framework upon which we will draw our understanding within this section and the overall text.

Event development phase

The event manager facilitates the development of event structures for governance, event networks, policies, volunteer practices and participation in a corporate social responsibility program

Event evaluation and renewal phase

The event manager facilitates the selection of event components to be evaluated, the completion of the evaluation tasks and the implementation of the evaluation recommendations

Event operational planning phase

The event manager creates and facilitates the development of written operational plans that are logical, sequential, detailed and integrated, along with contingency plans and the activation of a plan refining process

Event implementation, monitoring and management phase

The event manager facilitates the implementation of the written operational plans, monitors activities, looking for deviations, and manages all deviations from the plans

Figure 3.1 An event planning model

What is facilitation?

Bens (2000) defines facilitation as "a way of providing leadership without taking the reins" (p. 7). Facilitation theory assumes that learning will occur with the aid of one who facilitates the process of learning as opposed to one who simply provides knowledge to a group (Laird, 1985; Lambert & Glacken, 2005). Within this theory of facilitation, it is believed that since change is constant, the greatest teachers are those who have learned how to learn, and can lead others in self-directed learning and critical thinking (Lambert & Glacken, 2005; Peel, 2000). This style of leadership encourages the development of empowered learners and contributors to group processes, where the creation and dissemination of knowledge are dependent on all members of the group.

To be an effective facilitator and supporter of this theory one must subscribe to certain assumptions. According to Bens (2000, p. 8), believers in facilitation theory and practice assume that:

- People are intelligent, capable and want to do the right thing.
- Groups can make better decisions than any one person can make alone.
- Everyone's opinion is of equal value, regardless of rank or position.
- People are committed to the ideas and plans that they have helped to create.
- Participants can and will act responsibly in assuming true accountability for their decisions.
- Groups can manage their own conflicts, behaviours and relationships if they are given the right tools and training.
- The *process*, if well designed and honestly applied, can be trusted to achieve results.

Now that we have a general understanding of what is meant by the theory of facilitation, the role of an event manager acting as a facilitator can be explored.

Role of an event facilitator

If we look back to the event planning model shown in Figure 3.1, the event manager has an important role to play as a facilitator throughout all of the planning phases. As a facilitator, your job is to *get others to assume responsibility and to take the lead*. Rogers and Freiberg (1994, p. 21, after Lao Tzu) expressed this facilitation leadership role in the following way:

> A leader is best
> When people barely know that he exists,
> Not so good when people obey and acclaim him,
> Worst when they despise him.
> Fail to honour people; they fail to honour you
> But of a good leader, who talks little,
> When his work is done, his aim fulfilled,
> They will all say, "We did this ourselves."

A facilitator becomes the director of the performance, where each participant plays a central role (Vidal, 2004). By the end of this performance, with

30

the creation of group synergy, which should be one of the main goals of true facilitation, then participants will have had "the pleasure of working creatively and collectively to achieve some goals" (p. 394). Overall, facilitators aim to make specific processes easier during all phases of the event.

There are many specific skills, experiences and areas of knowledge that the event manager must possess to facilitate an event (Peel, 2000; Thomas, 2004). This array includes advancement knowledge that involves intuition about the processes which will help others "act on their feet" and make quick decisions with regard to the needs of a group or process (Peel, 2000). By making these processes easier, specific tasks will be completed, goals will be met and the team will feel a pleasurable synergy after a job well done (Vidal, 2004).

A good facilitator empowers the group and the individuals within it to rise to their own potential and have the confidence to be an equal player on the team so that no one becomes dependent on a "teacher." Everyone is shown to be their own developer of knowledge, and the strengths of each individual within the collective can be drawn out and their benefits maximized within the overall process (Peel, 2000).

Figure 3.2 offers a comprehensive outline of some of the specific roles that a facilitator would play during the event managing process.

A facilitator

- Helps the group define specific goals and objectives.
- Provides processes that assist members to use their time efficiently to make good decisions; helps group members understand these processes.
- Guides group discussion to keep things on track.
- Keeps accurate notes that reflect the ideas of the group members.
- Supports members in assessing their current skills and the building of new ones.
- Uses consensus to help the group make decisions that take all members' opinions into account.
- Supports members in managing their own interpersonal dynamics.
- Helps the group communicate effectively.
- Helps the group access resources.
- Creates a positive environment in which members can grow and work together toward attaining group goals.
- Fosters leadership in others by sharing leadership responsibilities.
- Supports and empowers others to facilitate.

Source: Bens (2000); Peel (2000); Vidal (2004).

Figure 3.2 The event manager as a facilitator

FACILITATING THE COMMUNICATION REQUIREMENTS

Greenberg (2002) explains that "Communication is the process through which people send information to others and receive information from them" (p. 217). This process can be a difficult one to facilitate, as it is made up of numerous interactions between various members of a team, all of whom bring their individual personalities, knowledge, skills and communication styles to the table. It is a key role of the event manager, then, to act as a facilitator and to make sure that communication lines are open, that members of the team feel that they are being supported, and that specific processes and requirements are articulated and managed throughout the overall process (Bens, 2000).

In organizational settings, the communication process can be extremely complex, depending on the design of the organization. In many cases, information may need to flow up or down through the "ranks" or be transmitted to certain individuals via other individuals (Greenberg, 2002). The complexity of these links can lead to communication breakdowns and confusion if not managed properly. The wonderful thing about facilitating a group of individuals with whom you are considered a part of the team is that most of the communication in this process will move horizontally. As Greenberg states, "Messages of this type are characterized by efforts at coordinating, or attempts to work together" (p. 201). By focusing and guiding group members' communication and decision-making processes in a structured form, a facilitator can reduce the chances of engaging in faulty processes and harness the strengths of the group. If the proper communication requirements have been articulated and set in place by the facilitator at the onset of the event planning process, the facilitator should fade into the collective, only to be called upon to manage problems and situations as they may arise.

As a facilitator, the event manager is constantly listening, thinking and reflecting throughout the process as problem solving and decision making are occurring between group members. In any group situation, decisions will need to be made, and any conflicts will need to be resolved. While the overall process of task completion is equally the responsibility of each member of the group, it is the role of an effective facilitator to guide the group to a synergy that is born of effective communication (Vidal, 2004). In this regard, historically a facilitator would act as a neutral party who reminds the group of the aims, guides the group communication requirements, sets specific strategies at the onset of the process and

32

- Be a supportive communicator.
- Focus on the problem instead of the person.
- Match words with body language and encourage group members to do the same.
- Encourage the group to acknowledge each other's ideas.
- Keep the conversation going.
- Encourage open feedback.
- Encourage the use of simple language.
- Paraphrase to clarify; repeat what people say to assure them they are being heard and to make sure each member of the group has understood and is clear.
- Walk the talk; don't say one thing and do the other, and watch for this behaviour in group members.
- Be a good listener and encourage members of the group to do the same; consider the use of a "talking stick" to ensure that everyone has a chance to speak and be heard.
- Stay neutral, and avoid sharing your personal opinion unless it is requested; focus on your *process* role of communication.
- Ask questions; this will invite participation, help to gather information, test assumptions and get to the root causes of problems.
- Synthesize ideas; encourage group members to comment and build upon each other's ideas.
- Stay on track; set time guidelines for each discussion.
- Summarize clearly.

Source: Bens (2000); Greenberg (2002).

Figure 3.3 Facilitation tips

interjects as necessary to guide the group back into synchronicity (Laird, 1985; Rogers & Freiberg, 1994).

Now that the importance of facilitating the communication requirements is understood, below are some helpful tips to consider:

Facilitating group communication requirements: the case of group rhythm and facilitation

According to the seminal work by Drucker (1946), "an institution is like a 'tune'; it is not constituted by individual sounds but by the relations between them" (p. 26). An event can exhibit institutional characteristics and requires the facilitation of the relations between the many individuals involved to create a coordinated tune.

Lulu Leathley, from Vancouver, British Columbia, Canada, is an individual who specializes in facilitating group rhythms (group drumming circles) and promotes the importance of facilitated communication in group processes. The teachings of Leathley position the facilitator's role as beginning with the act of being a conductor. In music, the goal is to reach a moment in the facilitation of group music-making where everyone (regardless of their musical background and experience) feels empowered and collectively reaches a place of group synergy. It is her goal to slowly fade into the background and become a part of the group so that the music created is dependent upon each person and no one becomes dependent on her as a leader. To accomplish this goal, she sets certain communication requirements (both verbal and non-verbal) at the beginning of the group drumming circle. She very clearly articulates the importance of listening to each other, making eye contact and getting in touch with inner intuitions and rhythms. In other words, she encourages and empowers group members to look inside themselves for the knowledge that she believes they already possess in order to create something that is a sum of all parts of the collective. Throughout the facilitation process, she encourages the group members to bring their own inner rhythms and strengths forward in order to contribute to the collective song. She makes sure to keep the rhythm going, despite the ups and downs, and provides ample room and encouragement for feedback. At the completion of a successful event, there is the energy of connection.

In music collaboration, there is an overall feeling by the musicians when everything culminates in a satisfying "click" (Sawyer, 2006). It is a challenge to attain this synergistic click as it takes the cooperation and ability of all group members working together to reach this goal. The facilitator's job is to communicate with the group both verbally and non-verbally in the beginning and then to re-enter and guide the group and *sense* what is needed throughout the process.

Experience in facilitation allows you to become quicker with your intuitive decision-making abilities, and your flexibility effect includes personalizing your knowledge, perceptions and ideas to create an advantage. A facilitator's role, therefore, is to use one's knowledge to facilitate the event process. This facilitation includes recognizing when certain group members are overpowering others, when people are not listening to each other or when the group is approaching a collective musical disaster. In this situation, Leathley responds and reacts to the needs of the group based on her own experience, knowledge, skills and intuition: this is her *flexibility effect* acquired as a music teacher and facilitator.

If the group has succeeded in coming together and clicking, there is an overwhelming sense of empowerment, pride and accomplishment as a collective at the conclusion of the event. As mentioned in the previous section, this is the sign that the event facilitator has been effective and successful in their role. Facilitating communication within the group process, then, can be seen as one of the most important roles of the event manager.

A sport, recreation or tourism event manager facilitates the communication processes. Their experience, knowledge, skills and intuition contribute to the ability to create a collective synergy in event production.

We have now reviewed the meaning of facilitation and the role of the facilitator, specifically regarding communication process requirements. We will consider another important role in facilitation, the transfer of knowledge.

Facilitating knowledge transfer

In addition to what has been described above, as a facilitator of a collaborative group effort, it is your job to make sure knowledge is transferred and built upon between group members. This transfer helps to ensure that the best and most informed decisions are made in the pursuit of task completion, drawing on the collective knowledge of the group. But how does the facilitator go about ensuring that their own knowledge is transferred to inform the field as a whole?

The sharing of knowledge with others is an invitation and assumes that other facilitators will in return share their knowledge, and as a result, the knowledge apex will broaden and expand. This broadening has very positive outcomes if we are to assume that the goal of sharing and receiving new knowledge is to continuously work toward honing our effectiveness and expertise as facilitators. Knowledge transfer is a long, steady, continuous process that needs to be completed over the entire time of the event, including all four phases illustrated in Figure 3.1.

Within a practical setting, let us revisit Lulu Leathley's facilitation of rhythm-based events. As a facilitator within a network of other facilitators, Leathley engages in many specific knowledge transfer strategies that enable her to inform her field, contribute to the expansion of the knowledge pool and broaden her own knowledge base. Some of these strategies include:

- building relationships and sharing dialogue about experiences with other facilitators;
- attending rhythm facilitation conferences;
- continuously attending training sessions with other facilitators with varying levels of experience;
- joining discussion groups and posting information on various websites;
- becoming an active member in the rhythm facilitators' guild;
- assisting others to develop facilitation skills by lending talents and experiences to mentorship programs.

In these activities, there is a climate of cooperation and support that aids in the important transfer of knowledge. As a result of this enthusiasm and support, the community of facilitators continues to grow and individuals are able to develop their *perspicacity* (quick advanced insights and understandings) based on the knowledge that is shared. There are many ways in which an event manager may facilitate this knowledge transfer, and we have already examined various examples within one particular case. We have also outlined the specifics of facilitation, the role of the event manager as a facilitator, the importance of communication and the methods by which communication requirements may be facilitated. Let us now begin a discussion on another area of interest in the development phase of the planning model, the facilitation of structures for governance when staging an event.

FACILITATING EVENT STRUCTURES FOR GOVERNANCE

(by Joanne MacLean)

Let us consider an event of huge magnitude; for example, the Olympic and Paralympic Games. Rio de Janeiro in Brazil hosted the 2016 Games; Sochi in Russia hosted the 2014 Games; London, England hosted the 2012 Games; and in 2010, the communities of Vancouver and Whistler welcomed the world to Canada for a massive winter sporting festival. Competition is generally conducted over a 17-day period, with another

10 days of Paralympic competition following. The event organizers have, as their mission, to inspire the world through this event. For example, the Vancouver Organizing Committee indicated that:

> [T]he mission is to touch the soul of the nation and inspire the world by creating and delivering an extraordinary Olympic and Paralympic experience with lasting legacies. The vision is to build a stronger Canada whose spirit is raised by its passion for sport, culture and sustainability.
>
> (Vancouver, 2010, 2007)

The London Olympic Organizing Committee had a motto of "Green and Secure" (scribd.com). This motto indicated an emphasis on safeguarding both the natural environment and the participants and spectators throughout the Games. Also, Rio had the following motto: "To deliver excellent Games, with memorable celebrations, that will enhance the global image of Brazil and promote sustainable social and urban transformations through sport, contributing to the growth of the Olympic and Paralympic Movements" (Rio 2016, 2013, para. 6). The missions, visions and mottos were to be achieved and expressed through organizing a variety of sporting competitions and cultural festivities. Thousands of employees and volunteers staged the Games, and the images of athletes from hundreds of countries around the world were televised and followed intently. Organizing the Olympic Games required an enormous planning process.

Now turn your attention to a smaller event staged in your community, such as a community tourism event or a team sport championship being hosted at your university or college. Even though it is smaller in magnitude and duration compared to the Olympics, the event still involves many of the same components.

Event components in sport, recreation and tourism can include elements such as:

- accommodation;
- accreditation;
- ceremonies;
- communications;
- competition management;
- drug testing or doping control;
- food and beverages;

- hospitality and protocol services;
- human resource management (volunteers and staff);
- media management;
- medical services;
- merchandising;
- officials' management;
- participant management;
- results and awards;
- security/safety;
- spectator services;
- transportation and parking services;
- ticketing.

In each case, a considerable amount of work is devoted to planning and staging a successful event.

Events within sport, recreation and tourism have levels of magnitude, appeal and complexity that require well-designed event structures which contribute to successful delivery. Very often, the structure and governance of event management are "silent," they are somewhat behind the scenes of the main program of activities that are consumed or watched. However, in reality, the elements of effective structure and governance are foundations to success. Successful events simply cannot be achieved without a structure for planning and delivering the event. This enables effective communication, decision making and appropriate amounts of flexibility among event managers. In order to understand this in further detail, the purposes of the following sections include:

1 defining the concepts related to event structures and good governance of event management;
2 outlining the theoretical dimensions of event structures that will enable the delivery of successful events, without identifying the specifics of that structure;
3 identifying principles that result in the creation of effective event structures;
4 applying the theoretical dimensions and principles of event structures identified above to different types of events currently popular in the business of sport, recreation and tourism.

By following the topics identified above, students will gain an appreciation for two important fundamental principles about facilitating event

38

structures for event management: first, different kinds of events require different event management structures that provide the appropriate management for the particular event; and second, we believe that event managers are better served learning the *guiding principles* that will enable them to make decisions about the most appropriate and effective structure for the event being planned, as opposed to duplicating the structure from another event. You may label these two fundamental principles *flexibility* and *specificity* regarding event management structures. The following sections will help you understand these and other principles and their application in creating effective event structures.

Event structures

So what exactly do we mean by the term *event structure*? This term refers to breaking down the tasks associated with delivering the event such that employees or volunteers have specific roles and an understanding of how these roles interrelate. The structure involves the positions of the head of each committee within the hierarchy or network. These individuals manage groups of individuals that have the authority to make decisions. Their position in the structure dictates the reporting relationships. Typically, event leaders publicize a management structure in the form of a chart with boxes and connecting lines outlining the task areas, with proximity between areas that need to cooperate and/or collaborate, and reporting directions.

Theoretically, the structure of an organization is usually examined from three points of view (Slack & Parent, 2006). The first viewpoint is *formalization* (the degree to which rules and regulations, policies and individual and committee roles are defined to guide the activities of event managers). The second viewpoint is *complexity* (the scope and number of different individual committees and sub-units required to deliver the event and the density of the hierarchy of authority involved). The third viewpoint is *centralization* (the degree to which decision making is controlled by those in charge of the event or delegated to individuals working at the level of committees or individual jobs). The event structure can be designed to be high or low in each of the areas of formalization, complexity and centralization depending on the type of event.

Event structures are developed to aid the governance of an event. Governance refers to exercising the authority to define policy regarding how the event will be run, who does what, and when and how it will be done. If an event is to be successful, then the structure created to deliver it must provide for effective transfer of knowledge and decision making. Facilitating event structures means that you have the knowledge necessary to create the most appropriate organizing structure for your event.

In addition to the theory discussed above regarding event structure, there are a number of other important theories that have been developed which aid in understanding effective event structures. The theoretical dimensions of event structures that we have chosen to include in this discussion involve systems theory, contingency theory and complexity theory. The following sections will briefly introduce each theory in the context of understanding effective event structures for good governance and successful event management.

Theoretical dimensions of event structures

Event structures vary considerably. For concrete local examples, examine how your educational recreational events are structured. Compare the recreational event structure to a local tourism event and a locally held elite sport championship. Each event can be unique in its structure. The structure dictates the hierarchy, which in turn influences the freedom to act in the process of making, relaying and implementing decisions and actions when staging an event.

When creating an event, you will need to consider a structure that will lead to the most effective and efficient delivery for staging the event. In order to achieve this goal, there are several theoretical perspectives that relate information about effective organizations and event structures. The theoretical dimensions outlined next are largely complementary, in that parts of each theory may apply in specific ways to the event structure you develop.

Systems theory

Systems theory stresses that event management structures rely on the environment within which they operate for many of the materials that will be required for hosting the event. Materials include a wide variety of items such as people, equipment, technologies and facilities to name a few. Systems theory suggests that the event will have three different systems working together: *input systems, throughput systems* and *output systems.*

40

In order to run an event, you must take in resources (inputs), create the event activities (throughputs), and generate end results for participants or others (outputs). The three systems interrelate and depend on each other for success. A change in one inevitably affects the other parts of the system. Any event you are organizing involves inputs or the acquisition of raw materials (competition facilities) and human resources (volunteers) to organize the event; throughputs might include the application of technology (a website designed for managing communication and registration) and information (the number of participants that can be accommodated); and outputs include the enjoyment of participants and the funds raised for the charity of choice. The overall event system interacts within its component parts and with its environment. Facilitators of events must understand that the application of systems theory identifies the importance of component parts of the organization structure depending on and influencing one another.

Contingency theory

A rational extension to systems theory in understanding the organizing structure and management of an event involves *contingency theory*. This theory suggests that the effective structure of an organization is contingent on contextual factors of the environment within which it operates, such as size, competition, strategy, resources and so on. This contingent structural situation can be explained further with the concept of *dissipative structures*. This concept implies that a structure can be reproduced or repeated if it is in a steady state (in equilibrium). However, achieving this steady state is difficult because structures tend to combine, be pulled apart, and then recombine again. This concept re-emphasizes that a structure is contingent upon the particular environment and needs of the event. As such, the design of the event structure and its units must "fit" with the environment and work well in coordination in order for the event to succeed. For example, in a tourism event, the structure of the organizing system will need to account for the number of participants, the age group and the cultural mix. Further, the size of registration may be wholly contingent on how many facilities exist, how much time can be acquired within facilities and the particular services that are available. These factors may be impacted by other events running proximal to yours in timing or location. Such factors are often termed constraints, and facilitators of events need to understand event constraints and contingencies in order to achieve optimal organizing structure, decision making and leadership. Overall, event facilitators should not expect to continue with the same operating structure and need to be open to organizational structural changes based on the concept of dissipative structures and contingency theory.

Complexity theory

In keeping with systems and contingency theories, *complexity theory* works to identify how organizations optimally adapt to their environments. Using this theory, managers focus on the required complexity of structure that can achieve the mission of the event while retaining the ability to adapt and make strategic decisions quickly. Complexity theory identifies the importance of complex adaptive systems, structures that commonly consist of a small number of relatively simple, partially connected structures. In our example, a simpler structure involving committees for scheduling, facility organization, registration and volunteers that connect to each other via a leaders' committee will be better able to communicate, make effective decisions and adapt to its environment.

Theories expand our understandings

In academic study, the word theory is used to describe the logical explanation for a phenomenon that has been studied systematically and is thought to expand our understanding. The theories briefly described above provide a foundation for understanding why and how event structures may be optimally designed. How can we facilitate effective structures? What makes one event structure effective and another ineffective? How do event structures come to influence good governance, such that the decision making, policy development and efficiency of the event are optimized? Understanding the above theories sheds some light on answering these questions. And from these theories, along with trial and error of what works in practice and the transfer of this knowledge, a variety of principles in event structures have been identified. Let's look at these in further detail.

Principles in event structures

Principles can be likened to rules or understandings that have resulted from theory and practice regarding how and why things work. In developing effective organizing structures for event management, a number of principles are identified that will help event organizers create the optimal structure for the particular event and environment within which the event

42

is being delivered. Identified below are some of the major principles applying to event structure development.

- *Form follows function.* This principle suggests that the type of structure created to manage the delivery of an event should be predicated on the purpose of the event and the definition of governance roles (for example, developing policy, managing, operating) within the event management design. Copying the event structure from a previously successful event does not necessarily result in a workable structure for another event. For example, using the structure developed to deliver the Olympic Games would be ridiculous when delivering a high school basketball tournament because the former event is so much larger and more complex than the latter.
- *Operating specialization.* Optimal event structures identify the activities required to deliver the event and cluster similar or like activities together into sub-units to encourage communication and decision making. By so doing, efficiency is created by maximizing interconnections among managers with responsibilities that impact one another, leading to more autonomous but interconnected work groups.
- *Increasing complexity increases both planning and time required for planning.* The more complex an organizing structure, the more planning is required to ensure that the structure functions optimally. It stands to reason that this will take more time than with a simple structure. An example of this principle is the organizing of the Olympic Games. Games operating committee structures are designed six to eight years in advance of the competition at a minimum, and the extent of planning is exceptionally broad.
- *Communications efficiency.* Planning does not take place in the brain of one person in isolation from others. Therefore, the structure for event management must create linkages and liaisons for individuals to communicate their activities and decisions, and this communication must be formally arranged in order to be efficiently enacted. The speed and number of communications can be enhanced depending on the type of event structure created.
- *Synergistic outcomes.* Synergy refers to the phenomenon of greater efficiency and outcomes that occur when two or more agents work together than could be achieved had each completed the same effects in isolation. Event structures that create opportunities for synergistic outcomes are said to be efficiently lean and more effective for task

accomplishment (Kilmann, Pondy & Slevin, 1976). The accruing synergistic outcome results from the idea that the overall accomplishment is more than a simple summation of output, meaning that the whole is greater than the sum of its parts.

Understanding the theories and principles relative to facilitating effective event structures is very important, but knowing how to apply the ideas presented to create actual event structures is perhaps even more critical for the success of the event and its managers. Next we move to a discussion of the application of key characteristics of the above theory.

Application of theory and principles in event structures

The theory and principles outlined earlier in this chapter regarding the development of effective event structures apply to both traditional and niche events. In practice, traditional events may involve more formality of structure compared to niche events. This is dictated by the governing body and its established policy regarding how the event is to be organized. Systems theory suggests that the environment within which the event is hosted should be considered for both traditional and niche events. The resources required to create the event, the anticipated outcomes of the event, and the event activities will also need to be considered. Contingency theory holds that the importance of fitting the event structure to both its purpose and environment, creating a structure that fits appropriately with the size, resources and intent of traditional and niche sporting events, is paramount. Complexity theory also establishes the importance of matching the structure for organizing the event to its environment and purpose in order to create a structure that matches the strategy and adaptability that might be required in the environment.

Being able to adapt to unforeseen problems, pressures and changes is a fundamental requirement for traditional and niche event structure frameworks. This can be optimized when the structure created for the event is directly linked to its purpose (for example, form follows function). While it might seem advantageous to use another successful event structure when planning a new event, it is actually a risky proposition. Linking form and function – creating an event structure that identifies the intent and governance roles that most specifically meet the needs of the actual event – is very important. While this is critically important for traditional sport event structures, it may be even more crucial with

44

niche events where the event structure is without the guidance of a governing body, established policy or other comparable events.

Similarly, creating a clear understanding of the operating specialization for the event and linking the activities of sub-units with common or dependent roles will encourage effective communication and create efficiency. This is the case with both traditional and niche sport events. The complexity of the event structure will surely impact the amount of planning that is required to enable effective communication and decision making along with the time it will take to make this a reality. Planning with the specific intent of ensuring coordination among the parts of the event organizing structure is an important role for event managers that can have a multiplied, synergistic outcome of much greater magnitude than the impact of the work of an individual or committee. Event leaders need to take a role in creating synergy among the parts of the event organizing structure, where the impact will be a positive result in both traditional and niche sport event structures.

Creating event structures so that good governance will result is the ultimate goal of understanding and applying the theory and principles discussed above to the management strategies for your event. A structure that is flexible provides for effective levels of communication, decision making and exchange of information among the individuals delivering the event. The structure created, while being specifically designed for the purpose of the event, will best serve the needs of event managers and contribute to overall success. Effective event structures for governance go hand in glove with facilitating effective event networks that bring additional groups or constituent organizations' relationships and resources together to contribute to the development of an event, our next topic of interest.

CONCLUSION

In this chapter, the key role of an event manager as a facilitator was introduced. A definition of facilitation was provided, along with the theory of facilitation. The role of the event manager was outlined as that of a facilitator who guides the development of event structure for governance established in the first phase of the planning model, the development phase. Further, systems theory, contingency theory and complexity theory were applied to the key role of event facilitation.

1 What does a person do when they "facilitate" event activities and what types of knowledge does one need to successfully facilitate?

2 How is facilitation different from teaching personnel involved in an event?

3 An event structure can be examined from three points of view: formalization, complexity and centralization. Describe these three points of view.

4 Describe systems theory, contingency theory and complexity theory and relate these theories to the development of event structures and the role of a facilitator.

5 What does the principle *form follows function* imply?

6 What are dissipative structures and how do they apply to event facilitation?

CHAPTER 4

THE EVENT PLANNING MODEL

THE DEVELOPMENT PHASE

MAUREEN CONNOLLY, LORNE J. ADAMS AND CHERI BRADISH

This chapter examines the first phase of a four-phase event planning model, the event development phase. The event manager is a facilitator of event activities throughout all of the phases. In the development phase, this facilitation role includes a plethora of areas. We begin with an assignment on facilitating event development in a number of these areas including event legacy statements, a staff training program, event contracts, permits and liability insurance, as well as an excellent event communication system. This is followed by an overview of the generation of additional development phase elements, including policy development, establishing event volunteer programs and participation in social responsibility.

FACILITATING THE ELEMENTS IN THE DEVELOPMENT PHASE

(by Maureen Connolly and Lorne J. Adams)

There are several elements in the development phase of the planning model. This section is based on the key premise that you cannot be an excellent event manager if you do not learn to think through the event hosting requirements and ensure that they are congruent with the particular event. This skill requires you to apply your knowledge and determine how you will obtain additional knowledge as you think through the requirements for a particular traditional and/or niche event. To help you work through the process to select an event and then generate an overview of the planning items for the development phase elements outlined below, you should consider the following:

47

- *Event legacy statements.* Develop three legacy statements for your selected event. Consider that event legacies are the catalysts for the post-event benefits and include areas such as grassroots development, advances in infrastructure, regional economic benefits, social advancement, trade, tourism investment, advances in regional marketing, increases in participation, volunteer skill development, and the debut of new events.
- *Staff training program.* Design an event staff training program. Consider the goals and objectives; policies; recruitment and interview process; general event training, including a venue tour; specific components; communication processes; retention and recognition activities.
- *Event contracts.* Determine a knowledge transfer strategy for advancing your understanding of event contracts. Where would you go to obtain a previous contract and/or to learn about the detail required in each contract? Develop a list of contracts needed for your selected event. Then, provide an overview of the key elements that need to be outlined within each event contract.
- *Event permits and liability insurance.* Think through the requirements for event permits and liability insurance for your selected event. Determine where you would go to obtain each type of permit and liability insurance; provide an overview of the data required to complete the permit and to obtain the insurance; specify the cost; and the timeframe needed to complete the paperwork and obtain a permit/ insurance documents for an event.
- *The event communication system.* Devise an excellent event communication system; provide a diagram illustrating who will be able to contact whom and how. Be sure to consider the communication requirements for all members on the event organizational chart, such as the event management team and event staff; think about how your event staff will communicate with venue staff, volunteers, participants, and with transportation, accommodation and emergency services.

Now that you have created your planning overview, set it aside and be prepared to re-address it in two weeks' time. You may be amazed at how you can keep advancing your work to achieve excellence in development phase elements as you continue to apply your advancing knowledge and your skill at thinking through requirements.

48

FACILITATING THE DEVELOPMENT OF EVENT GOALS AND OBJECTIVES

An event manager is responsible for facilitating the generation of event goals and objectives. *Goals* are overall statements that clearly outline what you expect to accomplish or achieve for the event. Multiple event goals can be established; for instance, goals can be established for each of the multiple components within an event such as accommodation, accreditation, transportation, the food and beverage component, etc. *Objectives* need to be established to indicate by whom, when, where and how each goal statement will be accomplished. The objectives, thus, provide the specific directions that guide the activities to make each goal statement become a reality. They can describe what needs to be accomplished, who is responsible, what is expected, when it is to be completed, the products or services needed, as well as the objectives for the financial requirements and timeframe.

Examples of goals and objectives are found in Appendix A.

FACILITATING EVENT POLICY DEVELOPMENT

As an event manager, you will come face to face with both established policy and the need to develop new policy. Sometimes you will feel constrained or limited by policy, and at other times, you will wish that you had a policy in place to help you deal with one of the contingencies that has arisen from an event you are managing. Such is the life of an event manager. You have to negotiate a world that is at once well-defined and perhaps restrictive in some matters, but ill-defined and fluid in others. As these issues arise, you will have a need to ask yourself whether existing policy helps with the present situation or whether it needs to be modified. You might also need to ask whether new policy needs to be developed or whether the issue can be dealt with without a formal policy.

The foundations of policy development include four general purposes or types of policies that are germane (Graff, 1997). Each policy type is relevant to your role as an event manager and they comprise:

1 policy as a statement of belief, position or value;
2 policy as a method of risk management;
3 policy as a rule;
4 policy as an aid to program effectiveness.

Event policy development involves the generation of statements or premises that direct personnel involved in an event. Policies direct (or guide) expected approaches, actions, accountability and the consequences of actions for the particular structure, network, staff and volunteers in an event. The combination of event policies provides the foundational framework for all actions and desired outcomes. The goal of policy development is to guide event personnel by providing direction in those key areas: approach, procedures and actions or protocols.

According to *Webster's New Collegiate Dictionary* (1985), policy is prudence or wisdom in the management of affairs – sagacity. Sagacity means discernment or the ability to do the right thing in the moment. Curriculum and policy are analogous allies. So ask:

- What are the intentions?
- What are the assumptions?
- Who or what are the resources, how will they be distributed and under what authority?
- What are the relationships necessary for things to work and what is the authority structure for advancing the relationships?
- What has or has not worked and how do I know?
- What or how shall I learn from this and what is the process for adapting for the learning?

These questions can also be used to initiate the development of policies. Answering questions such as those posed above can aid in revealing topics that can be used to develop policies for an event. Overall, policies are needed to provide the foundational framework for how committee members are to interact to be efficient. Procedural policies are needed to guide actions during the interactions. Protocol policies are necessary to provide rules of behaviour during the interactions. The intertwining of policy between and among these factors increases accountability. Additional examples of policy topics are found in Appendix A.

Facilitating policy congruence

When facilitating the development of event policy, consider the concept of congruence. It has been noted that congruence involves "the suitability or appropriateness of the chosen policy given the external and internal

50

operating pressures experienced" (Ghobadian, Viney & Holt, 2001, p. 387). This suitability requires an understanding of whether or not a policy can realistically be implemented based on the pressures when facilitating an event. In order to effectively bring a policy to fruition under pressures, an event manager must facilitate the advance of three equally important elements to achieve policy congruence: (i) a well-defined policy, (ii) clearly formulated and articulated strategies for implementation, and (iii) an implementation management strategy (James, Ghobadian, Viney & Liu, 1999). All three elements are important as they overlap each other and are dependent upon each other for successful policy development and implementation. A well-defined policy involves short and coherent statements that are easy to interpret consistently. The strategies for implementation must include an examination of the demand for event coordination. Further, there is generally a need to lower this coordination demand and, at the same time, ensure that the event has the capacity to coordinate the policy implementation requirements (Sarma, Herbsleb & van der Hoek, 2008). Additionally, an implementation management strategy involves streamlining policy-driven event processes and the sharing of expertise, as well as ensuring excellence in communication, a monitoring system and training in order to enact a policy.

Example: policy becomes praxis

As you read the following example, make a note of which policies need to be made more explicit, and where gaps may appear in written policy. The example makes clear the link to contingency theory. Once you have reviewed the example, based on your knowledge and thinking through the issues and how they affected the participants, you should be able to indicate the type and the context of policies that you would need as an event manager.

Further, be sure to consider two additional policy areas that are applicable to every event. These areas include policies based on the specific laws enforced within a country as well as the institutional customs. These laws and customs may change based on different countries' interpretations, and an event manager must be open to incorporating both of these areas within event policy praxis.

This example is an annual meeting and conference concerning those with disabilities. Approximately 120 participants included 65 young people with disabilities, an organizing team of 10–12, a conference services team of four, various support staff and 65 student volunteers. There was also significant liaison with the surrounding city and region.

As far as sport, recreation or tourism events go, a five-day, 350-person event is hardly extravagant; however, the contingencies were intriguing, to say the least. Chief among these were the heavy construction projects scattered across the area hosting the event, making entrances, exits, way-finding and overall access a challenge for non-disabled participants and a nightmare for participants with disabilities.

There were obvious explicit rules. The safety and dignity of all participants was a priority. People with disabilities were consulted on how needs were to be met. No effort was spared to make campus spaces accessible. Planning began 15 months in advance of the event. Unspoken rules were more subtle, of course. Assume that everyone has good intentions; all stakeholders get equal credit; no one argues or fights – we have mature disagreements; reputational impact is significant; promised activities will unfold as they have been described; all volunteers and support personnel will show up and know what they have to do. Deeper subtexts were anxiety over injuries, ignorance of the disabilities, fear of saying the wrong thing or being inadvertently offensive, food allergies, getting lost on the way to activities, missing buses and planes, and no-shows.

The larger system at work for this event to be successful was an authentic meritocracy; that is, a code of conduct where people do indeed work hard for the good of the event, feel a sense of pride in that work ethic and are publicly appreciated for that work ethic.

A lived experience features the people, places, objects, happenings, and other entities that need to be considered as the components of what is the "lived eidetic" as each of our bodies exists within space, time, and relation-ships. Within the conference there were several prominent happenings including opening ceremonies, various receptions, excursions to the surrounding region's tourist sites, a closing banquet, an annual general meeting, the conference sessions, keynote and plenary speakers, activities and a social program for youth delegates.

One youth delegate activity was sailing. The sailing activity had been organized months ahead of time, with the number of kids who needed special seats or partners being discussed, as was the number of boats available, along with the number of support personnel who needed to be present on site. There was one-to-one volunteer support for the delegates, but none of the volunteers had expertise in sailing. The City provided free bus transportation for the delegates and their volunteers, as well as medical support and coordinators for the three buses. Directions to the site were in hand. The weather was perfect. We had mistakenly assumed that the weather was our only uncontrollable contingency, and at the outset, it was cooperating. As one contingency after another presented itself, we realized in hindsight that we had not taken seriously enough the lived experience of body, space, time and relation. The saga unfolds.

The greater than typical numbers of persons using wheelchairs and ambulatory assists meant that boarding the buses took an hour longer than we had planned. Although we had phones, there was no phone contact at the site so we could not inform them of the late arrival. This is an example of non-disabled people underestimating the time it takes for a person with disabilities to access a transportation vehicle. Further, the delegates on the buses were experiencing the hour of waiting in a hot space in close quarters with other bodies, so the lived experience of that hour probably felt much longer and the bodily experience of sweating on vinyl seats with 30 of your close friends was also a less than exhilarating start to the activity.

Finally, the buses departed and air conditioning and the moving vehicles dismissed the previous frustrations. Directions to the site were excellent; getting from the site entrance to the boats was more complicated as there was no signage, no familiar humans; no obvious signs of a sailing activity for young people with disabilities. Thanks to innovative and observant volunteers, we were able to make our way to the dock where three boats and three sailing support personnel awaited 65 children and young people as the weather developed into the hottest day on record.

Results included dehydration leading to seizures and adverse medication reactions in several delegates (unanticipated lived-body responses); numerous non-event people in the general area volunteered their boats, drinking water and a variety of play objects (balls, Frisbees, kites). This was an unanticipated but welcome experience of lived relation. Once again, lived time reared its ugly head as waiting for turns felt endless; however, volunteers maximized the waterfront site, thereby utilizing lived space in an innovative and safety-conscious fashion. The coordinators learned from the earlier lived time bus-loading adventure and began a phased return to the campus once groups of delegates had completed their recreational sailing and tourism experience. As a planning team, we had woefully underestimated lived time and lived bodies and had over-estimated the lived relation preparedness of our sailing program team. Our volunteer and citizen lived space and relation contributions were pleasant surprises.

This one happening within a larger event is a dramatic example of how considering the lived body allowed us to plan, adapt and evaluate our behaviour. However, it did not allow us to turn back the clock and pretend that all was well and that our planning and policies had been adequate to the challenges of our highly (bodily) contingent population.

It must also be said here that even if our group had not been a group of children and young people with disabilities, several significant errors occurred long before the sailing day happened. I challenge you now to revisit these questions posed earlier in light of the event just described.

- What were the intentions?
- What were the assumptions?
- Who or what were the resources?
- What materials were needed?
- What were the relationships that were necessary for it to work?
- Were there any applicable laws and customs?
- What did not work and how did I know?
- What, or how, shall I learn from this?
- What can be done better next time?

Now, add to your reconsideration of these questions one final reflective activity: assume that your overall approach is a contingency-based model with a serious consideration of bodily contingency. Suggest one procedure and one protocol, along with required policies, that might have made a difference for the sailing day. Embracing contingency will allow you to anticipate and respond in ways that make your policies coherent and your events memorable for all the best reasons, including actions that promote dignity and respect.

One challenge in event management is the facilitation of the generation of policy statements that direct personnel in their expected approaches, actions, accountability and the consequences of actions. Overall, the practice of generating policies is used to guide activities within the structure of an event, including those of the multiple staff and volunteers. Another important area for consideration in the development phase of the

54

planning model is social responsibility. Participation in social responsibility can enhance an event and a discussion on this valuable area in event management is provided below.

FACILITATING EVENT VOLUNTEER MANAGEMENT

(by Lorne J. Adams)

Volunteers are as diverse as the society in which we live – rich and poor, employed and unemployed, professionals and labourers, moms and dads, young and old, friends. A volunteer provides their services and talents with no expectation of remuneration in return for their involvement, other than a sense of contributing to the greater good.

> Volunteering is the most fundamental act of citizenship and philanthropy in our society. It is offering time, energy and skills of one's own free will. It is an extension of being a good neighbor, transforming a collection of houses into a community, as people become involved in the improvement of their surroundings and choose to help others. By caring and contributing to change, volunteers decrease suffering and disparity, while they gain skills, self-esteem and change their lives. People work to improve the lives of their neighbors and, in return, enhance their own.
>
> (Volunteer Canada, 2006a)

A volunteer management program

Unless you are involved in an already established program, you may need to be the driving force behind establishing a volunteer program that will benefit both your event and the volunteers. Starting from scratch may seem a little daunting, but just like the rest of the concepts in this text, some careful planning will go a long way to ensuring that everyone's needs are met. Just as you have established values, goals and objectives for your project, the same thought processes will go into the creation of a successful volunteer program.

Why a volunteer management program should be developed
Quirk (2009) asked questions concerning the need for and value of the development of a volunteer management program. In response, I would

say that there should be some direct service value to your organization. In addition, this service value extends to the individual volunteer and the opportunity should be available to serve the larger community and to develop personal skills. It is through volunteering that you may make connections or linkages that would not otherwise be possible, or perhaps you simply have an increased profile locally and/or beyond. The management of the volunteers should not be left to chance, but should be a well-planned and organized program. To begin this program, a code for volunteer management is needed.

A code for volunteer involvement

An organization called Volunteer Canada has published a *Canadian Code for Volunteer Involvement: An Audit Tool* (2006b) that promotes "overarching values, guiding principles and organizational standards applicable to volunteer programs in non-profit and voluntary sector organizations" (p. 2). As such this code promotes:

- values for volunteer involvement (p. 3);
- guiding principles (p. 4);
- organizational standards (pp. 4–5).

Volunteer Canada (2006b) also outlined some national standards for volunteer involvement in this audit tool that provide a sound basis for mounting a volunteer program.

Support for the volunteer management program

A volunteer management program needs to be established with the full support of the organization, including the Board of Directors and the Executive Committee (Quirk, 2009). Obviously, a program cannot be successful if only a small segment of the organization is committed to the enterprise. As Penner (2002) has pointed out, both individuals and organizations harbour a certain amount of neophobia – fear of something new. The amount of stress that change induces is related to the size and impact of the change, the amount of preparation for the change and the level of input from those affected by the change. The introduction of a volunteer program therefore requires that your communication skills are well developed and that you are equipped to be an agent of change. The benefits of your new program will need to be well articulated and should answer questions such as:

56

- What are your short-term goals?
- What are your long-term goals?
- What benefits will the organization accrue from this volunteer management program?
- How much money will be required to support the program?
- What human resources will the program require?
- Where are volunteers needed?
- What specific skills will volunteers need?

As Hager and Brudney (2004a) indicate, "Benefits and challenges are two sides of the same coin" (p. 2). Being fully aware of both will aid you in gaining support from all sectors in the organization.

While they bring much to the table, "volunteers are not free" (Quirk, 2009, p. 2). This means that there is a need for financial and human resource support for the volunteer management program. It will be your job to determine what resources are needed for the program and you will also need to develop those resources. Even if your organization is small, someone is going to have to provide training and supervision to those volunteers. As more volunteers are needed, the level of supervision, reporting and accountability also increases. This may mean that someone will have to be assigned to those responsibilities and, further, you may need to hire someone to assume that responsibility. Either way, event managers must address the fact that there are direct and indirect costs for the volunteers. There may be some training involved for the person who will supervise volunteers. You may wish to send that person to training workshops or conferences. In addition, a volunteer recognition program is not without cost. As the event manager, you will need to account for these costs. You will need to assess whether those costs provide you with the benefits you hope for, and if the funds are not available, fundraising may be necessary.

The volunteer management program structure and processes
Next, you will need to think through how you would like the volunteer management program to function and how each volunteer role fits into the functional processes (Quirk, 2009). The functional processes can be established by asking the questions:

- To whom will the volunteers report?
- How will volunteers report?

Consideration of the benefits of a volunteer management coordinator could be valuable. Hager and Brudney (2004b) looked at the net benefits accrued by an organization in terms of the investment in a paid staff person who assumed volunteer management duties. Their research showed that the lowest level of net benefits was associated with not having a volunteer coordinator. Conversely, they found that net benefits to the organization increased as paid staff members (one-third time, one-third to two-thirds time, two-thirds time and above) devoted more time to volunteer management. They were surprised, however, to find that unpaid managers in the volunteer management role had net benefits just as high as those paid volunteer coordinators who spent a substantial amount of time on volunteer management. While they admitted that this phenomenon needed further study, it appears that in some organizations, an unpaid volunteer can be just as effective as a paid staff member. They hypothesized that unpaid volunteers have what Susan Ellis has called "the luxury of focus" (2010, p. 9). That is, those volunteers were not constrained in their duties by other organizational duties and commitments. They further explain that unpaid coordinators may have a special rapport with their volunteers, which may improve the experience and performance of the volunteer program. Having the right person in the right place appears to provide substantial benefit to an organization.

Volunteer roles
At this point an assessment can be made as to the specific tasks that volunteers will complete. Again, answering a number of questions can aid in the development of this activity, including:

- Are there tasks that could easily be passed off to a volunteer that would free up staff to do other activities?
- How do the volunteers assist us in achieving our mission goals and objectives?
- How many volunteers will be needed?
- How many different types of volunteers are needed and what specialized skills are required? What type of involvement will we be asking of the volunteers?

Hager and Brudney (2004a) have indicated that volunteers have different interests and ways that they can contribute. Their research indicated that organizations derive more benefits if they arrange for volunteers to perform a variety of functions within the organization. They concluded that using volunteers in a variety of assignments was positively related with net benefits, even though the "use [of] volunteers in various assignments incur[s] greater demands on management and greater challenges" (p. 8).

Volunteer recruitment and assignment

The volunteer assignments should fit the specific needs of the organization and the volunteer. In order to get started, one of the things you can do is to make a list of all the different types of volunteers your organization will need and then develop a profile of the individual best suited for that type of job. Think about where you might come in contact with that type of individual and what would be the best way to get in touch with them. Quirk (2009) recommends identifying "recruiters" who can ask their friends and contacts to volunteer. The key way volunteers get involved is from being personally asked (Quirk, 2009). This is a very powerful statement and reaffirms the need to constantly develop and expand your network. The more people you have in the network, the greater the resource pool from which to draw.

Before profiles can be matched, though, it is imperative that for each volunteer assignment, a clear and detailed position description must be created. Volunteers need to know specifically what their duties and responsibilities will be and what skills they need for a particular task. Volunteers should also be provided with a realistic estimate of the amount of time a particular assignment will entail. It is just as unfair to overestimate the level of time commitment as it is to underestimate the level of time commitment. Since volunteers tend to be interested in satisfying their own needs, a realistic statement about what personal benefits might be gained from volunteering should be included. In summary, recruitment messages need to be clear, realistic and outline the expectations for each assignment.

Another consideration in volunteer recruitment is the level of risk associated with each position. The risk can be to either the organization or to the individual volunteer. Obviously, we want to minimize the risk for all concerned, but we probably cannot eliminate it entirely. This may mean that new policy will have to be developed or that differential levels of screening and supervision will be required depending on the assessment of the level of risk. To that end, the Volunteer Canada Code (2006b, p. 20) recommends that "Screening procedures are delivered consistently with no exceptions made for certain individuals or positions."

As part of the recruitment process and in order to attract the best people, a list should be created of where best to post the call for volunteer positions. Some will require the use of broad-based media, while others, depending on the task, may need to be targeted at a very specialized audience.

As part of the recruitment process, as well as an application form, taking the time to develop meaningful interview questions will help the process immensely. Well-thought-out questions will allow you as manager to assess what the volunteer has to offer the organization and whether they match the profile you have developed for the particular position. Also, good interview questions and a well-conducted professional interview allow the potential candidate to assess their own level of fit with the organization and whether or not their individual needs will be met by this particular assignment. They should also know at this stage that screening is an essential process and that the level of screening is concomitant with the level of risk inherent in the position.

Volunteer training

People volunteer because they have an interest in your particular event or cause. It is fair to assume that by doing so they want you to succeed, for your event to be a success or your cause to be recognized. It is also fair to assume that they too want to succeed at whatever assignment they have taken on. As the event manager, you need to provide them with the tools (resources) and the training required for them and you to succeed. Once the interview and hiring process is complete, the volunteer needs to know about the mission, goals and objectives of the organization. That is, they need to understand where the organization is going and how it is going to get there. Understanding the *core values* and being given an opportunity to discuss them formally or informally increases commitment and motivation. Informed people are cooperative people and they may in fact become "advocates" for the organization, increasing your recruitment pool, your recognition in the community or your reputation.

A *policy and procedure manual* should be provided for each volunteer, or a copy should be made available via the website. Further, volunteers should be given an opportunity to review the manual and there needs to be a mechanism for questions and feedback. In particular, the policies and procedure specific to their assignment should be highlighted.

Additionally, if the event is involved in social responsibility, this needs to be incorporated within the volunteer training activities. It is imperative that all of the volunteers involved in the event are part of instituting the social responsibility activities in order to contribute to success

60

in the program. This topic will be addressed in full in the next main section of the chapter.

Given the type of assignment and level of risk, volunteers should be given adequate training for performing their duties. For some jobs, that can be as simple as an orientation meeting, along with a small fact sheet referencing specific tasks. These procedural guidelines are relatively simple and should be easy to follow. Other jobs, with elevated risk, may require specialized or even intensive training. This may mean that they are assigned a paid staff member as mentor or that they need to attend special training sessions. The goal is to be able to complete their assignment without putting themselves or others at risk.

Volunteers should also be made aware of where their job begins and where their responsibilities end. This is not to curtail the enthusiasm of the individual, but understanding the specific boundaries of a task prevents "job creep," communication problems and potential conflict. Going outside the intended boundaries may also increase the risk to the individual, others and the organization. Ongoing supervision and regular performance evaluation should, however, ameliorate the problem. This should also give the volunteer an opportunity to provide feedback and input for the organization. The popularity of reality TV shows like *Undercover Boss* have consistently pointed to the need for an opportunity to connect to the people "on the ground" doing the work and acting as the face and indeed spokesperson for the company. Training, supervision and feedback are big elements of satisfaction.

While it is unpleasant and not a desired outcome, there will be situations that require either a reprimand or in some cases outright dismissal. It is imperative that there is a well-delineated policy and procedure in place that clearly outlines what the grounds for dismissal are and how it will be enacted. These rules and regulations cannot be made up as they are needed, but must be predetermined. Each volunteer should be made aware of this at the time they are informed of the mission and goals, etc. Should the situation arise, it is imperative that the protocol is invoked and that the dignity of the individual is respected.

Volunteer retention and autonomy
I am not sure who said it, but some sports figure once said, "It is hard to excel at things you don't enjoy!" This quote is particularly germane to the notion of volunteer retention. How long do you persist at activities you don't enjoy? Given the wide array of activities available to provide us

with enjoyment, we simply quit the activity in favour of something else. Volunteer retention programs need to nurture environments that are conducive to keeping volunteers.

Organizations need to develop a culture that is both welcoming and respectful. As indicated above, many organizations could not get by without volunteers. To treat them as valuable contributing members of the team is to create a symbiotic relationship that allows everyone to flourish. This relationship can be created by simply "managing," or by walking around observing and speaking with people. Your presence, even occasionally, gives status to the work being performed and provides a sense that you are invested in it and you care. Opportunities to provide feedback both formally and informally provide a sense of being heard and valued. Input from volunteers can be incorporated into planning and evaluation. If volunteers are considered to be equal and contributing members of the team, the likelihood of retaining them is enhanced. Similarly, staff members who work frequently and effectively with volunteers should also be recognized for their commitment to creating a positive culture for the organization.

There are many things that might attract a volunteer's attention once they have selected your organization. We want to be able to keep them, particularly if there is a large investment of time, money and training. As Hager and Brudney (2004b) have indicated, to enhance retention, organizations should focus on "enriching the volunteer experience" by "recognizing volunteers, providing training and professional development, screening them and matching them to organizational tasks" (p. 1). Hager and Brudney go on to say that volunteers have been widely used to meet organizational needs for services and administration.

> Most charities could not get by without their volunteers . . . Turnover of volunteers can disrupt the operation of the charity, threaten the ability to serve clients and signal that the volunteer experience is not as rewarding as it might be.
>
> (Hager & Brudney, 2004b, p. 12)

Volunteer recognition

As we have indicated earlier, volunteers provide their skills, expertise and time with no expectation of monetary return. This does not, however, mean that we can abdicate our responsibility to acknowledge and recognize the significant contribution they make. As an event manager, you have an obligation to acknowledge publicly and formally the contribution of volunteers. This can be achieved in a number of ways, such as printed materials, in personal letters, in mass media, when speaking publicly about the event and when talking to volunteers in person.

Formal methods of recognition such as dinners, receptions, certificates, reference letters or letters of commendation need to be provided both consistently and in a timely fashion.

Informal methods of recognition also need to be delivered in a timely and appropriate manner. Something as simple as an article of clothing that links the volunteer to the organization and the event goes a long way to creating a culture that increases the likelihood of that person volunteering again.

A trained, motivated volunteer base that you can count on is an invaluable resource for an event manager. Like most other concepts in this text, that type of resource does not just happen. It takes pre-planning and attention to detail. It also calls upon your skills as a manager of people to ensure that volunteers feel they have made a worthwhile contribution and that their involvement is valued and acknowledged.

Additionally, event managers are now being tasked with facilitating social responsibility. An overview of this responsibility is the subject of the following section.

FACILITATING EVENT SOCIAL RESPONSIBILITY

(by Cheri Bradish)

> Being a responsible corporate citizen in today's sports marketplace means being a vigilant steward of the emotional and financial investment made by individuals, companies and community groups into your sports organization. It is recognizing, valuing and nurturing the partnership that is fundamental to that investment.
> (VP, Maple Leaf Sport and Entertainment, 2005)

Broadly defined and interpreted, *social responsibility* (SR), or corporate social responsibility, is regarded as an all-encompassing commitment of an organization to sustained community well-being both in theory and practice. More generally, SR can also be interpreted as an organization's commitment to behave ethically. As broadly interpreted, SR has come to be known and associated with a number of "giving back" concepts and practices, which provides for sport, recreation, tourism and event managers a number of different possibilities for demonstrating a commitment to community well-being. At its core, a *true dedication to SR MUST exist to make the commitment relevant and authentic*. Managers can adopt a number of related strategies under the greater SR umbrella. Doing so will facilitate sound and ethical business practice, which includes the principles of corporate reputation, cause-related marketing, strategic philanthropy, community relations and even sport for development.

Strategic philanthropy is understood simply as strategic giving, most commonly in the form of financial support. An organization adopts a cause (or causes) to support, which is in line with their mission and objectives, and supports that cause financially throughout the year.

Community relations also represent an effective outlet for SR practice. Here, through community outreach programs, a sport, recreation or tourism organization can develop stronger relationships with the community. The opportunity then exists to highlight the positive actions of both the company doing the supporting and the community services receiving the benefit. Community relations, media relations and public relations can all work together to develop and execute sound SR programs.

Sport for development is a concept whereby organizations understand and interpret sport and recreation as a vehicle for development– be it economic and/or community – and even, as is indicated in the International Olympic code of conduct, for peace for all nations. Partnerships with Sport for Development organizations, such as Right To Play (Figure 4.1) add a global element and a more international focus to an organization's overall SR commitment.

As an event manager, understanding SR gives you an advantage in terms of enhancing whatever event you may be organizing. Being aware of companies that have a well-developed SR plan is another tool you can add to your toolbox. Matching the right company to the event is your challenge, but once a match has been found, everyone, including you, stands to benefit.

On one level, if the company has been matched with the event, you may have access to resources, including human, technical, financial and materials, that you might not otherwise have. On another level, the prestige or visibility of your event may be enhanced by being linked to a company that is highly respected. On yet another level, there may be a "trickle down"

64

The organization Right To Play uses specially designed sport and play programs to improve health, build life skills and foster peace for children and communities affected by war, poverty and disease. Working in both the humanitarian and development contexts, Right To Play has projects in more than 20 countries in Africa, Asia and the Middle East.

Right To Play is a global-scale implementer of Sport for Development and Peace programs and takes an active role in driving research and policy development in this area and in supporting children's rights.

Right To Play focuses on four strategic program areas: Basic Education and Child Development; Health Promotion and Disease Prevention; Conflict Resolution and Peace Education; and Community Development and Participation.

Working with partners, funders and the local communities, Right To Play tailors every program to meet identified needs. Each program has specific goals, impacts and outputs. To build each program, it draws upon specially designed sport and play-based resources, as well as the expertise of program development, research, monitoring and evaluation, policy and country office teams.

The principles of the Convention on the Rights of the Child underpin Right To Play, and they ensure that its programs benefit the most marginalized children, including girls, street children, former child combatants, refugees and children affected by HIV and AIDS.

Right To Play's Team of Athlete Ambassadors is supported by an international team of top athletes from over 40 countries. These athletes inspire children, are role models for healthy lifestyle choices and help to raise awareness and funding for Right To Play projects. Led by four-time Olympic gold medalist and Right To Play president and CEO Johann Olav Koss, Athlete Ambassadors include Wayne Gretzky, Martina Hingis, Dikembe Mutombo, Haile Gebrselassie, Michael Essien, Frank Lampard, Anja Pärson, Chelsea Football Club and many more.

The global reach of Right To Play is extensive as it works in Azerbaijan, Benin, Chad, China, Ethiopia, Ghana, Indonesia, Jordan, Lebanon, Liberia, Mali, Mozambique, Pakistan, the Palestinian Territories, Rwanda, Sierra Leone, Sri Lanka, Sudan, Tanzania, Thailand, Uganda, the United Arab Emirates and Zambia.

For further information on Right To Play see: www.righttoplay.com/Pages/default. aspx

Figure 4.1 Right To Play

effect where some will say, "If X company is involved, then we should be involved as well."

The notion of giving back to the community creates a symbiotic relationship. The event gains support and recognition from the community, and the community stands to gain both tangibly (for example, economic infusion) and intangibly (such as reputation as a tourist destination).

Events that have a well-defined SR plan, and a commitment to the plan, can increase market share, strengthen their brand position, improve the corporate image and enhance employee morale. It may also lead to increased attraction from stakeholders.

While it has been recommended that you be aware of companies that have a well-developed SR plan, it would also behoove you to promote SR to targeted partners or stakeholders. By doing so, you can enhance the reputation and success of the event and create a win-win situation for the event and community.

CHAPTER QUESTIONS

1 What are the three equally important elements in event policy congruence? Also, how can these elements be accomplished in event management?
2 Discuss the impact of volunteers in the field of event management and the need to properly service the volunteers.
3 Describe practices within a volunteer life cycle.
4 Describe a minimum of three strategies outlined in this chapter that are used to reveal areas that require the generation of policy statements that direct personnel involved in an event.
5 What is social responsibility (SR)?
6 How can SR be instituted within events, and what value do you place on SR?

66

CHAPTER 5

THE EVENT PLANNING MODEL

THE EVENT OPERATIONAL PLANNING PHASE

CHERYL MALLEN

The second phase in the event planning model, the event operational planning phase, encompasses the creation of the written operational plans for the variety of event components. These plans include the guiding instructions for hosting the event. Examples of event components include: accommodation, accreditation, ceremonies, communications, drug testing or doping control, food and beverage services, hospitality services, media management, officials' management, participant management, volunteer management, results and awards, spectator services and transportation. This chapter details a number of mechanisms that contribute to operational planning success. These mechanisms comprise the cultivation of the operational planning network; the creation of logical, sequential, detailed and integrated plans; the inclusion of contingency plans; and the activation of a plan refining process. Finally, this chapter outlines key issues in operational planning and provides practice scenarios.

MECHANISM 1: THE CULTIVATION OF THE OPERATIONAL PLANNING NETWORK

To begin the operational planning process, an event manager must facilitate the formation of an operational planning network. The creation and utilization of this network requires an event manager to have the skills and sensibilities to facilitate the assignment of the best possible people, along with the correct number and combination of individuals with planning expertise to meet the operational planning requirements for the event. There is no single formula for assigning the network of individuals correctly; each situation is unique. However, if individuals are assigned incorrectly, problems that influence the efficiency and effectiveness of the plan may arise. The task of creating operational plans for each component requires an intricate combination of talented planners who can develop the operational plans for their own component as well as coordinate and cooperate with other event component personnel.

A simple exercise will demonstrate the complexity of assigning individuals to tasks. Consider subdividing the members of your class to complete a number of components of a plan that could be for a traditional or niche event. How would you subdivide the class? What elements would you consider in subdividing the group? There are many ways to assign network members including: dividing individuals into groups that have similar expertise; creating groups that offer a wide variety of expertise which could broaden the knowledge base; or creating groups that are devised based on whether they work well together. Individuals could be placed in groups based on their personal interest in the component. There is not one particular way to subdivide the group that can be applied to every situation. It is important for an event manager to develop an understanding of and sensitivity to the elements of assigning individual members of the network based on the particular context.

Individuals assigned to each event operational planning component make up a node. A node may be further subdivided into constituent nodes. For example, those planning the accommodation component can be subdivided into constituent nodes whereby each is responsible for the accommodation plans of a separate part, such as those for the event participants, another for the officials and a third node that manages the accommodation for the organizing committee members. Linkages between constituent nodes foster the interactions required to complete the overall accommodation planning tasks.

The linkages between nodes (including linkages within a component and between components) create a network of multilateral intra-organizational alliances. These linkages determine how members interact to establish plans, manage planning decisions and manage issues or problems. Each linkage is part of the structural design, creating a network alliance that can be unique in its application.

The design of the network alliance is crucial to the effectiveness in the development of successful operational plans. There are many influences that impact the design of a network alliance. To give examples of some of these influences, the characteristics found within contingency theory, complexity theory and agency theory can be applied to a network design.

Application of contingency theory and dissipative structures

Contingency theory indicates that there is no single correct way to structure the alliance linkages between the planning nodes. This is because, as contingency theory states, the search for one correct structure is simply not available in the world, as one system of organization cannot be found that "is superior to all others in all cases" (Owen, 2001, p. 399). The structure of each operational planning alliance must be efficiently designed for the specific needs of each event.

Dissipative structures are a characteristic of contingency theory. Dissipative structures imply that a structure can be reproduced or repeated if it is in a steady state (in equilibrium); however, achieving this steady state is difficult because structures tend to be continuously pulled apart and then recombined again. When recombined, the structure or elements may not be exactly the same. This means that an event manager must be open to change, and able to adapt for it. An event is, thus, expected to be capaable of being repeated at another time, even in the same venue, but the event manager must expect that it will not be repeated in exactly the same way. The event manager must respond to dissipative structures and the associated change. This means that previously designed event operational plans cannot be applied directly to a future event and that plans must be adapted to the particular environment, participants, sponsors, etc.

An application of the characteristics of contingency theory and dissipative structures during the event operational phase implies that an operational network design that worked for a previous event may not work for any other event. So, what guides the design of each network in the operational planning phase?

Wijngaard, deVries and Nauta (2006) hold that it is the authority and responsibility assigned with the tasks that determine a configuration or structure. This structure establishes expected behaviours of the event operational network members and the event planners that guide the network design. This means that an event manager needs to be sensitive to the event context in order to effectively configure the multilateral positions, the role of the members, the power, approvals, subdivisions and overall autonomy required for event operational planning. Further, an event manager must be open to changes due to the presence of dissipative structures. A combination of organic structures – whereby members have the authority to make decisions concerning their component – as well as hierarchical structures may be needed to suit a particular complex event environment. There is no single predetermined structural design that has been deemed best for operational planning for the event components. An event manager needs to be open to different intra-organizational network designs that may be needed for the various event components. Whatever structure is designed for an event, an event manager must monitor its applicability to the event activities and facilitate adaptations if needed.

Application of complexity theory

Complexity theory is also applicable in the event operational planning phase. Complexity theory indicates that a basic condition of our contemporary environment is that it is in a pivotal state (Doherty & Delener, 2001). This means that the environmental conditions include levels of "uncertainty, diversity and instability" (Stacey, 1996, p. 349). A stable state in the environment is not achievable because the "world is primarily made of dissipative structures" (Keirsey, n. d., para. 9). Dissipative structures involve a constant evolving of structures as they are being pulled apart and refitted by several forces, and this means one cannot be expected to be in a state of "equilibrium" (Keirsey, n. d., para. 9). Complexity in the environment means we cannot expect to work in an environment devoid of change.

An application of the characteristics of complexity theory indicates that an event manager must efficiently design the operational network alliance to be adaptable for conditions of change. An understanding that change is expected implies that once the network alliance is designed and instituted, the work of the designer is not finished. The network must be managed to cope with new or changing conditions.

A state of equilibrium cannot be expected within the event operational network. Change may involve the movement of network members within the nodes, the replacement of some members or the reconfiguration of how the nodes interact. Multilateral intra-organizational network alliances are made over time, and adaptations must also be made continuously to ensure that the design meets the flexibility demands for developing flexible operational plans to stage an event. This requirement can be a constant and time-consuming task for an event manager.

Application of agency theory

Agency theory pertains to two key issues that are applicable to the operational planning phase. Both issues deal with ensuring the cooperation of planning efforts. The first issue involves times when "the desires or goals of the principal and agent conflict [as] . . . it is difficult or expensive for the principal to verify what the agent is actually doing" (Eisenhardt, 1989, p. 5). An application of this issue means that the operational planning network needs to:

1 ensure that all parties understand their expected behaviour while in the operational planning phase;
2 encourage the group to work toward the collective goals and objectives;
3 work toward efficient group progress;
4 ensure excellent communication among the network members concerning the operational planning progress.

If excellent communication is not facilitated between network members, it can result in difficulty in understanding or verifying the progress being made by the multiple members in the network who are completing the operational planning. The second issue in agency theory involves "risk sharing that arises when the principal and agent have different attitudes toward risk" (Eisenhardt, 1989, p. 58). An application of this issue means that the network members must manage operating planning risk elements, such as the timing of the completion of operational plans, and be concerned with the impact of critical time periods.

MECHANISM 2: GENERATING WRITTEN OPERATIONAL PLANS

The event operational network members are assigned the task of generating the written operational plans that constitute guiding instructions for staging each component within an event. This task compels the members of the operational network to produce the directions for the delivery of the event (Wijngaard et al., 2006). These written operational plans establish the goals and directions for managing all functions for staging the event.

Generally, multiple operational plans are created in tandem. All members of an operational network within each node are required to have the expertise needed to meet the scope of responsibility for the planning function. This scope includes designing the written format for the operational plan and creating logical, sequential, detailed and integrated plans.

The written event operational plan: establishing a design format

To begin the task of recording the step-by-step instructions for the operational plan, a format is needed to achieve consistency and control (Wijngaard et al., 2006). This format guides how all written operational plans are to be laid out. Multiple formats have been used for sport, recreation and tourism events. There is no one correct format that can be used. The general rule for selecting a format is to ensure that all requirements of the plan can be expressed. These requirements can include a number of items such as:

- an executive summary;
- the timing of each planned activity;
- a detailed list of planned tasks;
- the authority for each planned element;
- event diagrams illustrating activity sites and the placement of key event items.

Any format selected must take into account the complexity and fluidity of event operational planning along with the requirements of what must be recorded within a specific plan to ensure that the elements are communicated in an easy-to-use manner. See examples of design formats in the operational plans provided in the Appendices.

Logical operational planning

During the creation of the written operational plans for the event, all members of the operational planning network must learn to determine and record the individual activities or tasks necessary to complete their particular component. *Operational planning includes the deliberate creation of suppositions, assumptions and conclusions for the development of a coherent and logical step-by-step written list of reasoned event activities*

72

to stage a successful event. The activity requires a "thinking through" process that is not a simple activity. This is because a concentration on each element within the component and the delineation of each logical step and the recording of the steps is a complex and time-consuming task. Goals can be established to guide members as they "think through" the logistical requirements.

Why a list to follow for operational planning is not provided
Many events that have previously been held have information that can be reviewed such as lists or outlines of event activities. This reference information may provide guidance for developing logical operational plans for an event. However, the reference information is contextually specific and does not take into consideration the unique nuances that may exist within other events. The information is tied to the structure of the operational network, the components and detailed actions that were designed for that event. Reference information is valuable only for gaining common knowledge about an event. The reference material does not replace an event manager's responsibility for thinking through each activity and developing advanced knowledge for the specific facility and activities of the current event. There are no shortcuts to the thinking through process for excellent – event-specific – operational plans.

Sequential operational planning

Each operational plan needs to itemize the event tasks in an ordered and reasoned sequence. The most common method used to achieve this end involves using the concept of time. For example, an operational plan can be subdivided to record all of the tasks that must be completed three, six or twelve months prior to an event, as well as the activities during the week prior to the event and a minute-by-minute list of tasks for each day of the event. As a parallel activity, separate sequential plans can be created to outline the specific items needed from the venue (such as rod and drape, tables, chairs), including the time and site at which they are required.

To help in the development of sequential operational plans, the concept of *weaving* is used. Weaving involves conceptually thinking through all of the requirements for each specific element of an event one at a time. For example, a network member can conceive and record the tasks necessary to complete the media management operational plans by conceptually weaving the potential requirements of one media member from the moment of arrival at the event parking lot until they depart. This weaving process is followed repeatedly to develop the multiple logical and sequential steps that must be recorded in the operational plan. A planner can *weave forwards* or *weave backwards*.

Weaving forwards involves recording elements as they will happen, in a progressive, unfolding process. In contrast, weaving backwards requires conceptually thinking of the end product and then backtracking to determine the step-by-step activities that were completed.

It does not matter if a planner conceptually thinks through the planning requirements by weaving forwards or backwards. The aim is to develop a process that assists in determining the sequential steps to stage the event.

Detailed operational planning

The amount of detail required in an operational plan differs from event to event and can be a difficult decision for an event manager. The plans need to be written in a clear format to ensure that other members in the network can read, understand and be guided to complete the tasks as outlined. The plan must provide clarity, limit emerging questions and reduce the potential for improper interpretations concerning the actions needed to produce the event. A detailed account of each task is necessary, but the difficulty lies in determining the appropriate threshold for detail. How much detail is required?

There are three threshold levels of detail in operational planning. Each level requires a different amount of detail in the written record concerning each event task. The three levels are referred to as level 1, level 2 and level 3 planning. The higher the threshold level, the greater the detail provided within the operational plan.

Level 1 planning provides the lowest level of planning detail. A level 1 plan exhibits a minimal level of detail to explain each task. Level 1 planning is open to questions concerning the clarity of the event tasks and does not provide a detailed step-by-step list of directions to avoid misinterpretations should others enact the plan. Consequently, level 1 planning is open to interpretations of those completing the implementation of the plans, and these interpretations may alter the planned activities.

74

Level 2 planning requires a higher or medium amount of planning detail. This level of planning provides general clarity and offers more detailed step-by-step directions to enact the plan. Level 2 planning answers the majority of questions one would have if implementing the plan. However, the plan is still open to some interpretations that may alter the planned activities.

Level 3 planning demands the highest level of detail. The level 3 plan provides clear instructions and includes the intimate requirements to complete the tasks. Level 3 planning is open to a limited number of questions and potential plan deviations, as minute details for the completion of each task have been provided.

An event manager must facilitate an understanding of the sensitivities of the detail required for a particular event. There is a subtle difference between providing instructions and offering too much detail to the point where the network members do not read the plans. For example, select a familiar task and consider at which point you could be given too much detailed instruction that would inhibit your ability to complete the task.

Next, integrating the multiple plans for the various event components is necessary.

Integrated operational planning

The development of each component operational plan begins as a separate entity, but a key to successful event management is the integration of the multiple detailed plans. Integration, interlacing or intertwining event elements creates multiple coherent, cohesive and smoothly flowing plans for the overall event.

An example of integration for an accommodation plan is the interlacing of elements from the transportation plan within the accommodation plan. This integration can help to coordinate elements such as the transportation drop-off and pick-up sites at the accommodation venue. The integration can also ensure that transportation coincides with the accommodation check-in time arrangements. Integrating elements from the accreditation plan can also assist in the distribution of accreditation and room assignments all in one coordinated effort.

A successful integration process relies upon a key operational factor. This factor is the *establishment of integration exchange opportunities* for the operational network members. The integration process must be designed to provide an adequate number of exchange opportunities on a regular basis, and must be adaptable to allow intermittent integration exchanges to meet the integration workflow requirements. Generally, there is a large amount of planning detail and the integration process is complex (Matusik, 2002). An event manager facilitates an integration process and ensures that multiple exchange opportunities are arranged, if required. Common strategies for integration can include messages, bulletins, announcements, charts, drawings, diagrams, sketches, maps and reports. A particularly crucial strategy for integration is to set up production meetings between the members from different components. These meetings provide opportunities to discuss and coordinate items that are important to more than one component. *Network theory* indicates that operational network members can exchange planning data without the use of a hierarchy. The success of an event is, however, contingent upon the extent to which the event manager can facilitate the transfer of operational data across the planning nodes. The flow of the operational planning knowledge is contingent on the structure and strategies established to disseminate the transfer.

Other mechanisms that aid the development of excellent event operational plans involve establishing meeting agendas and the inclusion of contingency operational plans. The meeting agendas and contingency operational plans can be developed simultaneously with the event operational plans.

MECHANISM 3: ESTABLISHING MEETING AGENDAS

The operational planning activities generally indicate the need to establish meetings with the multiple groups involved in the event. These meetings may involve, for example, meeting with personnel from the venue, the media outlet, and/or the accommodation site. The event manager must think through the requirements for each meeting and devise an agenda to guide the meeting.

An agenda for a meeting between the event manager and the venue personnel can include items that are diverse and include areas such as:

- date, time and site of meeting;
- those to be in attendance at the meeting;
- welcome and introductions;
- confirmation of date booked and venue rooms/areas to be utilized;

- confirmation of parking requirements for event staff, special guests and the associated costs;
- venue access for move-in activities, including the specific gate/doors and times they will be open; security available during move-in activities; the move-out timeframe;
- venue services, such as the availability and cost of an electrician, the electrical service available, the need for electrical extension cords; the ushers, food services, event marketing assistance and use of tables, chairs and red carpets;
- financial requirements, including deposits and the final payment timeframe.

Now, identify five items that should be added to this venue meeting agenda. Also, create a list of additional event staff members who should be at this meeting and what they could discuss at the meeting.

A meeting agenda with the event manager and the contracted media outlet (i.e. television station producer) can also span across a number of items such as:

- event overview (including the details to be provided to the media outlet prior to the event, such as the event activities and their time-frame, who will be involved in the opening ceremonies, and background information on key event participants);
- media truck arrival/departure times, along with the parking space required;
- food and beverage requirements for media staff (including site, times, menu items and who is responsible for paying for this service);
- media electrical requirements and who is responsible for paying for these services (the event or the media outlet);
- seats that need to be removed from being for sale due to camera positions/platforms;
- specifics about what will be televised (i.e. the anthem singer, awards ceremonies, intermission activities);
- sponsors and their contracted media requirements;
- access or accreditation requirements.

Think through the requirements and add five agenda items to this list along with an overview of event staff who should also attend this meeting.

A final example involves an agenda for a meeting between the event manager, the event accommodation manager and the accommodation personnel that includes items such as:

- the number of rooms booked and the date/time that a final count must be provided;
- the number of people per room;
- who will be paying for the rooms and the payment timeframe;
- who is responsible for paying for services such as the mini-bar, movies and room service;
- signage;
- parking availability and cost;
- hospitality rooms.

Again think through the requirements and add five agenda items to this list.

MECHANISM 4: THE INCLUSION OF CONTINGENCY PLANS

To enhance planning preparedness, contingency plans involve two key elements. The first is to conceive potential deviations from the operational plan that could occur. The second is to predetermine action steps to reduce the chance of the deviation; or should it occur, to manage each deviation. The outcome of contingency planning is a back-up plan. Contingency planning can help to develop a greater level of preparation for any event. However, contingency planning cannot ensure that all deviations will be foreseen. There will usually be unexpected deviations from the operational plans due to the complex nature of events. The more contingency situations predicted and planned for, the more time the operational planning members provide to the network members to manage deviations that were not predetermined.

Before moving forward, it is important to take a minute to consider how *contingency theory* relates to or is different from contingency planning. As previously noted, contingency theory tells an event manager that there is no single organizational structure that is considered superior; and the associated dissipative structures reveal that whatever structure is chosen, the elements are constantly being changed, pulled apart and reconfigured – ranging from slightly to significantly changed. Consequently, the concept of contingency planning is related to contingency theory as it is framed with an understanding of the pressure for structural change. This means

78

that operational plans cannot be designed and then be expected to remain in a state of equilibrium without change; instead, the event manager must design their event plans anticipating that change will occur with respect to the structure, that plans will need some level of structural adaptation to manage the change, and that they must monitor and manage change throughout the process. Contingency planning differs from contingency theory as the planning focuses on organizing steps based on a possibility occurring, while the theory outlines the characteristics that produce structural contingencies.

Generally, to begin contingency planning, a contingency meeting is held. The objective of a contingency meeting is to host an open forum for operational network members to express their ideas concerning potential deviations from the plan that could occur. Each event component or sub-component hosts a contingency meeting to discuss the potential plan deviations for that specific component. Examples of contingency issues include concerns about equipment malfunction, what to do should a hot water pipe unexpectedly burst or a protest about a social issue be staged at the venue on the day of your event.

Facilitating a contingency meeting requires an event manager to keep members on the task of determining deviation ideas and to prepare a written record of these ideas (and not moving into how to manage each deviation). Contingency meetings allow members to be creative about what could potentially go wrong at an event. It is important to facilitate the meeting to allow the ideas to flow and hold the assessment of practicality concerning a potential deviation until the next step of contingency planning.

After a contingency meeting, the operational network members develop action steps for coping with each deviation should it occur. Contingency action steps are created in the weeks and months after the initial contingency planning meetings have been completed. Each contingency issue can be integrated within the operational plan or can be added as a supplementary or contingency operational plan. An important next step in contingency planning, thus, is determining which contingency will be mitigated prior to the event (and how this will be completed); and which contingency situation will be planned for but not instituted unless necessary.

A key component in contingency planning involves ensuring that the design of the communication system is excellent. What does an excellent communication system involve? It involves thinking through elements such as:

- the communication equipment, including cellular phones, landlines (hardwired phones) and walkie talkies;
- the recording and distribution of cellular phone numbers to the appropriate people;
- the recording and distribution of landline phone numbers;
- finding a suitable place to provide the phone numbers: a common place is on the back of the accreditation pass for managers and others who require the numbers (if there is a plastic sleeve used for accreditation, the list of phone numbers can simply be slipped into the back of the sleeve);
- obtaining walkie talkies, making sure that the batteries are charged and a headset and extra battery are given to the user, organizing a sign-in and sign-out sheet (as they can go missing);
- testing the communication system to determine the people who can easily converse, ensuring access by key individuals to those making decisions concerning plan adaptations and to medical, security and emergency personnel – this is critical;
- putting in place a backup communication system (i.e. bullhorns – considering how many are needed and where they can be placed);
- providing training for utilizing the communication system – for instance, which groups will utilize which channel on the walkie talkie? What are the communication protocols (i.e. what if someone is conducting personal chatter and no one else can contact the individual when needed?);
- recognizing that each communication system is unique and that the equipment, system and protocols must be designed for the particular event.

A critical element in contingency planning involves emergency planning.

MECHANISM 5: EVENT EMERGENCY PLANNING

Every event manager should know how many minutes it will take to clear a section of the venue, as well as the full venue, in the event of an emergency. Additionally, they should know how to make this evacuation happen quickly and have pre-established sites where the participants are

80

to go once evacuated. It is important that the communication system for informing participants in the event of an emergency and the instructions for an evacuation are pre-established. This includes pre-set visuals and signage, verbal statements and the establishment of an excellent communication system, as well as a backup communication system. As event manager, therefore, you should work directly with the facility manager to adopt the specific emergency procedures that have been established and practised by the facility staff. The facility's emergency policies and procedures should be integrated within the event operational plan, and importantly, all staff and volunteers should be trained in these procedures. This process, however, may not be applicable for a niche event that does not utilize a traditional venue. This niche situation means the event manager may be positioned to be uniquely responsible for the facility manager's role in developing the emergency policies and procedures. Knowledge in this vital role is crucial. It is recommended that event managers in this position advance their common and advancement knowledge in facility emergency management by reading pre-established policies and procedures; by talking with facility managers and by developing relationships with the right people. These relationships extend from police and fire services to medical and emergency personnel. Always utilize the professionals in emergency management to review your operational plans for emergencies and consider their advice.

MECHANISM 6: PLANNING FOR EVENT POLITICS OR THE "GAME-WITHIN-THE-GAME"

Events can be rife with politics among organizers, sponsors, participants and others. This can be referred to as the "game-within-the-game" (GwG). This is where those involved utilize their particular role in the conduct of the event for their own purposes, to promote themselves or their special interest. Who plays these games? Those playing the political game can be found anywhere in an event, and cannot only be a distraction from the business of planning and running the event, but also have the potential to detract from or even sabotage the success of the event. Every event is different and the GwGs can be unique to the event activities and individuals associated with the event. Consequently, the event management team must expect the GwG to occur and be prepared to identify situations where it can or has occurred and develop mitigating strategies for managing it should it arise.

Sometimes the GwG can benefit the organizers. For instance, an individual may be thrilled to be part of the organization committee of an event in order to advance their personal skills and résumé. This could provide additional motivation for this person to work hard and be very committed to their assignments which would be beneficial to the event. Or, conversely, this individual may only sign up to work at the event with the intention of putting it on their résumé without much interest in completing their tasks – they show up, but end up being detrimental to the overall effort, and this usually results in someone else having to take on their tasks as well as their own which stretches the available resources in a negative manner. Something as trivial as a volunteer being assigned a walkie talkie may prompt that individual to refuse to complete their tasks because others have been assigned this communication equipment. This may make them feel that they are not as valued by the event staff.

Therefore, the role of an event manager must include seriously considering potential GwG scenarios for their particular event and alerting the management team to also consider the potential of such activities for their component. Further, the event manager must ensure that there are operational plans to mitigate and manage such activity. This is necessary as GwGs can be a distraction, can interrupt planned event activities, and can monopolize the media attention that focuses on the event.

MECHANISM 7: THE ACTIVATION OF PRODUCTION MEETINGS TO REFINE AND COMMUNICATE THE PLANNED ACTIVITIES

Once a logical, sequential, detailed, integrated operational plan is developed along with the contingency plans and emergency plans, they must be refined for use. One method to achieve that goal involves hosting a meeting with key representatives from each component and facilitating a production meeting for refining the plans. In this meeting, the representatives review the integrated plans and refine the details into a coordinated and efficient effort.

The refining process is intended to add detail to the plan and eliminate any questions that may arise when the plan is implemented. An example of a refining process was illustrated by the 2002 Salt Lake Olympics Organizing Committee (SLOC). This committee instituted a peer review process as a refining technique along with what they called an "Executive Roadmap" (Bowen, 2006). The peer review process included an exchange

82

of operational plans for consideration by others within the event operational network. Reviewers searched for gaps in the detail provided in the operational plan, ensured clarity in the planning statements and determined any questions arising when reading the operational plans. The roadmap consisted of an executive summary of the key timelines that needed to be met and was used for quick reference. Skilled event planners completed the refining process to meet the goal of planning excellence.

PRACTICE TO ADVANCE YOUR OPERATIONAL SKILL DEVELOPMENT

To aid in your skill development, at the end of this text, in the Appendices section, there are examples of operational plans for you to review. Review these documents to learn more about the details necessary in an event operational plan, and consider any questions that arise if you were responsible for implementing the planning actions.

Practise operational planning

The best way to develop operational planning skills is to understand the planning process and to practise operational planning. See Figure 5.1 and complete an operational plan following the instructions. Further, see Appendix B for examples of operational plans. But remember, your operational plans must be adapted for your particular event and the uniqueness of your venue, event structure, activities and resources, including human, financial and technological resources.

Complete the following practice assignment using the following process:

1 Select an event (you will be completing operational plans for a media conference for this event).
2 Read the assignment scenario below and then develop two or three planning objectives for the media conference.
3 Think through the requirements and generate an operational plan for the media conference (see the guiding framework provided below).
4 Develop contingency plans (for a minimum of five event contingency issues) and place these at the end of the operational plan.
5 Record the process to be used to refine the operational plan.

▼

The assignment scenario

You are responsible for managing the media conference for a major tourism event (event of your choice). This media conference is to be held mid-morning, one day prior to the launch of the event and is to be held at a major hotel in the down-town area of your city or town. Create a written operational plan for managing the key elements to complete the media conference. Be sure to include the invitations for four key media outlets to attend, including one media outlet from each of the following: newspaper, radio, television and web-based media. Further, the operational details must include setting up the media conference room or area in the hotel, managing the media as they arrive, checking credentials, providing accreditation, the provision of the media conference activities and a media question period. Remember the operational plan must include all communication requirements (for example, communicating to the venue staff the requirements for tables, chairs, microphones, platforms, rod and drape, the hanging of signage and security). Build into the plan the speakers representing the event along with the media opportunities such as personal interviews and photo opportunities. Assume you have the funding to support all of your activities. *The chart below is only a starting point.* Expand the operational planning details as you think through the requirements.

Planning Objectives:
Objective 1:
Objective 2:

DATE	ITEM	WHO IS RESPONSIBLE?
Eight months prior to event	***Media personnel preparations:*** What will be in place for: – Media policies, procedures and processes (consider television, radio, print, social and online media) – Media accommodation preparations – Provision of media shuttles – Provision of media accreditation – Media television production truck management – Media parking (including space for media production trucks) – Media venue requirements – In-house electrical requirements for media	Media Coordinator and Volunteers A, B and C
Six months prior to event	***Pre-event media release:*** – Media release contents – Distribution plans for media release	

84

Five months prior to event	**Media information package:** – Contents (consider accreditation, media centre, shuttle, site details, parking, team practices, competition details, environmental sustainability plans, and a contact for further information)
Four months prior to event	**Design of media centre:** – Media centre requirements – Media centre volunteer requirements – Media security plans – Media food and beverage – Media signage (consider signage to be placed inside and outside the media centre and how the signage will be held in place) – Media check-in process
Three months prior to event	**Assignment of media space:** – Consider television booths, radio booths, online and social media space, photographer sites and camera positions and seats that must not be filled (due to camera positions)
Three months prior to event	**Volunteer management:** – Determine pre-event volunteer requirements – Event volunteer roles (specific duties) – Communication system
One month prior to event	**Contingency plan development:** Contingency A: Contingency B: Contingency C: Contingency D: Contingency E:

Figure 5.1 Operational plan: practice assignment

CONCLUSION

In the second phase of the planning model, the operational planning phase, network members complete intensive operational plans that include timed activities for each event component. The strength of an event operational plan is determined by the logical and sequential process, the amount of planning detail provided, the integration forged between the planned components, the extra preparedness based on the contingency plans and the process of refining the plans prior to their use. Facilitating quality operational plans can be developed with practice. The concept of quality in event operational planning is discussed further in Chapter 10, "Facilitating quality in event management." Overall, the operational plans are created in preparation for the next phase in the planning model, the implementation, monitoring and management phase.

CHAPTER QUESTIONS

1 What are the characteristics of contingency theory, complexity theory and agency theory and how do these characteristics guide an event manager in the event operational planning phase?
2 Describe the difference between level 1, level 2 and level 3 planning.
3 How does contingency theory relate to and differ from contingency plans?
4 What do contingency plans provide, and why are they important in event management?
5 What is a plan refining process and how does it assist an event manager?
6 Describe three key issues in the event operational planning phase and then outline how an event manager can act to overcome these issues.

CHAPTER 6

THE EVENT PLANNING MODEL

THE EVENT IMPLEMENTATION, MONITORING
AND MANAGEMENT PHASE

LORNE J. ADAMS

This chapter emphasizes the role of the event manager in making the operational plan work when it counts most – at the event itself. While many people may be aware of the detail within the operational plan, no one knows it as well as you, the event manager. That is why you will be called upon to facilitate the work of the people who implement the plan, to monitor the various elements of the event, as well as manage and provide guidance for the unforeseen problems that may arise. How you manage all of this will determine not only the success of the event, but also your success as a quality event manager.

A lot will be asked of you as the event unfolds. Understanding yourself and your role is critical to the success of the event. You will not be a dispassionate observer; you will be totally immersed in the event and all it entails. You will also bring your unique set of skills and abilities, predispositions and biases with you. They are as much a part of the event as the people and systems that you are attempting to manage.

IMPLEMENTATION: EXECUTING THE PLAN

Implementation involves the execution of the plan by moving the planned operational concepts and processes from the members who completed the planning to the myriad event staff and volunteers who are tasked with executing the plan (Buchanan & O'Connell, 2006). Facilitating the implementation of the operational plans does not take place in a passive world; it is purpose-driven, goal-oriented and dynamic as we live in a unique change-based time (Mallen, 2006). The forces of change demand that we react and manage the repercussions of that change. In this environment, implementation is not easy. The first step entails coordinating and getting all of the people implementing the plan on the same page.

DISSEMINATING IMPLEMENTATION REQUIREMENTS AND HOLDING PRODUCTION MEETINGS

A much broader group or team will be responsible for implementing the plan than that which created the plan. They need an opportunity to hear, understand and assimilate the plan in their unique area of responsibility and in the larger context of the overall plan. *Production meetings* are held to provide this opportunity. There are several key elements required in the art of hosting production meetings. These meetings include a variety of event invitees who are involved in the integral act of implementing the event operational plans. These meetings need to have a pre-established detailed agenda, offer supplementary materials that ensure understanding of goals and objectives of the organization, as well as the event, delineate the specific roles and responsibilities and offer facility tours to ensure that all of those implementing the event plans know the facility.

Who is involved in these meetings? In some cases when the event is small, it is possible to involve everyone in the production meeting. However, as the size and complexity of the event increase, the less practical and possible it is to involve everyone. Your plan should have identified managers for each event component. It is essential that these people are in attendance. They in turn will be responsible for holding implementation meetings with the staff and volunteers who make up the network members associated with their unique area of responsibility.

What does hosting a production meeting entail? To begin, a detailed agenda needs to be developed. This will help you prescribe an adequate amount of time for the meeting and an agenda. You want to maximize the use of people's time and keep them focused. A detailed agenda with some general guidelines allotting time for each item helps to maintain attendees' focus and will allow for a logical progression to the meeting.

Be considerate of people's time; be sure to provide the agenda in enough time for participants to review and analyze the material. This is a subjective guideline. If you send it too early, you risk having it set aside and forgotten;

if you send it too late, people may be reviewing materials as the meeting unfolds. This will lead to needless discussion and can derail a meeting quite quickly. As a rule of thumb, 7–10 days of advance notice is a reasonable timeframe for many people.

Supplementary materials should also be provided with the agenda. This includes providing the written operational plans. Once again, as these are the people who are going to train others and keep them on track, a high level of detail is required here. Throughout the plan, each member's personal responsibilities should be highlighted in some way. This can be as simple as the use of bold text or a coloured highlighter. This personalized plan takes time, but for each member it is a focusing agent. Also, the inclusion of an executive summary can minimize questions. In addition, providing an organizational flowchart will help to delineate responsibilities and establish a context for each node involved in the plan. Finally, a diagram of the facility with detailed and accurate instructions will further the understanding of locations and placement of equipment. The pictorial representation will save a lot of verbal explanations that could be misinterpreted.

When members attend production meetings, you should never assume that everyone has read the material provided in advance. People don't intend to derail a meeting, nor do they deliberately attempt to hold up the process by shirking their responsibility to review the material. However, they may have busy, complex lives, and sometimes even the well-intentioned have to deal with issues not associated with your event, no matter how important it may seem to you. As the facilitator, it is your responsibility to provide a verbal review to ensure that they understand the written operational plans and the specific tasks for which they are responsible.

Production meetings provide opportunities to ensure that each member implementing the plan understands the goals and objectives of the event. They must also know their own responsibilities, including required actions. Creating specific responsibilities limits the possibility of someone thinking that someone else was responsible for a particular task, and thereby increases accountability.

It is also important that team members understand the interrelatedness of their role with other elements of the plan. They need to see how what they are doing contributes to the larger plan, and that what they are doing is valued. When it becomes clear that what they are doing is not an end in itself, but an important part of a much larger whole, commitment and motivation are enhanced.

In addition to written materials and their discussion at the production meeting table, a tour of the facility or facilities to discuss elements at the site in the context of the operational plan is essential. During a tour, managers of each event component may be able to assess specific needs or problems, such as access to electrical outlets, the sound system, running water, internet and so on.

At the end of production meeting(s) and facility tour(s), component managers and the constituent managers within each component should be aware of the specific goals of the event, their unique responsibilities and how they fit into the overall plan. They should also be familiar with the venue(s) and be prepared to motivate and train those who will report to them. Their questions should have been answered and, if you have done a good job, they will be excited about getting started.

MONITORING THE DYNAMIC AND FLUID OPERATIONAL ENVIRONMENT

During implementation, you as the facilitator need to focus on the details of the plan using a "zoom lens." Two key areas of focus are monitoring the issues of timing and progress. For example, you need to monitor whether enough time has been allotted for getting essential materials to the venue in a timely manner so that people are not sitting around waiting to do their work. Also, have you allocated enough time for set-up and to test the equipment? If people need to be at two or more venues at specific times, is there enough time for travel between each venue? Monitoring involves questioning to determine if people are attending to the task that will lead to successful implementation of the plan in the time scheduled.

As a facilitator, it is important that you see and are seen by the event staff and volunteers. You should employ an operating principle that involves "the five Ps of implementation." Use your *presence* and *profile* to support *positive* and *productive performance*. Presence is the concept of management by walking around. When you are present, it is easier for dialogue to occur. Implementers can ask you questions, and you in turn can question them. This will reduce ambiguity in the first instance, and in addition, provide the sense that what they are doing is important and a worthwhile contribution. Your presence also reinforces your perception

90

of attention to detail. Ultimately you will have a working knowledge of all phases of the plan.

Your presence also raises the profile of the specific components. If it is deemed important enough for you to visit them, it raises the value of that unit to the people completing the task. Like it or not, as an event manager, you have a profile, and you can use that profile in positive, productive ways. When you have taken the time to visit, ask and respond to questions, a subtle process of accountability has been introduced. If you have addressed the concerns of the front-line workers, have listened to their suggestions and provided your vision of the project or event, people will be more committed to doing the work and doing it well. They are people, and you are seen as a person, not an object. If workers have the sense that everyone concerned is important to the eventual success of the project, they will be more committed to ensuring that success with their productive performance.

MANAGING OPERATIONAL PLAN IMPLEMENTATION

As the event manger, it is your responsibility to facilitate the management of deviations from the operational plan that may happen for any reason. This will be a tough task. According to Wijngaard, deVries and Nauta (2006), tacit knowledge is required to make judgments on the precision of performance. Tacit knowledge, you will recall, is related to advancement knowledge. As this text has pointed out, tacit knowledge has been acquired through personal experience. It is the know-how you have acquired over the years as a student, as a volunteer, as an emerging professional. It is that "job sense" that comes from having been there. Schön (1983), in his book *The Reflective Practitioner*, refers to professionals being able to work "in the indeterminate zones" that their training has not explicitly prepared them for. This requires an application of knowledge. Several tips (adapted from *How to Stay on Course: Sensing and Responding to Deviations from Plan* [various authors, 2006, pp. 1–19]) can assist you to keep implementation on track:

- Determine deviations from the operational plans through a variety of mechanisms, such as periodic progress reviews, anecdotal reports or direct observation.
- Create a climate in which people are not afraid to report implementations in a timely way, including arising problems and issues.

- Do not wait for progress reports; be out on the front lines of implementation, observing and asking questions.
- Every implementation plan contains risks – some unforeseeable. Create a contingency plan for all foreseeable issues and be prepared with a strategy to assess and manage unforeseeable issues.

Once you have noted that there is a deviation from the plan, you will require the knowledge and ability to develop a strategy for bringing things back on track. A skilled and knowledgeable event manager is needed to handle issues, to create a decision-making process and complete the adaptations to ensure that the planned activities conform to timelines and acceptable levels of completeness. The decisions on how to manage issues must be aligned with the overall objectives and priorities of the event. You will need to determine ahead of time the process to be used, who will be involved, a strategy to resolve conflict, and an implementation stage; you will also have to be mindful of time constraints and the need to act quickly.

Overcome foreseeable failure when managing deviations from the plan

You need to be conscious of the fact that managing deviations from the operational plan can invoke a predictable response that can result in a negative impact for the event. You need to overcome this predictability to improve your decision-making abilities during event implementation. This predictability was revealed by Dörner (1996), as he outlined in great detail how well-intentioned, intelligent people can experience difficulty in complex, dynamic systems. He developed a game with a hypothetical population and simulated the real-world environment, and found that participants responded in a consistent and patterned manner.

His research indicated that participants tended to *act without prior analysis of the situation*; that is, they accepted things at face value without much consideration of prior events or history that were germane to sound decision making. The lack of an immediately obvious negative effect of an action deluded them into thinking that their decision had solved the problem. Participants *failed to anticipate side effects and the long-term consequences of a particular course of action*. In addition, participants *failed to take into account the lag time between action and consequences* and were forced to react quickly at a future point as a consequence of their prior decision. This "domino effect" was repeated in the simulations,

92

and in most cases, compounded the problem or created new ones that needed to be handled with increasing urgency. In Dörner's terms, problems increased exponentially, not in a linear fashion, and created a catastrophic conclusion. In his words, participants demonstrated "an inadequate understanding of exponential development and an inability to see that a process that develops exponentially will, once it has begun, race to its conclusion with incredible speed" (p. 33). Dörner (1996) concluded: "People court failure in predictable ways" (p. 10).

When you consider that events are run under strict time constraints, Dörner's (1996) work is worth remembering. Certainly, no one intends to fail, nor would you actively court that outcome. However, if you do not understand yourself or the system (event) with which you are dealing, the possibility exists that your desired outcome will not be achieved. In addition, when you are called upon to make decisions, it is worth noting that decision making is not a single activity, something that takes place at a particular time. Decision making is best described as a process, one that takes place over time and is "replete with personal nuance and institutional history" (Garvin & Roberto, 2001, p. 1).

It would behoove you to go back and look at the material on complexity theory, contingency theory and systems theory (see Chapters 3 and 5). Knowledge of theories will help you make the decisions that will need to be made during the implementation of an event. In addition, consider how you will analyze situations (including taking into consideration the history, side effects and consequences of actions).

Predetermine the decision-making team and process

When managing deviations from the written operational plan, the decision-making team must be predetermined. Basically, you are answering the questions, who's in and why? There is no magic formula for this or guidelines for answering these two questions. There will be key players that your advancement knowledge will make obvious. Certainly, anyone who will be directly impacted should be considered.

The process that the decision-making team works within must be predetermined.

▪ Who gets brought into the issue?
▪ How are they informed?

- How much time is needed to assemble or obtain a decision?
- How quickly must the decision be disseminated?
- Is there a need for a dispersed decision process (teleconference)?
- How will the decision-making process unfold (consensus, simple majority, majority, referral to an ultimate decision maker)?
- How will conflicts in the decision-making process be handled?

As we have already indicated, any response to a plan deviation needs to relate to the vision and goals of the event. Mintzberg, Raisinghani and Théorêt (1976) described a process model as a situation whereby the goals are clear, but the methods to attain them require decision making. These researchers indicate that decision making in a process model includes an environment whereby "the entire process is highly dynamic, with many factors changing the tempo and direction of the decision process" (p. 263). In a process model, the decision-making process has historically been divided into three areas: *identification, development* and *selection* (Mintzberg et al., 1976). Identification provides the recognition of the situation and communication through the system that a decision is required. Development involves the search for options as solutions. Selection includes the evaluation of options and the finalization of the chosen decision for implementation.

Once a decision is rendered, a decision-making implementation process must be followed. This process determines how decisions will be implemented. The following questions need to be asked:

- Who will implement the decision?
- What processes will be put in place to ensure that the decision is being acted upon?
- What monitoring will be put in place to ensure that the decision is achieving its desired outcome?

The process to implement decisions must be facilitated for efficient and effective application of decisions. To help to achieve this state, programmed decisions are created.

Programmed and non-programmed decisions

As you have spent many hours developing the plan for your event, you will have asked yourself the question, "What if. . .?" on many occasions.

94

In event management, a significant portion of decision making in the operational network is prescribed and automatically implemented at a designated time. The prescribed decisions are stated in the contingency operational plans. When the situation(s) arises, the decisions are enacted. These decisions are considered to be programmed or pre-established.

In contrast, there will be situations when the decision making is not programmed. During these situations, the communication system that was pre-established becomes vitally important to achieve operational network membership negotiation, coordination, decision making and cooperation, and for the integration of actions within the overall operational plan. According to Wijngaard et al. (2006), when completing operating plans that fall outside the programmed decisions, a pattern of decision making and work functionality is established that requires support from the system. Facilitating the communication system is a priority in order to manage non-programmed decisions.

INHERENT IMPLEMENTATION, MONITORING AND MANAGEMENT ISSUES IN OPERATIONAL NETWORK PRACTICE

In operations management, be sure to allow staff and volunteers to "contribute significantly to the performance of the system" (Wijngaard et al., 2006, p. 408). These event members are positioned within the planning and control framework to implement tasks and manage emerging issues and problems. These members, thus, need some level of autonomy. Yet, "this autonomy adds also to the unpredictability and ambiguity of the system of control" (Wijngaard et al., 2006, p. 395). This is because, although the planning and control elements eliminate as many potential situations as possible, they "can never be complete; there are too many tacit elements in the situation to control" (Wijngaard et al., 2006, p. 405).

Clearly, operational implementation performance cannot be fully controlled and the concept of control may even be a misnomer in a dynamic and fluid environment. However, as an event manager, you will be looking for *scope control*. Scope control asks that people stay within the confines of the project and do not add or introduce elements that are not part of the overall plan. While we attempt to control as much as we can and operate within the parameters of the plan, "basically the system is not 'closed'. That is, the system is open to all kinds of unexpected influencers" (Wijngaard et al., 2006, p. 395).

If planning and control frameworks can never provide full control, then the system is open to providing inadequate planning and control (Konijnendijk, 1994). This inadequacy includes ambiguity, which in turn provides opportunities for individual interpretations of planned tasks (Wijngaard et al., 2006). Without the possibility of full control, the planning and control frameworks can offer what Wijngaard et al. (2006) call "perceived control" (p. 405) and a base line from which deviations can be determined. This implies that full control is not possible and that the event environment will involve handling arising issues.

Maintaining control is a complex issue in events, but regardless, it is your job to ensure the required level of quality in the control aspect of the event. In addition, it is your task as a facilitator to anticipate and manage your stress levels when attempting to obtain some semblance of control over the event implementation aspects. Knowledge of strategies for this can be developed by watching those in the field and how they handle these situations.

Issue: operational plan detail and implementation performance

If the operational plans are not detailed in nature, or if circumstances arise that require deviations from the operational plans, then there is a need to allow for a degree of operational freedom, and the importance of decision making increases. In order for members of the operational network to be effective in their decision making, the operational network members implementing the plan need "a good understanding of the system to control, the specifics of the actual situation, as well as of the underlying rationale of the planning and control framework" (Wijngaard et al., 2006, p. 398). In addition, the operational network members adapting the plan need a solid understanding of the event goals and expected outcomes.

If the operational plans are detailed in nature, the operational network need only initiate the steps as prescribed. A detailed plan limits the degree of decision making and operational change or freedom to make changes.

Issue: implementation knowledge and performance

One of the issues that may impact implementation performance is the knowledge level of the operational team members. You will need to ascertain whether the implementation network members understand and have a working knowledge of the overall event requirements and objectives. Obviously you cannot give a test to ensure that this is the case, but they should be given a number of opportunities and forums to facilitate the demonstration of their depth of knowledge and understanding of the event requirements.

An initial way to help ascertain if the level of knowledge has been transferred to the implementation network members is simply to check the attendance records in the minutes of production meetings. For instance:

- Have the members attended the meetings regularly so they can learn the requirements and the objectives?
- If they have missed meetings, what steps have they taken to obtain the information provided at the meeting? What steps have you taken to assist those who have missed access to the information?

Another issue that arises is the implementation team's knowledge regarding their role(s). As the event manager, this might be a good time to look in the mirror and ask yourself questions. The questions may include:

- How well did I facilitate the process to ensure that every member understands their role?
- Did I make assumptions because of my own deep familiarity with what is required?
- Did I use language that is clear and understandable?
- Was a timeframe allotted to every task, and was it realistic?
- Was the integration process completed?

The answers to these questions illustrate the complexities within the role of event facilitation.

Issue: deviations from the plan

There are any numbers of reasons why an activity may not be completed as planned. Some of the issues that may contribute to that outcome are now highlighted. One of the most obvious problems is that an operational team member(s) adapts the role or the event due to an individual's level of understanding, or lack thereof. Further, sometimes people take it upon themselves to alter the activity for reasons known only to themselves, perhaps because of prior experience: "it's the way it's 'always' been done"; "it's not the way we used to do it"; "I can make it better" and so on.

One of the main contributors to activities not being completed as planned is the communication system and the communication skills of the members. In addition, communication is a key factor in the capacity of the intra-organizational network members to function as a team. Communication assists in improving the level of cooperation present to complete tasks. Your role is to facilitate the communication process to ensure that general communication problems are overcome. These problems can advance if information is withheld, if information is available to only a select few, or if decisions that affect a particular role or task are not communicated.

Issue: implementation conflict

Conflict may not be inevitable, but any time you bring a group of people together to work toward a common goal, the potential exists for conflict to occur. "Ironically, one of the important characteristics of a well structured team – diversity of thinking, backgrounds and skills – is itself a potential source of conflict" (HBS Press & Harvard Business School Press, 2005, p. 8). One of the purposes of bringing people together is to examine options, to engage in critical thinking and collaborative thinking, and ultimately, to embark on the best course of action. Obviously, this kind of focus can engender great debate and people can have widely divergent thinking. As meetings unfold, there may come a time when, in trying to decide between two alternative positions, people become entrenched in one camp or another. The longer this goes on, the greater is the likelihood that conflict will result. Garvin and Roberto (2001) point out that conflict comes in two forms – cognitive conflict and affective conflict.

- *Cognitive conflict* is the kind of healthy debate that is focused on the task at hand. It is substantive in nature, open to other alternatives and ultimately is designed to solve problems. The exchanges can be quite intense, but they are not personal; they are about the exchange of ideas with the ultimate goal of coming up with the best possible plan.
- *Affective conflict*, on the other hand, is personal. It may arise from a clash of personalities, a visceral dislike for someone or a defensive reaction to criticism. When you have interpersonal conflict, people

98

are less likely to cooperate, to listen to new ideas, to move the project forward. They may become entrenched in a particular position, as noted above, and are less accepting if a decision is made that is at odds with their firmly held stance.

To promote cognitive conflict and to reduce affective conflict, Garvin and Roberto (2001) provide a framework comprised of the "three Cs" of effective decision making: *conflict, consideration* and *closure*. As they point out, each of these needs to be handled carefully. The conflict portion has been outlined above, but bears repeating. As an event manager, you want to facilitate as much cognitive conflict as possible, while at the same time minimizing affective conflict.

The second "C," consideration, is a fairly simple concept, but one that in practice is often ignored. As I have pointed out, when there are two sides to an issue, one side will be chosen and the other set aside. Obviously, then, some people are going to have to support and implement a course of action that they did not, at one point in time, prefer. The concept of consideration is sometimes referred to as due diligence or procedural justice. At its heart, it refers to a sense of fairness. It is a far different thing to be heard, to express your views and ideas, than it is to be considered. "Considered" indicates that your ideas have been listened to carefully, have been weighed in the context of what must be done, and that your ideas are clearly understood.

Consideration requires the facilitation of members who listen actively, ask questions, take notes, ask for explanations, are patient during explanations of positions and keep personal opinions or preferences to themselves. At all costs, avoid looking as if you already have made up your mind.

Consideration also means that once you have decided, you communicate what the final choice is and why it is the best course of action. Making reference to the input you have received and how it impacted your choice will go a long way to achieving acceptance by the group.

Providing closure is also a balancing act. Debate cannot go on incessantly, nor should it be halted prematurely. In many cases, the event itself will dictate the timeframe by which a decision is to be rendered, but even if that is the case, there is a need for closure. It is a skilful facilitator who knows when to "call the question." The skilled and experienced event manager knows when enough information has been gathered, when repetitiveness is apparent and when to avoid the trap of paralysis by analysis.

Issue: implementation communication

Throughout this text you will find both explicit and implicit exhortations to communicate frequently and effectively. Effective communication is essential at every stage for an event manager. So much has been written about communication that it is beyond the scope of this text. However, I encourage you to constantly work on the development of your communication skills. Be an active listener and all that it entails, including use of eye contact, bridging, paraphrasing, body language, asking the right questions, being non-judgmental, not personalizing issues and so on.

Finally, be generous with your praise. Publicly acknowledge the accomplishments and successes of those who are carrying out the plan. Additional suggestions for facilitating the implementation, monitoring and management phase of the event management planning model are offered by Scott McRoberts at the end of this chapter (Figure 6.1).

CONCLUSION

Clearly, a lot is expected of an event manager facilitating the event implementation phase, and your skills will be tested. Event managers need to understand themselves and the complex systems that are part of any event. It is also quite clear that careful pre-planning and well-articulated goals and processes are essential to a successful event.

You need to be aware that decisions you make will have both short-term and long-term effects on the eventual success of the event. Event managers have the ultimate responsibility of monitoring and managing the implementation effort. You will be called upon to use direct observation and tacit knowledge. As you will be responsible for keeping operational plans on track, you are also responsible for putting in place the processes for implementing, monitoring and ensuring that deviations are managed. Be cognizant of the two different types of conflict that were discussed (cognitive and affective) during your facilitation activities. Also, remember the importance of improving communication skills.

100

CHAPTER QUESTIONS

1 Describe a production meeting (including why the meeting is held, who participates in the meeting and what is accomplished at the meeting).
2 What are two key areas of focus when monitoring an event?
3 Describe the five Ps of implementation.
4 What can you do to overcome foreseeable failure when managing the implementation of events?
5 There are inherent issues when implementing an event; what are the issues and how do they influence an event?

Facilitating communication

The facilitation of an effective communication process is crucial for an event to run properly. Experience indicates that the majority of communication issues arise in the first hours of the opening of an event. This can often cause mass confusion over the communication lines (such as radios, walkie talkies, or clear coms) established for an event. From my experience at a National Collegiate Athletic Association (NCAA) Men's Basketball Championship and the San Francisco International Children's Games, where over 400 volunteers and 100 staff were involved in each event, at least a third of the operational network members needed to be connected to the communication system radios. Therefore, an event manager must facilitate the proper use of the communication system as a key element in helping to resolve situations in a fast and timely manner. In addition, the proper use of the communication system keeps the airways clear in case of an emergency.

Facilitating motivation and direction

Sport, recreation and tourism events that last for longer than one day require an event manager to facilitate a high level of morale and energy throughout the members of the operational network, and this can be a challenge. You may be aware of the phrase, "It's all about the first impression." However, in event management, it is also the reverse; the last impression of the event is also vitally important to participants, spectators, sponsors and all partners. It is important for the event manager to consistently facilitate the interactions with network members staging the event in order to maintain professionalism from the first to the last day of the event.

One way to facilitate a high level of motivation is to constantly show a presence. The event manager must be available and responsive to network members' issues. This involves facilitating the care and concern of each member for a fair and effective process for providing breaks or rotating positions. It is also the event manager's role to provide a sense of appreciation throughout the event. A simple comment such as "Good job!" can mean a lot to a member.

Facilitating appropriate direction to operational network members during the staging of an event is also an important role for an event manager. The following are a few strategies for facilitating direction with a process for continuous dialogue to aid production.

After an initial briefing meeting prior to the start of an event, a daily production meeting can be held. This meeting can be offered at the end of the event day or held in the early hours each morning of the event. It is important that this meeting be facilitated to stay on the agenda topics and to be conducted in a short time period (such as in one hour).

Another process can be a debriefing page posted for members to review. This provides members with an overview of changes and can confirm activities as well as being presented as an inspirational and upbeat message to aid morale.

Whatever process is used, it is important that an event manager facilitates event changes with the operational network members and eliminates the occurrence of repeated problems. An event is conducted in an environment of change and interpretations that can lead to issues or problems. A process for continuous dialogue needs to be established and facilitated to allow key personnel the opportunity to collectively provide input on the current state of the implementation, monitoring and management of an event, and to provide positive suggestions for moving the event forward.

Facilitating through credentialling issues

A key challenge in event management involves the credentialling or accreditation process at an event. This can be a large issue if an event anticipates a significant media presence. The following are suggestions for alleviating credentialling issues:

Facilitate a process to develop an understanding of the number of individuals who may attend, but have not registered for a credential or accreditation pass; and a system for managing these individuals upon arrival. It is important to have a plan in place as well as personnel to deal with this issue. It is also important to monitor the process and to adapt to be able to provide additional personnel should they be needed or to reassign members should there be only a few unregistered individuals arriving.

There will be credentials that have misspelled names or provide the wrong access within the event venue. Having a credential machine on site with a dedicated and qualified person to operate the machine will help to resolve these issues in a timely manner.

Subdivide all credentials alphabetically and spread out the distribution sites of each group of alphabetical credentials to make the process efficient without a lot of congestion.

Facilitating personality issues

It is important for an event manager to facilitate the management of common situations that arise due to the personalities of the members within the operational network. There are three common issues that every event manager should be cognizant of and be prepared to manage: the fan versus the worker scenario;

personality conflicts; and the need to rotate members to other positions for the purpose of advancing their experience.

The *fan versus worker scenario* is common in the majority of events. Volunteers apply for a role in an event because they have an interest in the product. This situation can produce one of two potential outcomes. The first outcome is a terrific operational volunteer who, because of their interest in the event, maintains professionalism and attention to their position or duties. The second outcome is a member who becomes a spectator and is looking for access to participants, autographs and perks, which means that they do not pay attention to their position or duties. It is important for an event manager to establish, communicate and facilitate the rules for participation at the outset and create a zero tolerance policy for infractions. These infractions are witnessed in all types of events and can have an adverse effect on the motivation, direction and professionalism of others involved in the event.

Personality conflicts abound in event management. It is important for an event manager to position members within their strengths and to manage personality conflicts as they arise. Long hours at an event can lead to short fuses or those who are impatient with others with whom they are working. Other conflicts arise from individuals who think tasks should be completed in a particular manner that differs from what is in the operational plan. Facility managers must be cognizant of these types of situation and facilitate the efficient and effective management of the conflicts in a timely manner. One way to establish a process that helps to alleviate such conflicts is to rotate members within a series of positions.

Facilitating *a rotation of members* between a series of event positions is a good way to meet the needs of members who ask to expand their experiences and develop their skills, and to help keep members alert during events that are staged over many days as well as to alleviate personality conflicts. A process that does not impede the outcome of a successful event must be developed to offer the opportunity to "shuffle" event operational members to a new post or a series of new posts. While doing this, it is important that event managers be cautious, as they must first provide the training to cover the new duties and must involve the members in the production meetings that update the members. In addition, the member must be flexible and competent to manage a changing environment of tasks.

Learning the strengths of the members is difficult, especially when there are potentially hundreds of members involved in staging an event. In some situations, there may be members who are better suited to positions that require continued interaction with people, whether it involves celebrities, event members or consumers. Having an upbeat and positive member who can think on their feet will only reflect positively on the event as a whole. Furthermore, you may be able to determine if an individual is better suited to one specific task, one which may not involve decision making. Therefore, rotating members is a difficult activity to facilitate and, once begun, it requires constant monitoring and management. If facilitated effectively, a rotating process can leave event members happier and more experienced in the end.

Overall, the role of the event manager is very complex. The environment is forever changing. It is important that the event manager facilitates the event implementation, monitoring and management activities to ensure that the vision of the event is accomplished. Therefore, the vision must be conveyed to all event operational members, and they must be reminded of the vision throughout the staging of the event, especially as common implementation issues are being managed.

Remember, an important person in the entire process is the event manager. This means you must facilitate your own process to maintain control of your emotions, remain calm, be positive and present a positive perspective while managing all implementation issues. This includes presenting an attitude that situations can be solved positively, in a timely manner, with demonstrated professionalism and confidence. The manner in which an event manager conducts themselves highly influences the operational network members and ultimately the outcome of the event.

An important element for an event manager is to enjoy the facilitation process and to see the fruition of well-prepared tasks or activities happen over many tireless nights. Relaxation techniques aid an event manger to worry about only the elements they can control, and to have an overall perspective of the event to be able to determine which elements these are.

Figure 6.1 Suggestions for facilitating the implementation, monitoring and management phase of the event management planning model (by Scott McRoberts, Athletic Director, University of Guelph, Guelph, Ontario, Canada)

104

CHAPTER 7

EVENT OPERATIONAL PLANNING ISSUES AND STRATEGIES

NICOLE GRECO AND CHERYL MALLEN

Events in sport, recreation and tourism are rife with emerging issues. The purpose of this chapter is to define issues management and to present some mitigation and management strategies offered by event managers from the industry, including best practices and/or legacies. The aim is to understand issues and best practices in event management and to think through management strategies in the process of learning to manage issues.

ISSUES MANAGEMENT

Issues management is defined as the process by which a corporation can identify, evaluate and respond to issues that impact events significantly (Johnson, 1983). Issues management has been identified as a managerial function that consists of identifying, analyzing and responding to social and political concerns (Heugens, 2003; Nigh & Cochran, 1987). Johnson (1983) recognized decades ago "that the earlier a company can identify a potential threat, or opportunity, and commit itself to appropriate action, the more likely it will be able to influence an issue" (p. 22); this is the process of issues management.

In recent years, issues management has matured and grown in significance (Lawal, Elizabeth & Oludayo, 2012). Wartick and Heugens (2003) stated: "most commentators now agree that issues management excellence requires the proficient execution of three interrelated activities" (p. 9). Their description of these best practices for issues management is as follows:

> The first of these is environmental scanning . . . which involves mapping the business environment for weak signals appearing on

the corporate radar. The second activity is issue interpretation . . . which corresponds to keeping a close eye on previously detected issues to see whether they evolve into something requiring significant managerial attention. As a third activity, organizations must select an issue response pattern through which they actively address the most urgent and threatening of the previously identified and monitored issues.

(Wartick & Heugens, 2003, p. 9)

The combination of these three activities constitutes the best practices of most issues management systems (Wartick & Heugens, 2003).

Best practices

Dembowski (2013) described best practice as "the process of developing and following a standard way of doing things that multiple organizations can use" (p. 12), stating also that "best practice is the optimization of the effectiveness of an organization" (p. 13). In addition, Voss (2005) suggested that best practices lead to superior performance and capability, which in turn will lead to increased competitiveness. The continuous development of best practices is supported as a valuable endeavour, as multiple research studies show links between the adoption of best practices and improved performance (Cua, McKone & Schroeder, 2001; Fullerton, McWatters & Fawson, 2003; Jayaram & Droge, 1999).

Best practices can be framed with *coordination theory*. Malone and Crowston (1990) defined coordination theory as "a body of principles about how activities can be coordinated, that is, about how actors can work together harmoniously" (p. 358). The theory originated in the late 1980s from the field of computer sciences and draws upon a variety of different disciplines including organization theory, management science, economics and psychology (Malone, 1988). Crowston (1997) indicated that organizations which perform the same tasks or activities can do so with differing processes or patterns that aid in coordinating the completion of the tasks. Understanding the patterns generated, and ensuring that the coordination process is easy to enact, can aid in devising best practices. Additionally, best or excellent practices can lead to positive event legacies.

Events as legacies

Preuss (2007) defined an event legacy as "irrespective of the time of production and space, legacy is all planned and unplanned, positive and negative, tangible and intangible structures created for and by . . . [an] event that remain longer than the event itself" (p. 211). Preuss built his definition on the work of Cashman (2006) who categorized legacies into fields such as economics, infrastructure, information and education, public life, politics and culture. Meanwhile, Horne (2010) suggested two types of analysis for legacies: the first focused on the impacts or outcomes of the event for material development (economic, technological, urban infrastructure); and the second addressed the ideologies in media representations of the locations and the many groups involved and the relationship of these to national identities. This second type offered representational types of legacy that included intangible effects based on an awareness and imagery of host cities and countries. It is evident that the term "legacies" has been used in a variety of ways throughout literature to highlight the different legacies of events. To perform with excellence, and to leave event legacies, event managers must first plan and execute the event, including managing the arising issues.

Event issues and management strategies

The event management literature revealed a general lack of research focusing on operational planning of events, particularly in the areas of event issues and management strategies. Parent, Rouillard and Leopkey (2011) examined the topic, albeit from the government perspective of coordinating the Olympic Games. Other comparators, therefore, were not available. This chapter was, thus, based on a recent research project conducted by Greco (2016) which was framed using the work of Parent et al. (2011). Her research specifically sought to determine the key issues and management strategies in the event management industry. The quotes from event managers are part of the research process conducted by Greco. An overview of her research process is outlined in Figure 7.1 at the end of this chapter, and additional research in this area is encouraged.

Greco's examination of event managers and their issues, as well as strategies for issues management, revealed a number of prominent event management issues. Examples of these emerging issues included the following categories: timing; accountability/authority; knowledge management; funding; relationships; and turnover of staff and volunteers. It is important that event managers understand the types of emerging issues in event management, as well as how to devise mitigation or management strategies for handling them in a manner that advances the success of an event. Examples of event issues, as well as management strategies, will now be presented.

Timing issues

Timing issues were the most prominent issues encountered by event managers in the industry. Timing issues are described as "unmovable deadlines, decision making pace speeding up" (Parent et al., 2011, p. 350). There were several types of timing issues that were revealed in the research. One timing issue involved the *timing of formal agreements*. It was noted that if formal agreements are *not done early enough in the process, then the event has no leverage with the host committee and/or local stakeholders such as hotels*. It was revealed by an event manager in the industry that "if you wait to negotiate them after you've won the [event], hotels are going to jack up the prices on you because they know you have no choice now." A strategy identified to help solve this issue included developing and providing templates of details well in advance of agreements and ensuring that the process is completed as early as possible. Additionally, it was noted that one organization "provides a template for such agreements and the agreements must be signed at the bid phase. This way when a host is granted the rights to host the [event], agreements are already in place."

One timing issue involved *not communicating in a timely manner*. This could mean that staff or volunteers may get so consumed by their event activities that they do not consider others involved, and may not respond to their inquiries in an appropriate timeframe. Event managers in the industry indicated that discussions needed to be held with event staff and volunteers concerning established communication protocols. These protocols can ascertain elements such as the appropriate timeframe expected for a response, as well as the process to be used for responses, in order to mitigate this issue.

Another timing issue involved *the time it takes for a decision to get made*. An event manager in the field noted that, "If I need approval to book flights and right now the flights are on sale – so I'm trying to save the organization money, but then their flight isn't approved until a month later when the seat sale is gone." Thus, the ability to facilitate timely decisions is important. This implies that the issue and strategy management decision protocols must be established to clearly articulate areas such as who can make a decision, the process for requesting a decision, and the impact of the timeframe. This issue is also linked to the accountability/authority issue discussed below.

A further timing issue was *not accomplishing tasks outlined in the strategic plan in the timeframe that has been established for them to be completed.* This issue means that an event manager must facilitate a strategy to provide feedback based on the monitoring and management of event activities. This feedback must ensure that staff and volunteers understand the timeframe as well as the impact of missing the timeframe established. Staff can also be positive motivators who encourage tasks or activities to meet the scheduled time requirements. Also, two-way feedback is important. This means that an event manager must establish a process and be open to hearing from those completing the tasks. These individuals can outline the reasons for delays, the impact of the current resources, and can provide strategies to overcome the hurdles that are impacting the accomplishment of tasks or activities in the established timeframe.

A final timing-related event management issue involves the *timing of staff hiring.* It was noted by event managers in the industry that delayed hiring has an impact on work, but also that hiring too early impacts event finances. Event managers must facilitate the timing of hiring to be optimal for the budget and work requirements. Overall, an event manager must be continuously cognizant of time and facilitate the pace of planning activities, including agreements, communication and decisions to be completed within the set timeframe.

Accountability/authority issues

The second most prominent event management issue category found in the Greco (2016) study involved *accountability/authority,* which was described by Parent et al. (2011) as "assigned roles and responsibilities, who has the final say, [and] who has the power to make decisions" (p. 351). One issue within this category involves *role clarity – if roles are not clear, issues arise.* All of the individuals who play a role in the operations of events are stakeholders, and it is important that their roles are clear in order to assist in the successful execution of events. Industry event managers suggest the need to "revise manuals and organizational charts with clearly defined roles and responsibilities for each area." This implies that human resource management strategies are needed to mitigate these types of issues.

Another accountability/authority issue involves *different stakeholders not responding to communications [being accountable]*. Industry event managers have found that sometimes staff/volunteers or participants "don't avail themselves of the information that is available and that is sent to them." A mitigation strategy involves putting instructions in writing; and additionally, hosting production meetings to review instructions verbally. Alternatively, if the instructions were provided in a verbal format initially, then follow-up written material is necessary. This issue has direct links to the issue above regarding the timing of responses. This implies that communication is both an important timing and an accountability/authority issue.

A further accountability/authority issue involves *making decisions based on wants and not on needs* and *decisions being made without consultation*. Overall, the prominence of these accountability/authority issues should be noted by event managers in order to prepare for the significant impact these issues could have on an event.

Knowledge management issues

Parent et al.'s (2011) description of knowledge management involves: "learning, information sharing/keeping people informed, information bottleneck, monitoring, knowledge transfer, communication inefficiencies, freedom of information, reporting, centralization of information, corporate memory" (p. 351). Communication and information were key words utilized in the description of these issues. In this category, Greco (2016) found that the key issues were: *not enough communication takes place*; there is the *assumption that everyone knows the necessary information*; *information does not flow from one function/department/area/position to another as well as it should* or what Parent et al. (2011) describe as "information bottleneck"; and the *misinterpretation of information*. This means that communication was implicated in issues based on timing and accountability/authority as well as knowledge management – this makes communication a crucial issue for event managers, and advancement knowledge for managing communication is a key skill. Event managers, thus, must facilitate the establishment of regular communication strategies to ensure that operational participants feel abreast of the latest information, protocols and decisions, and to ensure clarity in the interpretation of instructions. Regularly established meetings are considered

110

to be best practices, and suggestions from industry event managers include: "monthly meetings with set agendas"; "file-sharing capabilities"; and considering "conference calls." This sharing of information can aid in engaging staff and volunteers in their roles.

Funding issues

Events would not be possible without the financial support necessary for the implementation of planned activities. The description of funding as an issue category provided by Parent et al. (2011) was "budget, economic situation" (p. 350). Issues in this category indicate that *there is never enough funding*; that events struggle *trying to balance the financial requirements of hosting*; another issue is the *loss of revenue streams*. Industry event managers suggested that it is important to: "Have a clear understanding of your budget"; "Be smart and creative to stretch your budget"; and "Spend money in the right places. You can't cut corners on certain elements." This means that event managers need advancement knowledge in managing event finances.

Relationship issues

The issue categorized as relationships was described by Parent et al. (2011) as "trust, fairness, openness about issues, embeddedness, right people around the table, individual/personal, intra/inter-departmental, intra/inter-governmental, involvement of community and/or other stakeholders, integration, temporary vs. enduring" (p. 352).

In event management, these relationships stem from the need to coordinate operational plans within, as well as between, event components.

A key relationship issue in event management involves *conflicting personalities among staff and/or volunteers*. An event manager in the field emphasized that, "You're dealing with many personalities; different skill sets, different experiences and then you're building a team with them . . . not everyone . . . works well together." This issue means that the fostering of an environment of cooperation for coordinating operational plans can be one of the greatest challenges an event manager faces. Cooperation problems stem from the variety of personalities, the different skills, abilities, and knowledge of the operational network members that are required to develop component plans and then incorporate them into the multiple component operational plans.

Industry event managers provided some of their best practices to help solve the issue of *conflicting personalities among staff and/or volunteers* in the relationship category. Numerous strategies were suggested, including having good policies and principles around a respectful workplace; having a strong leadership and human resources department; and bringing the issues forward and having staff and volunteers provide their ideas for a resolution. It appears that different event managers have solved the issue of conflicting personalities in a variety of ways. This suggests that there is no one specific best practice due to the complexity that stems from the differing personalities and how they must be handled.

In addition, relationship issues emerge due to increasingly remote or dispersed work opportunities. This issue stems from the wide footprint of major events that can lead to the use of communication technology to coordinate activities as events can operate out of many different venues. Coordinating off-site activities requires additional communication and demands clarity within the communications.

Another relationship issue involves the government as a partner. Event managers in the industry indicated that there are two key political situations arising from this relationship that should not be ignored. The first relationship issue is that *government leaders change positions throughout the course of planning and executing an event*. Second, there is the issue that *the government may not view the event as a high priority*. Suggested mitigation strategies from event managers in the industry revolved around building – and importantly, maintaining – relationships with key elected officials and explaining the economic impacts of the event to government personnel.

Turnover of staff and volunteers
The study by Greco (2016) found that the turnover of staff and volunteers is a key issue; this involves the *loss of quality staff – the management concern of how to replace them*. According to event managers, the best way to solve this issue could be impacted by different organizational factors such as whether completion bonuses are offered, the ability to hire from within, and/or the expertise required for the position needing to be filled. However, no single best practice to help solve the issue is available. Further, it is important to note that a strategy for the introduction and training of new staff and volunteers is crucial for making them productive sooner and keeping them longer. This means that an event manager must not just hire, but must facilitate a "turnover" training program to be operationalized throughout the event planning process. This program should include areas such as ensuring that new personnel understand

the event goals, objectives, the roles, decision-making process, timing, communication expectations and protocols. How often these training programs must be activated depends on the turnover rate.

CHAPTER SUMMARY

This chapter provided an overview of the management of event operational planning issues. Event operational planning issues were outlined, including the issue categories of timing, accountability/authority, knowledge management, funding, relationships and turnover of staff and volunteers. Industry event managers offered suggestions for managing some of the issues and/or their best practices. Those reading this chapter are encouraged to think through the operational planning process and to determine additional types of issues. In particular, readers are encouraged to work in the event industry in order to understand the types of emerging issues and the management strategies that worked or did not work well and the reasons for that.

CHAPTER QUESTIONS

1 Define the concept of best practices in event operational planning.
2 Outline five key event management operational planning issues discussed in this chapter. State your established strategy for mitigating or managing each issue.
3 Define coordination theory and outline how it applies to event management.
4 Define the concept of an event legacy and state how these legacies relate to event management issues.
5 Think through the operational planning process and determine three additional issues that must be managed in the process of event management. Also, devise strategies for mitigating or managing each issue.

There was such limited research on event issues and strategies that this chapter would not have been possible without the completion of a specifically focused research project. This research utilized a modified Delphi technique. This technique is outlined and additional research in this area is encouraged.

A modified Delphi research technique (Greco, 2016)

According to Day and Bobeva (2005), the Delphi technique is "a structured group communication method for soliciting expert opinion about complex problems or novel ideas, through the use of a series of questionnaires and controlled feedback" (p. 103). Dietz (1987) outlined the basic process for the Delphi technique as follows:

> First, a panel of experts on the topic(s) under study is created. A series of questionnaires is sent to each member of the panel, soliciting both a forecast for each event being studied and a brief statement as to why the panellist has made that particular forecast. The second round questionnaire . . . [provides] summaries of the overall panel response on the previous round and a brief summary of the reasons offered for each forecast. The third round questionnaire provides panellists with information from the second round, and so on.
>
> (Dietz, 1987, p.80)

In this study, a modified Delphi research technique was utilized. First, in-depth interviews were completed, then the interviewees were provided with the results via a questionnaire that solicited further data; and this was repeated with another questionnaire. Three feedback rounds with respondents is common practice in a Delphi study, and the participants remain anonymous (Costa, 2005; Day & Bobeva, 2005; Mallen, Adams, Stevens & Thompson, 2010; Powell, 2003). Overall, Martino (1983) outlined that the value of the technique was that the total information available to a group can be many times that possessed by any single member, and the number of factors that can be considered by a group can be at least as great as the number which can be considered by a single member.

The interview and questionnaire framework

The interviews and questionnaires were designed with a focus on operational planning and execution issues arising in the management of a major sport event and the strategies used to address these issues. The framework followed an adaptation of Parent et al.'s (2011) eight strategy types: (i) communication processes; (ii) decision-making frames; (iii) engagement; (iv) flexibility; (v) formalized agreements; (vi) human resource management procedures/principles; (vii) strategic planning; and (viii) structural framework.

The Delphi participants

The typical instance sampling (Tracy, 2013) included male and female managers responsible for the operational planning and execution of previously held major sport events. Martino (1983) stated that experts are considered to be experts in the sense that they know more about the topic to be forecast than do most people. Martino suggested selecting a slightly higher number of panellists than the

114

researcher deems necessary due to the possibility of panellists dropping out. Previous Delphi studies have utilized anywhere from 17 panellists (Costa, 2005) to 31 panellists (Mallen, et al., 2010). Dalkey, Brown and Cochran (1970) determined that starting with 15–20 panellists was a suitable number. This research study had 15 participants. The average number of years of industry experience of the participants was 15, with participant experience ranging from 5 to 33 years, and the participants held titles such as Director, Tournament Director, Assistant Director, Senior Manager, General Manager and Chief Executive Officer, among others.

Panellists were contacted via email to request their participation with email addresses obtained via event websites and official event documents where available. Participation in the three rounds had a high retention rate of 66.6 percent.

Data analysis

Upon completion of interview data collection, this study followed a five-step analysis process. These steps involved:

1 human coding;
2 identifying themes, including identifying the operational planning and execution issues within the themes. The initial themes consisted of context-based issues outlined by Parent et al. (2011) and comprised time, geography, funding, other resources and political situation; the other issue types included accountability/authority, activation/leveraging, knowledge management, legal, operational, planning, power, relationships, social issues, structure and turnover (Parent et al., 2011) – this research is also open to additional issue types;
3 determining the strategies used to manage the issues, following Parent et al.'s (2011) strategy types previously outlined – this research is also open to additional strategies;
4 a comparison between issues and strategy management;
5 examining what went well in terms of issues management or best practices.

Stage A analysis occurred between rounds one (interviews) and two (first questionnaire) of the modified Delphi technique and involved the following three steps: (i) human coding; (ii) identifying themes, including identifying the operational planning and execution issues; (iii) determining the strategies used to manage the issues. Stage B analysis took place following completion of round two (first questionnaire) and three (second questionnaire). During this stage, the data was analyzed based on the participants' rankings of the issues identified during Stage A. Stage C analysis took place following the completion of round three (second questionnaire) and the analysis was based on the participants' ratings of the frequency of utilizing strategies, in order to determine best practices in operational planning. Step four of analysis comprised a comparison between issues and strategy management; and finally, step five examined what went well in terms of issues management or best practices.

Figure 7.1 The research process for determining event issues and strategies (by Nicole Greco, 2016)

CHAPTER 8

THE EVENT PLANNING MODEL
THE EVENT EVALUATION AND RENEWAL PHASE

SCOTT FORRESTER AND LORNE J. ADAMS

This chapter focuses on the evaluation and renewal phase of the event planning model. It discusses the background knowledge in evaluation and renewal for the event manager and the decisions required before evaluating. It is important to note that preparation for the evaluation and renewal phase begins in the development phase of the planning model and continues through all phases.

BACKGROUND KNOWLEDGE FOR THE EVENT MANAGER

Event managers need to understand what evaluation is, why evaluation is necessary and how evaluation is different from research or assessment. One needs to know the key evaluation questions, general steps in evaluating the event and decisions required by the event manager in order to successfully facilitate the process of conducting event evaluations.

Henderson and Bialeschki (2002) indicate that there are three components that are necessary in order to conduct evaluations. The first necessary component is the *purpose*, the second is the *data* and the third involves *decisions*. The purpose refers to why the evaluation is being undertaken in the first place, or what, specifically, about the event is being evaluated.

Identifying the purpose of the evaluation involves establishing evaluation questions that determine the framework in which to evaluate the event. As Henderson and Bialeschki (2002) suggest, "it is essential to clearly identify what questions are to be addressed or what criteria to evaluate before data are collected for an evaluation or research project" (p. 18).

The data refer to the information that will be systematically collected in order to address the purpose. Last, the decision-making component involves determining the "significance," "value" or "worth" of the event based on the analysis of the information (data) collected in relation to the purpose of the evaluation. These decisions come in the form of conclusions, interpretations stemming from the data analysis, as well as recommendations, proposed courses of action regarding what needs to be done or could be done based on the conclusions. These findings often suggest how the data might be applied in practice and subsequently inform the renewal phase of event planning.

EVALUATION CONSIDERATIONS

A review of the evaluation literature indicates that there are two main types of tools available to you as an evaluator. These are quantitative methods and qualitative methods. As part of formal evaluation methods, both types of evaluation are useful for events. While there are many texts devoted to delineating their differences, a rule of thumb is that *quantitative methods* are numerically based (such as the number of attendees, revenue raised, tickets sold, etc.), while *qualitative methods* are opinion-based (such as how much you enjoyed the event, what was your experience).

In addition, as an event manager, you might wish to take advantage of two different types of evaluation, *formative* and *summative* evaluation. These types of evaluation can be differentiated based on their timing. Formative evaluation takes place while the event is ongoing and tends to be process-oriented. Summative evaluation typically takes place after an event has concluded and tends to examine whether or not the event achieved its goals and objectives. The advantage of formative evaluations is that they can take place at any time and allow for changes to take place as the event unfolds and perhaps before something becomes a problem. For example, in formative evaluation, we could ascertain whether or not volunteers are satisfied with their position, and whether or not they are getting the support they require. Summative evaluation as a post-event process allows the event manager to make judgment decisions about whether or not the goals and objectives have been met. For some, this type of evaluation allows for assessment of accountability and decision making about whether or not an event should be renewed. In short, it allows you to identify what worked, what did not work and what needs to be improved.

Why is evaluation necessary?

Evaluating the event is a necessary step in the event planning model so that data-based decisions can be made regarding the merit, worth, value or significance of the event, which then allows the event manager to make informed decisions regarding the disposition of the event. The event manager can also use evaluations to justify the allocation of resources, scrutinize the competing interests and analyze the finite budgets that most events operate under. Results from well-thought-out, carefully and systematically executed evaluations are essential to sound decision making. Event managers are increasingly being held accountable for numerous aspects relating to the production of an event, such as human resource and volunteer management and security, to name a couple. In general, regardless of what aspect of the event is being evaluated, the purpose of evaluating the event is to measure the effectiveness of the event in terms of meeting its stated goals and objectives, and to measure the quality of the performance of the event, such as whether or not the event was profitable. Henderson and Bialeschki (2002) in their summary of evaluation identified five key purposes:

1 *Determine accountability.* This involves establishing the extent to which the allocation of resources, revenue and expenses, marketing, promotion and sponsorship efforts, activities and processes "effectively and efficiently accomplish the purposes for which an [event] was developed" (Henderson & Bialeschki, 2002, p. 25).
2 *Assess goals and objectives.* Events can be evaluated in terms of whether or not the goals and objectives were met for the event. This may also help to determine the appropriateness of the stated goals and objectives and whether they need to be modified for future events.
3 *Ascertain outcomes and impact.* The extent to which festivals, conferences, conventions or local, regional, national or international sporting events have encouraged tourism can be measured by the economic impact of the event through examining the direct and indirect financial benefits from tourist expenditures on a local economy. Or the event manager may wish to determine the impact that a local festival has on the quality of life in a community.
4 *Identify keys to success and failure.* Evaluating the event may also serve the purpose of identifying what worked well and why, what didn't work well, why it didn't work well and how that could be avoided or improved upon in the future.

5   *Improve and set a future course of action.* Evaluations can also help
     to identify ways in which particular aspects of an event can be
     improved as well as assist in the process of making decisions regard-
     ing the implementation, continuation, expansion or termination of
     an event.

In addition to these five key purposes, evaluation can also identify and
solve problems, find ways to improve management, determine the worth
of the event or its programs, measure success or failure, identify costs and
benefits, identify and measure impacts, satisfy sponsors and authorities
or help the event gain acceptance or credibility or support (Getz, 1997).
Another summary, this one by Chelimsky (1997), outlines three key functions of evaluation. The first is the development or the provision of eva-
luative help to strengthen the event and to improve event performance.
The second is accountability or the measurement of results or efficiency,
which provides information to decision makers. The third key function is
knowledge or the acquisition of a deeper understanding surrounding the
factors and processes underpinning the event which contributed either to
its success or its failure. Regardless of the specific purpose, evaluation is
a key component in the event planning model.

Key evaluation questions

In addition to ascertaining whether or not the event was successful in
achieving its goals and objectives, there are a number of other questions
that evaluations can answer. Evaluation questions typically fall into one
of five recognizable types according to the issues that they address (Rossi,
Freeman & Lipsey, 1999):

1   *Questions about the need for the event* (needs assessment). Needs
     assessments are often used as a first step in determining the initial
     ability to host an event or when designing a new event or restructuring
     an established event.
2   *Questions about event conceptualization or design* (evaluating
     program/event theory). Evaluating the conceptualization or design of
     an event involves explicitly stating in written or graphic form the
     theory guiding the event and then measuring how appropriate it is.
     This is most essential when planning brand-new events and when
     pilot testing events in their early stages.

3   *Questions about event operations, implementation and service delivery* (evaluating event processes). Process evaluation provides information for monitoring a specific procedure or strategy as it is being implemented so that what works can be preserved, and what doesn't work can be eliminated.
4   *Questions about the outcomes and impact of the event* (impact evaluation). Impact evaluation examines both the intended and unintended impacts of the event.
5   *Questions about event cost and cost-effectiveness* (evaluating efficiency). Evaluating event efficiency involves examining the benefits of the event in relation to the costs incurred by the event. Cost–benefit analysis can be used to evaluate the relationship between event costs and outcomes or impacts (benefits) by assigning monetary values to both costs and outcomes or impacts. Cost-effectiveness analysis also uses event costs and outcomes, but examines them in terms of the costs per unit of outcome achieved.

FACILITATING THE PROCESS OF EVALUATING THE EVENT

In order to effectively facilitate and manage the event evaluation process, there are a number of questions that the event manager has to consider before undertaking such an endeavour. The following questions are adapted from McDavid and Hawthorn (2006) in order to achieve a better fit within the context of evaluating events:

Key questions to ask

What type of event is it, and where is the event in terms of the program life cycle?
Is it a traditional or niche event? If traditional, what type of sport (see overview on traditional events in Chapter 1), and staged for what reasons (recreational, competitive and/or tourism), and at what level (local, regional, provincial or state, national or international)? Or what type of niche event is it (festival, banquet, conference, convention, stampede or other type of show)? Also, if niche, what is the history of the event, how did it evolve and is the event growing, remaining stable or declining? Regardless of whether or not the event is traditional or niche, the event manager should consider where the event is in relation to its life cycle.

That is, has the event lost its impact or freshness; does it appear to have gone flat or lost its appeal?

Who are the key stakeholders of the evaluation?

The term "stakeholders" refers to all individuals, groups or organizations having a significant interest in how well an event operates. For example, those with decision-making authority over various aspects of the event, sponsors, administrators, personnel, participants, clients, visitors, political decision makers, members of governing bodies, community leaders or intended beneficiaries all have a vested interest in the event. As most evaluations are typically user-driven, the event manager should identify early in the process the stakeholders, and consider their information needs when designing the evaluation project.

What are the questions or issues driving the evaluation?
That is, what is the goal or purpose of the evaluation?

Before evaluating the event, McDavid and Hawthorn (2006) recommend that event managers should know: who wants the evaluation done and why; are there any hidden agendas or concealed reasons for wanting the event evaluated; and what are the main issues that the evaluation should address (need, event design, event operations and delivery, outcomes and impact, cost and efficiency). While different stakeholders will have varying views and agendas, it is important that the event manager be aware of these groups and views when designing the event evaluation in order to avoid contaminating the data.

What resources are available to evaluate the event?

While most resources are typically dedicated to the production of an event, there is typically a scarcity of resources available to evaluate the event. When planning the event evaluation, the event manager should consider what resources will be required in order to effectively evaluate the event. These resources could be related to money, time, personnel, necessary expertise required, organizational support or any other resources that the event manager would need in order to effectively evaluate the event.

Have any evaluations been conducted in prior years?

Evaluation projects are different each time they are conducted. In order to reflect the uniqueness of the situation and the particularity of what is being evaluated, event managers can take advantage of evaluations of similar events in other settings or evaluations conducted in prior years. Rather than simply accept evaluations that have been conducted previously, the event manager should take into consideration the following questions. What issues did the evaluation address? What was evaluated, and how similar is it to what is currently being evaluated? Who conducted the evaluation? Who were the stakeholders? How credible is the evaluation? What measures were used, and what aspects are applicable to the current evaluation effort?

What kind of environment does the event operate in?
You will recall that complexity theory suggests that organizations adapt to their environment by creating event structures that are not overly complex and are also contingent upon the contextual factors of the environment. Questions relating to the size of the event, competition with other events, available resources or the degree of formalization, complexity or centralization in the event structure all need to be taken into consideration when preparing to evaluate.

Which research design strategies are suitable?
While the details of different quantitative or qualitative research designs are beyond the scope of this chapter, "an important consideration for practitioners is to know the strengths and weaknesses of different designs so that combinations of designs can be chosen that complement each other" (McDavid & Hawthorn, 2006, p. 30).

What sources of evidence (data) are available that are appropriate given the evaluation issues, the event structure and the environment in which the event operates?
Given the research design of the evaluation project as well as the approach to evaluating the event, what data should be collected in order to address the evaluation questions? Event managers should consider whether there is any existing data that can be used to serve their evaluation purposes as well as whether quantitative or qualitative data will best meet the needs of the evaluation effort.

Which evaluation approach seems appropriate?
The event manager will probably not be able to answer this until they have a foundational understanding of the strengths and limitations of different evaluation approaches.

122

Should the evaluation be conducted?

After reviewing the previous issues, the event manager must still decide whether or not to evaluate the event. One must consider, however, that "it is possible that after having looked at the mix of evaluation issues, resource constraints, organizational and political issues, research design, and measurement constraints, the [event] evaluator . . . recommends that no evaluation be done at this time" (McDavid & Hawthorn, 2006, p. 32). There is no sense in wasting the significant amounts of money, time and resources needed to evaluate the event if the results of the evaluation are not going to be used.

DECISIONS REQUIRED BY THE EVENT MANAGER BEFORE EVALUATING

In order for event managers to be able to successfully facilitate this phase of event planning, there are a number of elements that must be determined regarding evaluation. The evaluation should be conducted in the context of a theoretical framework and might include the following: informal versus formal evaluations; formative versus summative evaluation; what to evaluate; quantitative or qualitative approaches to evaluation; and dealing with political, ethical and moral evaluation issues.

ROLE OF THEORY IN EVALUATING EVENTS

When evaluating an event it is important to view the event from a theoretical perspective.

Systems theory suggests that event structures can be created and managed (as well as evaluated) by understanding the inputs, throughputs and outputs required to deliver the event. While it may not be feasible to evaluate all the resources (inputs), activities (throughputs) and outcomes (outputs) of the event, it is important to view the event from a systems perspective.

Process theory involves using the overall event plan to describe the assumptions and expectations about how the event is supposed to operate. These assumptions and expectations should be examined before evaluating the event in order to determine whether or not the expectations for the event were met and if aspects of the event operated as they were supposed to.

Contingency theory can also help event managers realize that the choice of organizational structures and control systems depends on, or is contingent on, characteristics of the external environment in which the event operates (Jones, George & Langton, 2005). That is why no two evaluation studies are identical. Even if the event has not changed dramatically from previous years, aspects of the external environment probably have. This in turn influences the operation of the event, which needs to be accounted for when evaluating the event from year to year. So, while evaluation projects are not designed to develop or test theory, systems theory, process theory and contingency theory can help event managers to develop a deeper understanding of the event and assist them in focusing on what aspects of the event to evaluate.

WHAT TO EVALUATE?

Before deciding whether to conduct a formative or summative evaluation, the event manager needs to determine what exactly is being evaluated. Henderson and Bialeschki (2002) discuss "five Ps of evaluation" in relation to what aspects of an event could be evaluated. These include *personnel*, *policies*, *places*, *programs* and *participant outcomes*. They further suggest that programs can be evaluated based on inputs, activities or outputs of the event. The inputs are the resources used to implement the event. Activities are the organizational processes within the event, and outcomes include such items as the economic impact of an event.

McDavid and Hawthorn (2006) observed that evaluating program effectiveness is the most common reason for conducting evaluations. They also suggest several other aspects of events that can be evaluated, such as event efficiency (including a cost–benefit analysis of the event), the cost-effectiveness of the event or how well the event was implemented. Event managers should be aware that basically any aspect of an event can be evaluated, including the development and implementation of the event plan, outfitting of the venue, ticketing and accreditation, security, communications, information and signage, transportation, parking and so on. Before making any decisions with respect to evaluation approaches or data collection strategies, the event manager must clearly determine what aspect of the event is being evaluated, why it is being evaluated and the criteria to be used to evaluate it.

124

APPROACHES TO EVENT EVALUATION

Goal-based approach

Although two main types of evaluation, formative and summative, have previously been distinguished based on the timing and intended uses of the evaluation, numerous evaluation models have been developed over the years. Among the first was the goal-based model developed by Tyler (Isaac & Michael, 1981) in the 1930s. The purpose of this goal-based, goal-attainment approach (Henderson & Bialeschki, 2002) or evaluation by objectives (Worthen, Sanders & Fitzpatrick, 1997) is to determine whether or not the event is achieving its goals and objectives. In this approach, goals and objectives are used as the criteria by which the event is evaluated. Goals are a broad statement about what is to be accomplished (Rossman & Schlatter, 2003), whereas objectives are specific statements that describe how the goal will be accomplished. Goal-based evaluation can be used with either outcome or organizational objectives. Outcome objectives examine the impacts or effects of the event on individual behaviours in one of four behavioural domains: (i) cognitive (such as thinking, knowledge); (ii) affective (such as feeling, attitudes); (iii) psychomotor (such as movement, acting); or (iv) social (such as how people relate to each other). Organizational objectives refer to internal processes within the event and relate to both the operation of the event and the amount of effort to be expended in the delivery of the event. In order for this approach to be effective, the goals and objectives for the event have to be well written. As Rossman and Schlatter (2003) recommend, objectives should be: specific, clear and concrete for understanding, measurable for objective assessment, pragmatic (attainable and realistic) and useful for making programming decisions. In addition to being one of the most common approaches used, the advantage to goal-based approaches for evaluating an event is the objectivity that this approach provides for establishing accountability. The drawback to using this approach is that the event needs to have well-written goals and objectives.

Goal-free approach

In response to the criticism of goal-based approaches to evaluation; namely, that they do not take unintended outcomes into consideration, Scriven (1972) developed the goal-free approach. This approach seeks to discover and judge the effects, outcomes and impacts of the event without considering what they should be. When facilitating the use of this approach, the event manager should begin with no predetermined idea of what might be found. The overall purpose of this approach is to find out what is happening with the event. According to Henderson and Bialeschki (2002), in this approach, the evaluator will

> usually talk to people, identify program elements, overview the program, discover purposes and concerns, conceptualize issues and problems, identify qualitative and/or quantitative data that needs to be collected, select methods and techniques to use including the possibility of case studies, collect the data, match data and the issues of audiences, and prepare for the delivery of the report.
> (Henderson & Bialeschki, 2002, p. 72)

The advantage to this approach is that it examines actual effects of the event (regardless of whether or not they were intended) and allows for in-depth analysis, usually through the collection of qualitative data. The drawback to this approach is that it can be very time-consuming and some effects may be difficult to measure.

Responsive approach

In response to criticisms that evaluations were not being tailored to the needs of stakeholders, Stake (1975) developed the responsive model of evaluation. This approach stresses the importance of being "responsive to realities in the program and to the reactions, concerns, and issues of participants rather than being preordinate with evaluation plans, relying on preconceptions and formal plans and objectives of the program" (Worthen et al., 1997, p. 159). Stake (1975) suggested that an evaluation is responsive if it "orients more directly to program activities than to program intents; responds to audience requirements for information; and if the different value-perspectives present are referred to in reporting the success and failure of the program" (p. 14). The purpose, framework and focus of a responsive evaluation "emerge from interactions with constituents, and those interactions and observations result in progressive focusing on issues" (Worthen et al., 1997, p. 160). When taking a responsive approach, the event manager must continuously interact with individuals from various stakeholder groups. The manager needs to determine what information is needed and must present it in a way that will result in understanding.

Empowerment evaluation

Fetterman, Kaftarian and Wandersman (1996) developed the empowerment evaluation model. This model uses evaluation concepts, techniques and findings to foster improvement and self-determination. The focus of empowerment evaluation is on programs. It is designed to help program participants evaluate themselves and their programs in order to improve practice and foster self-determination. The evaluator–stakeholder relationship is more participatory and collaborative than Stake's responsive evaluation. As a result, evaluators taking this approach work toward building the capacity of the participating stakeholders to conduct evaluations of their own. This approach enables managers to use the results from evaluations for advocacy and change, and to experience some sense of control over the event being evaluated. The process of empowerment evaluation "is not only directed at producing informative and useful findings but also at enhancing the self-development and political influence of the participants" (Rossi et al., 1999, p. 58).

The content, input, process and product (CIPP) model: a systems approach to evaluation

The CIPP model (Stufflebeam, 1971) is intended to provide a basis for making decisions within a systems analysis of planned change. The CIPP model defines evaluation as the process of delineating, obtaining and providing useful information for judging decision alternatives. This definition, in effect, incorporates three basic points. First, evaluation is a continuous, systematic process. Second, this process includes three pivotal steps: the first is stating questions requiring answers and specifying information to be obtained; the second is acquiring relevant data; and the third is providing the resulting information as it becomes available to potential decision makers. The manager can then consider and interpret information in relation to its impact upon decision alternatives that can modify or improve the event. Third, evaluation supports the process of decision making by allowing the selection of an alternative and by following up on the consequences of a decision.

The CIPP model of evaluation is concerned with four types of decisions:

1 planning decisions, which influence selection of goals and objectives;
2 structuring decisions, which ascertain optimal strategies and procedural designs for achieving the objectives that have been derived from planning decisions;
3 implementing decisions, which afford the means for carrying out and improving upon the execution of already selected designs, methods or strategies;
4 recycling decisions, which determine whether to continue, change, or terminate an activity or even the event itself.

In addition, there are four respective kinds of evaluation: context, input, process and product – hence the acronym CIPP.

Context evaluation yields information regarding the extent to which discrepancies exist between what is and what is not desired relative to certain value expectations, areas of concern, difficulties and opportunities, in order that goals and objectives may be formulated. *Input* evaluation provides information about strong and weak points of alternative strategies and designs for the realization of specified objectives. *Process* evaluation provides information for monitoring a chosen procedure or strategy as it is being implemented so that its strong points can be preserved and its weak points eliminated. *Product* evaluation furnishes information to ascertain whether the strategies, procedures or methods being implemented to attain these objectives should be terminated, modified or continued in their present form.

Event managers can use the CIPP model of evaluation as a framework for ensuring a complete and comprehensive evaluation of any event or aspect of it. Utilizing the CIPP model as a guideline, event managers can evaluate not just the outcome of the event, but the entire planning process, the event itself and the intended and unintended outcomes of the event. The CIPP model is designed to evaluate: the selection of goals and objectives; optimal strategies or program designs for achieving these objectives; methods to improve the execution of already selected program designs, methods or strategies; and whether or not to continue, modify or terminate the event or aspects of it.

Professional judgment approach

Should the event manager feel that they do not have the necessary expertise required to facilitate the event evaluation, one option, and another approach, would be to hire an outside professional consultant. If a high degree of objectivity is required or if the evaluation requires expertise beyond that of the event manager, then they may want to consider hiring an external expert. This may be the case if the event manager is interested in undertaking some sort of economic evaluation of the event. Hiring a professional consultant means that the event manager needs less time to evaluate the event and is generally easier for the organization. In addition, the event manager obtains the results from a neutral, external expert. This adds a degree of objectivity to the evaluation process which may be important where there are political issues surrounding the event. On the other hand, hiring an expert can be expensive and the external consultant should have a degree of familiarity with the event, which may reduce the pool of experts that the event manager has to choose from.

Which approach to use

The decision regarding which evaluation approach to use should be based on the purpose of the evaluation as well as what is being evaluated. If experts and standards exist, *professional judgment* might be best. If goals and measurable objectives exist for a program, evaluating by using those goals and objectives (*goal attainment*) as the foundation will be preferable. If one is interested in finding out what is happening without comparing to established goals, the *goal-free approach* may be superior. If the event manager is interested in evaluating one component of the event in relation to the inputs, throughputs and outputs, then a systems approach such as the *CIPP model* will enable them to choose the elements to examine in relation to the broad purpose of the event. Regardless of the approach taken, event managers should also ensure that the evaluation is responsive to stakeholders. Evaluation reports are utilized for making decisions to improve the event; to continue, modify or terminate the event or aspects of it; and, in the process of so doing, to help clients or participants evaluate themselves and their events.

As well as evaluating an event, managers need to consider the renewal of an event into the future.

EVENT RENEWAL: THE THREE HORIZONS

McKinsey & Company (2009) devised an overview on the concept of business growth over time that entails what they called "the three horizons." Each horizon is applicable to event management. An application of the three horizons framework means to act on hosting a sport, recreation or tourism event, as well as simultaneously positioning the event for growth over the next five years and beyond. Each of the three horizons are as follows:

- *Horizon 1* is concerned with the dominant focus or current business activities over the time period of one to three years. In event management, this means focusing on hosting the event. This focus can include a number of areas to ensure event excellence such as communication, resource management (people, finances and technology management), along with event marketing and sales.
- *Horizon 2* is concerned with the activities that will ensure that business growth will continue in three to five years' time. In event management, this means a focus on ensuring that an event is not stagnant in terms of growth over the medium term. This focus includes areas such as obtaining evaluation feedback from spectators about the event and using it to redesign future marketing and sales strategies; testing new rules today to be incorporated within the event in the future; testing new technologies for future use; and/or redesigning elements of the event for future application.
- *Horizon 3* is concerned with business activities for the distant future (five to ten years). Keeping an event relevant over the long term can be difficult. This horizon involves activities that will position the event for a viable long-term future. In event management, this can involve revamping the event for the needs of an upcoming generation and continuously incorporating elements that are on-trend.

If all three horizons are developed simultaneously, an event has a better chance of maintaining growth over the current term, the medium term and the long term.

CHAPTER SUMMARY

This chapter focused on providing the event manager with the background knowledge to successfully facilitate the evaluation phase of event planning.

130

In so doing, evaluation was defined as the systematic collection and analysis of data in order to make judgments regarding the value or worth of a particular aspect of an event, and distinctions were made between the terms evaluation, research and assessment. The chapter also explained why evaluation is necessary and identified several key evaluation questions. Five general steps when evaluating an event were detailed. The chapter outlined a number of decisions that the event manager needs to make in order to successfully facilitate the process of conducting event evaluations. Finally, the chapter presented the three horizons framework for event growth over time.

CHAPTER QUESTIONS

1 Why is evaluation necessary in event management?
2 What questions does the event manager have to consider before evaluating a event?
3 What are the five key evaluation questions according to Rossi et al. (1999)?
4 List and describe six approaches to evaluating an event.
5 Describe each of the three horizons and how each acts to guide an event manager to build event growth.

CHAPTER 9

SAFEGUARDING THE NATURAL ENVIRONMENT IN EVENT MANAGEMENT

CHRIS CHARD, MATT DOLF AND GREG DINGLE

"There is no business to be done on a dead planet"
(Hollender & Breen, 2010, p. 114)

This chapter focuses on the roles and responsibilities of event managers to produce a quality event while simultaneously considering the impacts of events on the environment. The call to manage events in a more environmentally sustainable manner will surely be amplified as there is increasing pressure to (i) reduce direct harm caused to the environment, (ii) satisfy ethical interests of stakeholders (both internal and external), (iii) integrate risk management, (iv) communicate in a credible manner, (v) ensure that events can operate in a safe and healthy environment, and (vi) meet new legal requirements.

In this chapter we will look at sustainability; specifically we will focus on *environmental sustainability (ES)* and consider why ES is important in event management. Next we will outline the various roles and responsibilities for event managers in designing events in a more sustainable way. Finally, we will introduce environmental impact assessment methods for events and specifically outline three approaches: life cycle assessment (LCA), carbon footprints and ecological footprints.

WHAT IS ENVIRONMENTAL SUSTAINABILITY?

In this chapter, the term "environmental sustainability" (ES) follows the well-established definition by the United Nations (UN) Brundtland

132

Report (1987). This report sets out ES as the capacity of an organization to safeguard the natural environment by "meeting the needs of the present generation without compromising the ability of future generations to meet their own needs" (p. 1). Clearly, this definition offers elements of choice as both the present and the future must be considered in any organizational decision making. Entwined in these "now" or "later" considerations, sustainability requires that organizations evolve and broaden the metrics to assess long-term success. However, we also note that estimates of the number of definitions of sustainability vary between 100 and 200 (Moscardo et al., 2013; Parkin, 2000), so this plurality of views offers the opportunity for a nuanced understanding of this concept. For example, Parkin (2000) argues that "sustainable" means that

> something has the "capacity for continuance." Sustainability is therefore a quality. It is an objective not a process. Something either has or has not got the quality of sustainability – the intrinsic capacity to keep itself going more or less indefinitely. We want the environment to have it, so it can support life. It is the growing number of indications that it has not got it (most worryingly manifest in climate change) that have prompted current concern.
> (Parkin, 2000, p. 4)

These contrasting definitions nevertheless illustrate the degree of consensus around the critical importance of ensuring that the natural environment is at the heart of sustainability efforts.

The terminology is evolving too. Robinson (2004) argues that while "sustainable development" is more commonly used by private sector and government organizations, the term "sustainability" is gaining widespread use among non-governmental organizations (NGOs) and academics. This is because the word "development" is tied to growth, whereas sustainability refers to the concept of preservation, or absolute limits. Robinson suggests that sustainability is seen more as a "value change" and sustainable development as a "technical fix." Although the terms *sustainability* and *sustainable development* are often used synonymously in practice, along with other common terms such as "corporate social responsibility" and "triple bottom line," the philosophical distinctions are important. There is a growing consensus that achieving gross domestic product (GDP) growth, or growth in the value of a country's goods and services, while at the same time shrinking resource use is extremely difficult (UNEP, 2011). Interestingly, Jackson (2009) proposes that prosperity can be achieved without GDP growth; however, this type of progress needs to be vetted. In the meantime, event managers need to be cognizant of the challenge to achieve financial growth on the one hand, and on the other, to improve quality of life through lower resource use and lower environmental impacts.

ENVIRONMENTAL CHANGE, VULNERABILITY, AND THE NEED FOR RESILIENCE AND ADAPTATION FOR SPORT, RECREATION AND TOURISM EVENTS

While the sustainability of the natural environment is of critical importance in broader sustainability discourse, it is also clear that the sustainability of humans, and our various institutions – including those in sport, recreation and tourism – are of equal importance. Indeed, these industrial sectors are as fundamentally dependent on natural resources as others (e.g. finance, retail, manufacturing), and in some ways are directly – or indirectly – dependent in ways that other industries are not. Specifically, much sport, recreation and tourism activity depends on natural resources for the basic elements of its success. For example, it is clear that sport depends indirectly on natural resources for the design, building and operation of the facilities in which it is staged (Kellison, 2015; Mallen & Chard, 2012; Nguyen, Trendafilova & Pfahl, 2014).

However, it is also clear that much of the sport, recreation and tourism sectors depends directly on ecosystems to provide the right environmental conditions that make them both possible and popular. In this way, sport, recreation and tourism are similar to other nature-dependent industries such as agriculture, aquaculture and forestry (Amelung & Moreno, 2012; Linnenluecke, Griffiths & Winn, 2013). For example, outdoor sports such as downhill skiing, snowboarding and a variety of football codes – including soccer, rugby union and American football – all depend on the global climate system to provide the stable and sufficiently cold local climates for their success. Equally, sports such as tennis, golf, baseball and cricket depend on the stable warm climates that are essential for their success, while sailing sports are dependent on nature for the winds that enable competition. Similarly, recreation and tourism activities (e.g. aquatic activities, visits to national parks) are also dependent on nature to provide either the natural attractions for such activities and/or the stable environmental conditions that enable these. This fundamental nature-dependence – which includes climate-dependence (Packard & Reinhardt,

2000; Scott, Gössling & Hall, 2012) – underpins significant elements of the sport, recreation and tourism sectors. Yet it also highlights the potential for the significant vulnerability of these sectors to changes in the natural environment, the need for building resilience for their physical sites, and adaptive capacity for the organizations that manage them.

Global environmental change (GEC) is a phenomenon supported by a vast body of scientific evidence (Rockström et al., 2009; Steffen et al., 2015; UNEP, 2005, 2007, 2012a, 2012b), and consistent with this, it is now recognized that the concepts of *vulnerability, resilience* and *adaptation* are important to understanding the human dimensions of this change (Janssen & Ostrom, 2006). While vulnerability (Füssel, 2007b; Gallopín, 2006; Smit & Wandel, 2006) has a number of definitions within GEC literature, Adger's (2006, p. 269) is perhaps the most appealing: "the state of susceptibility to harm from exposure to stresses associated with environmental and social change and from the absence of capacity to adapt." Such harms may be either direct and short-term ones, or long-term ones (Winn, Kirchgeorg, Griffiths, Linnenluecke & Gunther, 2011). In the context of GEC, vulnerability for sport, recreation and tourism may also be in the form of direct and short-term harm (e.g. damage to sport facilities, national parks or tourist precincts from natural disasters like hurricanes or forest fires); or longer-term and/or indirect (e.g. higher insurance premiums; higher operating costs; increased adaptation costs from changed regulatory or market conditions).

Resilience (Füssel, 2007b; Gallopín, 2006; Janssen & Ostrom, 2006) has been defined as "the capacity to absorb shocks and still maintain function" (Folke, 2006, p. 253). When applied to organizations, resilience has been described as a range of coping strategies (Linnenluecke & Griffiths, 2015). In the context of present global environmental changes, resilience in sport, recreation and tourism is a quality that has already been demonstrated (e.g. New Orleans tourist operators recovering from Hurricane Katrina in 2005; National Parks in California recovering from forest fires; Suncorp Stadium recovering from the 2011 Brisbane floods). In contrast, adaptation (Füssel, 2007a; Gallopín, 2006; Linnenluecke & Griffiths, 2015) – which has also been defined in various ways – has been described as "an adjustment in social–ecological systems in response to actual, perceived, or expected environmental changes and their impacts" (Janssen & Ostrom, 2006, p. 237). In essence, such adjustments are aimed at enabling such a system (e.g. a household, group, organization or country) to "better cope with" changed conditions, hazards or risks (Smit & Wandel, 2006, p. 282). For sport, recreation and tourism, adaptation may come about in different ways (e.g. outdoor sports introducing new playing surfaces in response to climate change; recreation centres or tourism operators reducing energy use in response to a carbon-pricing regulatory regime).

Overall, sport, recreation and tourism providers need to be able to adapt to change within natural, regulatory and market environments and develop resilience to such change.

ASSIGNMENT A: EVENT DECISION MAKING FOR ENVIRONMENTAL SUSTAINABILITY

Suppose you are a manager of an annual golf event that is the cornerstone fundraising vehicle for your charitable organization. The tournament has been held at the same nearby golf course for the past six years. While no contracts exist, there is a "general understanding" that the tournament will be held at the same golf course for the coming year; your volunteers and staff have operated under this assumption in all planning. Two months before the event, however, you are approached by the general manager (GM) of a new private course located 50 minutes north of your town. The GM offers financial incentives to move the event to their course; the proposal would increase net revenues from the event by 50 percent. As you contemplate the change of venue, other considerations spring to mind such as the increased travel for volunteers, staff and participants to attend the event, the longer hours for volunteers, the impact that the loss of the event could have on the local golf course, and negative image issues arising from deserting the local golf course at the last minute. Last, the GM tells you that the new club is experiencing a host of environmental challenges with pesticide use and water run-off to the local pond.

Clearly, the financial benefit of changing golf courses is evident, but how will you weigh these against the other social and environmental issues?

As can be seen from the scenario above, decision-making frameworks based entirely on the "bottom line" only account for the financial consequences of actions and are insufficient for contextualizing social and environmental considerations. Fundamentally, sustainability is about

136

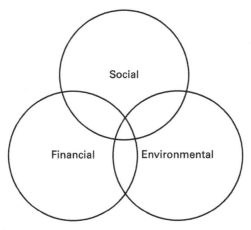

Figure 9.1 The three overlapping spheres of sustainability

managing three Ps: people, planet and profit! Figure 9.1 provides a visual representation of sustainability in action; here, understanding the interactions between economic, social and environmental contexts forces managers to recalibrate their thinking, managerial decisions and organizational assessment.

THE TRIPLE TOP LINE AND THE TRIPLE BOTTOM LINE

The "Triple Top Line" and "Triple Bottom Line" are each examples of paradigms that embrace this wider scope to organizational management and assessment. In traditional business accounting, the top line relates to incoming revenue for an organization, while the bottom line is what is left of this revenue after expenses have been accounted for. Similarly, the Triple Top Line moves "accountability to the beginning of the design process" (McDonough & Braungart, 2002, p. 252), by encompassing financial, social and environmental concerns. Essentially, the Triple Top Line focuses the event manager's lens on every aspect of planning for an event. For example, knowing that there will be $150,000 in revenue for a youth soccer tournament is not enough; we should know "how" the $150,000 is generated, socially and environmentally. Likewise, the Triple Bottom Line assesses the "bottom line" results of an event: how did the event perform? Again, consideration is given to the three sustainability measures. For example, considering our youth soccer event, if the event manager shows $28,000 in net profit, financially the tournament is deemed a success. However, if environmental degradation and social injustices occurred to achieve these fiscal gains, a Triple Bottom Line approach would account for these deficiencies.

McDonough and Braungart (2002) note that frameworks such as these are great tools for integrating sustainability into the business agenda by balancing traditional economic goals with social and environmental concerns. The key word here is *balance*. Of vital importance when interpreting Figure 9.1 is the need for *all* of the spheres to be strong. A common misconception of sustainable management is that it is *only* focused on environmental concerns. This is simply not true! Environmental sustainability at the expense of economic viability is in itself unsustainable. Randjelovic, O'Rourke and Orsato (2003) address this point, noting the "need to develop competences . . . which can create economic value *and* reduce environmental impacts/risks" (p. 251).

Hannah Jones, Nike's sustainability chief, addresses the concept of organizational sustainability by noting the desire of increasing value for shareholders, while simultaneously enhancing value, – socially and environmentally – for the multitude of organizational stakeholders. The thought process at Nike is that ES does not, and should not, come at the expense of increasing shareholder value. "We can do well and do good at the same time," said Jones (Hollender & Breen, 2010, p. 121).

WHY IS ENVIRONMENTAL SUSTAINABILITY IMPORTANT IN EVENT MANAGEMENT?

Barrett and Scott (2001) note that every organization, small to large, must consider environmental issues, such as transportation, personal and organizational consumption and waste management. Examples abound concerning "an increasing growth in the consumption of natural resources combined with a corresponding ferocious growth in the volume of waste" (Ingebrigtsen & Jakobsen, 2006, p. 389). The United Nations Environment Programme (2007) GEO-4 report notes clear evidence of environmental change facing the world today and, of particular importance, the report clearly assigns responsibility for these environmental changes to "human activities" (p. 8).

If we accept that the actions of all individuals collectively contribute to environmental change, then surely responsibility to enhance sustainability

138

is the duty of everyone: governments, businesses and citizens. Indeed, it can be argued that every event manager should be held accountable for their actions with respect to sustainability. Here, accountability is defined as "being called to account for one's actions" (Mulgan, 2000, p. 555).

Indeed, where no accountability is taken by any individual party for a mutual entity, the outcome may be the deterioration or destruction of said entity. In the case of ES, that entity is a vibrant planet. While this assertion may seem dramatic, Perelman (2003) noted that "in a complex world where the environment is now at the breaking point, the continued experiment with this dangerous system of organization represents a grave risk to everybody and everything" (p. 221). As Meegan Jones, Australian delegation head of ISO 20121, emphasized:

> Business as usual within the events industry can't continue. Our industry can't keep producing mountain ranges of rubbish, or leave clouds of CO_2 in legacy. No matter the type of event, every coming together of people for a purpose can be done so with consideration for sustainability.
>
> (Jones, 2011, n.p.)

ROLES AND RESPONSIBILITIES FOR ENVIRONMENTAL SUSTAINABILITY IN EVENT MANAGEMENT

The United Nations Environment Programme (UN, 2010, n.p.) lists a number of ways in which sport events can impact the natural environment, including:

- development of fragile ecosystems or scarce land;
- noise and light pollution;
- consumption of non-renewable resources;
- consumption of natural resources;
- emission of greenhouse gases;
- ozone layer depletion;
- soil and water pollution from pesticide use;
- soil erosion during construction and from spectators;
- waste generation from construction of facilities, and from spectators.

Recognizing this problem, it has been argued that event managers should be responsible for playing their part in protecting the natural environment

(Mallen & Chard, 2011). Some sport organizations have begun to embrace such responsibility. For example, the environment is now recognized as the "third pillar" of the Olympic Movement alongside sport and culture (Cantelon & Letters, 2000). Indeed, the Olympic Movement's Agenda 21 report highlights the commitment of the organization to environmental sustainability. Other examples of organizations embracing event management environmental sustainability initiatives in sport can be found, including the "Green Goal" work done by Fédération Internationale de Football Association (FIFA) on the World Cup (FIFA, 2006); the Football Association's FA Cup initiatives (Collins, Flynn, Munday & Roberts, 2007); the newfound focus on sustainability by the National Football League (NFL) and its flagship Super Bowl event (Scharwath, 2012); the 2010 Commonwealth Games (Sobhana, 2009); and the London 2012 Olympic and Paralympic Summer Games (Tian & Brimblecombe, 2008).

At a micro-level, Hums (2010) notes that "students need to know the actions they can take with their events and their facilities to contain the impact of sport on the environment" (p. 5). So it appears that environmental sustainability in event management is gaining support from the university classroom to the Olympic boardroom. At a practical level the question remains, who is ultimately responsible for ES and how might this responsibility be proactively and effectively managed?

ASSIGNMENT B: ACE CORPORATION TRIATHLON GROUP (ACTG) SUSTAINABILITY OWNERSHIP AND ACCOUNTABILITY

Imagine you are the marketing manager of the Ace Corporation Triathlon Group (ACTG). At a recent managers' meeting, which included the heads of finance, legal affairs, human resources, operations, information, and yourself, the mandate from the president of ACTG is to move environmental sustainability to the forefront of the company's event delivery for the coming year. After the meeting, everybody is excited about integrating ES into their division's practices.

At the following managers' meeting, the president asks for an update on the company's sustainability initiatives. Who steps forward to

---

140

give the breakdown of ACTG's progress on this initiative? If challenges are put forth by the management team, who "owns" these event management environmental sustainability initiatives, who will be charged with the task of finding solutions?

While environmental sustainability is certainly in its embryonic stage for event management, work has begun to move initiatives forward on the managerial agenda. For example, the Sport Event Environmental Performance Measurement (SE-EPM) model designed by Mallen, Stevens, Adams and McRoberts (2010) provides a comprehensive framework for evaluating a sport event's environmental performance. Key items of consideration within the framework include:

- the environmental organization system (environmental policies, environmental management committee, involvement in environmental programs);
- the environmental activities, stakeholder disclosure and relationships (information transfer, disclosure and communications);
- the environmental operational countermeasures (proactive initiatives such as renewable energy sources utilized, recycling, reduction, environmental training);
- environmental tracking (are items such as energy use and waste reduction being measured?);
- indicators and measurement items: inputs and outputs (paper, raw materials, CO_2).

The benefit of frameworks such as the SE-EPM lies in its utility to guide event managers on ES initiatives. Moreover, a clearly defined rubric to guide assessment on event environmental performance can assist event managers in making individuals accountable for their assigned ES projects. This type of guideline should serve event managers well in the coming years. Indeed, as the introduction of formal policies becomes commonplace, such as ISO 20121: Event Sustainability Management System (www.iso20121.org), the future of event management, and the requirements asked of the event manager will change. Here, the requirement to be compliant in terms of sustainability will be mandated and policies to ensure observance of set standards will need to be integrated into event planning decisions.

141

MEASURING TO MANAGE: INTEGRATING ENVIRONMENTAL IMPACT ASSESSMENT OF EVENTS

Even as a growing number of events incorporate qualitative environmental management, few carry out quantitative assessment or modelling (Jones, 2008). Decisions are therefore often based on intuition, visibility and ease of implementation, rather than on an empirical understanding of major contributors to environmental harm.

There is a famous management axiom: "You can't manage what you can't measure." In monetary terms, we rely on budgets and accounting procedures to make planning decisions and to reflect the value of goods and services. As we have discussed earlier in this chapter, the environmental and social costs are not fully captured in current financial valuations. For example, the value of water loss from a water-stressed region is not reflected in the price of goods and services. As event managers, we therefore need additional indicators to make decisions about how we organize our events and to answer questions such as: What is the biodiversity impact of fertilizers used on our soccer fields? How much will installing solar panels on our stadium reduce the impact of electricity use? Should we build temporary or permanent venues?

It is common to see events target waste reduction and recycled paper as part of their "green" initiatives. But are these the most important things on which to focus? Arguably not, since we know that Canada's greenhouse gas (GHG) emissions in 2010 showed that the impact of waste was 3 percent, compared to 81 percent for energy (of which 24 percent was transport) and 8 percent for agriculture (Government of Canada, 2010). While not ignoring the symbolic importance of the visibility factor of trash and the expectation of fans to see recycling bins, organizers need tools to help them focus on the areas where they can affect the greatest change. This section will discuss the emerging method of life cycle assessment (LCA) and two commonly used environmental metrics applicable to sport events: the carbon footprint and the ecological footprint.

Life cycle assessment

Sport event organizers can take advantage of a multitude of environmental sustainability assessment methods, tools and indicators (Ness, Urbel-Piirsalu, Anderberg & Olsson, 2007), but no internationally accepted

142

agreement exists on how governments, let alone events, should measure and report on impacts. We will focus on life cycle assessment (LCA) as a promising method for measuring environmental impacts over the life of a product or service: from cradle to grave. Life cycle assessment is being widely adopted by both the public and private sectors to assess impacts, report on performance and as a basis for policies and regulations (Finnveden et al., 2009). Specifically, it can be a powerful tool for deciding between alternatives: *does product/solution A or product/solution B have the lower environmental impact?*

According to the International Organization for Standardization (ISO, 2006), which sets out the ISO 14044 (www.iso.org) guidelines and requirements for carrying out an LCA, two of the key features of this method are:

1 life cycle stages: raw material acquisition, production, use, end-of-life treatment, recycling and final disposal;
2 phases for carrying out an LCA study: goal and scope definition, inventory analysis, impact assessment, and interpretation.

It is useful to understand each phase in a bit more detail (see Figure 9.2).

- *Goal and scope* defines the purpose of the study, the system boundaries and the major assumptions.
- *Inventory analysis* defines the inventory of data, environmental inputs (resources) and outputs (emissions, wastes) of the system under study, and the methods for data collection and analysis.

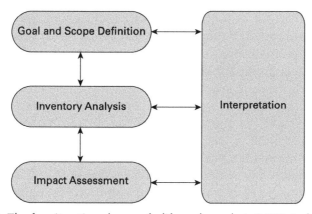

Figure 9.2 The four iterative phases of a life cycle analysis (LCA) study according to ISO 14044

- ■ *Impact assessment* translates the inputs and outputs into indicators of potential environmental impact (e.g. human health, climate change, ecosystem quality).
- ■ *Interpretation* provides meaning to the results of the inventory and environmental impact assessment relative to the goals of the study.

Thinking with a life cycle perspective encourages both producers and consumers to consider the upstream and downstream impacts in the supply chain. For event management, this means not only understanding the environmental harm caused on-site by activities, such as air quality affected by transportation emissions; but also the off-site impacts from purchased food, materials and the generated waste. Life cycle assessments are used for a widening range of applications including business strategy, product and process design, environmental labelling and product declarations. A key strength of LCA is its ability to characterize environmental impacts across multiple damage categories, such as human health, ecosystem quality, climate change and resource depletion (Jolliet et al., 2003). While LCA focuses on environmental impacts, it can be complemented by a broader set of life cycle management (LCM) tools including life cycle costing (LCC) and social LCA.

There are, however, some considerations with using LCA for event management. First, LCA results should not be used as a basis for comparison unless system boundaries, data sets, assumptions and included processes are the same; we need to compare apples with apples. Second, the complexity of an LCA can be resource-intensive if it requires extensive data collection and expertise. This can be a challenge for events with limited budgets or staff time. A third consideration is communication; while we all understand the value of a dollar, it can be challenging to interpret the importance of one tonne of carbon or one litre of polluted water. This leads us to a fourth issue – how to select between opposing results, such as: which is more important, carbon or water? The answer of course depends on many issues such as geographic location, water scarcity, stakeholder values, placing importance on current versus future impacts and so on. Life cycle assessment can be a powerful planning tool for events, but brings with it a need for increased expertise, education, stakeholder buy-in and resources to implement it effectively.

144

Carbon footprint

A carbon footprint measures the global warming potential (synonymous with climate change potential) of a defined activity resulting from associated greenhouse gas (GHG) emissions over a given time horizon that is usually 100 years (Wright, Kemp & Williams, 2011). The potential impacts for a number of GHGs (some common ones are carbon dioxide, methane and nitrous oxide) have been characterized by the United Nations Intergovernmental Panel on Climate Change as carbon "equivalents" (IPCC, 2007). The unit of measure is therefore the mass of CO_2 equivalents: kg CO_2-eq. The carbon footprint is the most widely used "single" environmental impact category in the sports industry, with a host of major events such as Vancouver 2010, London 2012 and the FIFA World Cup 2010 integrating it into their event management strategies. For instance, the United Nations Environment Programme estimated that the global warming impact of the FIFA 2010 World Cup in South Africa would total over 2 million tonnes of CO_2-equivalent emissions, with 65 percent due to international travel, 17 percent due to national travel and 13 percent from accommodation energy use; the actual footprint was 1.65 million tonnes (UNEP, 2012b).

Some benefits to applying a carbon footprint approach are as follows: it is a widely used and understood benchmark for environmental impacts; it has also become fairly well known and is therefore easily communicated to the public realm; it has the advantage of being applicable globally since global warming is not regionalized; and it benefits from a strong consensus in the scientific community on the existence of the problem and on the characterization of impacts (IPCC, 2007). A key drawback of events management using a single-indicator approach, however, is that it does not provide a full and contextual understanding of other impacts such as water use, land use or resource use (Collins, Jones & Munday, 2009; Weidema, Thrane, Christensen, Schmidt & Løkke, 2008).

Ecological footprint

The ecological footprint method developed by Wackernagel and Rees (1996) puts a focus on the carrying capacity of the earth. By estimating the total human consumption of resources and comparing it to the rate at which the planet can replace them, it can calculate whether our activities are meeting or exceeding its regenerative capacity. The unit of measure is the bioproductive area in hectares required to maintain human consumption. This can also be communicated in terms of the number of "planet earths" required to support our activities. According to the 2014 World Wide Fund for Nature (WWF) Living Planet Report, the human population currently exceeds our regenerative capacity by using the equivalent of 2.6 earths (WWF, 2014).

London 2012, for example, embedded the ecological footprint as a measure for achieving its sustainability platform of a "One Planet Olympics." Collins et al. (2007) applied this assessment framework to measure the impact of the FA Cup Final international soccer match in Wales. They were able to show that spectators at the event increased their ecological footprint seven times over the daily average for a Welsh citizen.

Whatever environmental impact assessment measures managers choose to use, it is vital to become literate in the concept of examining impacts with a life cycle approach and across multiple indicators. As new tools develop for the event industry, managers can increase the sophistication level of their assessments and demonstrate increased accountability to their stakeholders.

ASSIGNMENT C: USING A CARBON FOOTPRINT TO MINIMIZE THE ACCOMMODATION IMPACT

You are organizing a baseball tournament for eight teams of 15 people each. You are in the process of selecting a sponsor hotel to house the teams during the seven-day (and seven-night) event. One option, the Dandelion Inn, is certified with a "green hotel" program, partly because its owners have achieved significant reductions in energy use, water use and waste generated compared to the industry average. However, they are located 10 kilometres away from the venue. A second sponsor choice, the Meridian Hotel, is an industry average hotel and is located only one kilometre away. In either case, you need to send a shuttle bus to the hotel twice a day to pick up and drop off the teams. A recent LCA study tells you that the Dandelion Inn has an impact of 6 kg carbon dioxide equivalents (kg CO_2-eq) per person per night, and the Meridian Hotel has an impact of 12 kg CO_2-eq per person per night. You also know that the shuttle bus travel impact is 0.050 kg CO_2-eq per person per km.

Hotel	Hotel carbon footprint	Travel carbon footprint	Total carbon footprint
Dandelion Inn	kg CO_2-eq	kg CO_2-eq	kg CO_2-eq
Meridian Hotel	kg CO_2-eq	kg CO_2-eq	kg CO_2-eq

Figure 9.3 Scenario data chart

1   Determine the hotel, travel and total carbon footprints of each option. Which has the lowest impact?
2   What other ES considerations are there for an event manager when selecting hotels?
3   How else could you lower the carbon footprint of accommodation?
4   What are the considerations regarding applying carbon as the only environmental impact category?

To determine the hotel carbon footprint:

Dandelion: _____ people × _____ nights × 6 kg CO_2-eq / person / night = _____ kg CO_2-eq

Meridian: _____ people × _____ nights × 12 kg CO_2-eq / person / night = _____ kg CO_2-eq

To determine the travel carbon footprint from hotel to venue:

Dandelion: _____ people × _____ km × 0.050 kg CO_2-eq / person / night = _____ kg CO_2-eq

Meridian: _____ people × _____ km × 0.050 kg CO_2-eq / person / night = _____ kg CO_2-eq

Figure 9.4 Guidelines for determining the carbon footprints in Assignment C

CHAPTER SUMMARY

Alexander (2007) captured the inherent challenge for many managers considering changing business operations to implement ES practices: how to convince those who currently enjoy economic success to enter into a process that could reduce their financial standing. From a similar perspective, Lothe, Myrtveit and Trapani (1999) noted that:

[A] conflict does not exist when the environmental strategies save on raw materials, reduce government penalties, make waste into positive gross margin products or increase sales because "green" is marketable . . . A conflict does exist, however, when the environmental strategies require extra investment.

(Lothe et al., 1999, pp. 314–315)

The call to manage events in a more environmentally sustainable manner will surely increase in the future. Reducing the direct harm caused to the environment is the responsibility of everyone. Clearly, event managers have a part to play in ES. Indeed, managing events with consideration for each of the three spheres of sustainability should be a priority for every event manager in the future.

CHAPTER QUESTIONS

1 What is the difference between "sustainability" and "sustainable development"?
2 What are the three perspectives that are used to describe, manage and assess sustainability?
3 "If you cannot measure it, you cannot manage it." Describe how this can be applied to ES initiatives in event management.
4 In your opinion, who or what department within an organization should "own" ES?
5 Consider a road race and think of the multiple environmental sustainability initiatives that an event could adopt. Think of at least five other event management ES initiatives.

To determine the hotel carbon footprint:

Dandelion Hotel: 120 people × 7 nights × 6 kg CO_2-eq/person/night = 5,040 kg CO_2-eq
Meridian Hotel: 120 people × 7 nights × 12 kg CO_2-eq/person/night = 10,080 kg CO_2-eq

To determine the travel carbon footprint from hotel to venue:

Dandelion Hotel: 120 people × 280 km (10 × 7 × 4) × 0.050 kg CO_2-eq/person/night = 1,680 kg CO_2-eq
Meridian Hotel: 120 people x 28 km (1 × 7 × 4) × 0.050 kg CO_2-eq/person/night = 168 kg CO_2-eq

Hotel	Hotel carbon footprint	Travel carbon footprint	Total carbon footprint
Dandelion Inn	5,040 kg CO_2-eq	1,680 kg CO_2-eq	6,720 kg CO_2-eq
Meridian Hotel	10,080 kg CO_2-eq	168 kg CO_2-eq	10,248 kg CO_2-eq

Figure 9.5 Answer to the scenario assignment concerning the choice of hotel

148

CHAPTER 10

FACILITATING QUALITY IN EVENT MANAGEMENT

CRAIG HYATT AND CHRIS CHARD

How do you define "quality" with respect to an event manager and their role as a facilitator? In this chapter, we will examine how various theorists have defined quality over time. The theoretical concepts of quality will then be applied to the role of the event manager facilitating the staging of an event. The challenge to define quality for the role of the event manager will be discussed, and quality statements to guide an event manager will be developed.

Every event manager wants to produce a *quality* event. While this seems a fairly simple and straightforward concept, you must remember that most events have at least four different sets of stakeholders: the participant performers or athletes; the staff and volunteers; the sponsors; and the spectators or tourists. Each set of stakeholders can emphasize different criteria when analyzing the quality of the event; defining quality, therefore, is complex.

CAN AN EVENT MANAGER MEET ALL OF THE REQUIREMENTS FOR QUALITY?

Each of the sets of event stakeholders can have different needs when it comes to quality requirements. For example, the athletes or performers may indicate that quality is based on the equipment, staging, and amenities in the locker room. To the volunteers, a quality event may involve obtaining experience that advances their personal skills and provides them with event clothing. The sponsors may indicate that quality involves having unlimited product sampling opportunities or being able to mingle with clients in a hospitality area. The spectators may want short lines for quick access into the venue and for food and beverages, and excellent sight lines from their seats. Within each of the four stakeholder groups, quality is a relative concept. Each person involved in an event will have a personally determined idea as to what quality means. This fact challenges event managers. If an event manager wants to know if they have produced a quality event, understanding definitions of quality is a good place to start to manage this challenge.

WHAT IS QUALITY?

For decades, both academic theorists and industry practitioners have attempted to define quality. During the first half of the twentieth century, the service industry was not as prevalent as it is today (especially in the sport, recreation and tourism industries), and the manufacturing and purchasing of durable goods had advanced to be a prominent concern. Here, quality was discussed predominantly in terms of the fabrication of hard goods. During the second half of the twentieth century, there was a gradual shift in the focus of developed countries' economies from manufacturing to services. The rise of the service industry, including event management, meant a change in how quality was conceptualized. We will consider these two perspectives briefly.

Quality is defined as ruggedness and longevity in the manufacturing industry

Initially, quality was thought of in terms of ruggedness and longevity and was often expressed in terms of meeting measurable specifications for the size and strength of manufactured parts. This meant that quality was the responsibility of the inspectors who assessed the completed goods prior to leaving a factory – quality controllers. This type of quality process enabled mistakes to be caught and fixed without the consumers ever knowing that they once existed.

Definitions for quality in the service industry

Unlike manufactured goods, services are simultaneously produced and consumed, making it very difficult to catch and fix service mistakes without the consumer's knowledge. In this environment, services often

150

require the knowledgeable input of the consumer to ensure a quality outcome. This means that quality is no longer expressed just in terms of physical specifications; it is now conceived in terms of meeting the expectations of the consumer.

EXPANDED MEANINGS OF QUALITY

Reeves and Bednar (1994), in their study on the evolution of the meaning of quality, concluded that the essence of all the various definitions of quality resulted in only four basic categories: *quality is conformance to specifications*; *quality is excellence*; *quality is value*; and *quality is meeting and/or exceeding customers' expectations*. Further, Yoshida and James (2011) promoted three additional definitions of quality: *aesthetic quality*; *functional quality*; and *technical quality*. Each of these seven definitions of quality will now be discussed.

Quality is conformance to specifications

Defining quality as conformance to specifications provides product or service providers, as well as consumers, with a standard that can be agreed upon. Here, "Quality is the degree to which a specific product conforms to a design or specification" (Gilmore, 1974, cited in Garvin, 1988, p. 41). If the product's quality is called into question, the specifications are examined. If the product meets the specifications, it is of quality. If it does not meet the specifications, it is not.

In 1979, this definition of quality was expanded by corporate executive Philip Crosby when he presented a broader definition which would be applicable when one is not just concerned with a product. He defined quality as "conformance to requirements" (Crosby, 1979, p. 17). Crosby explained that whatever it is we are examining for quality – including "quality of life" –must be broken down into its component parts so that each component part can be specifically defined in such a way as to make it measurable. If each component part is compared to a predetermined acceptable measure and meets that specification, the entire entity is considered to be of quality. As he stated:

> Those who want to talk about quality of life must define that life in specific terms, such as desirable income, health, pollution control, political programs and other items that can each be

measured. When all criteria are defined and explained, then the measurement of quality of life is possible and practical.

(Crosby, 1979, p. 17)

Consequently, over time, the concept of quality as conformance to specifications has expanded to apply not only to products, but also to services.

Quality is excellence

Quality conceived as excellence requires something to be as good as it can be. If an alternative is found to be better, yours is no longer thought to be of quality. When Henry Ford introduced his Model T Ford as a "universal car," he said it must have certain attributes (Ford & Crowther, 1922). This first attribute concerned the quality of materials used:

> Quality in material to give service in use. Vanadium steel is the strongest, toughest, and most lasting of steels. It forms the foundation and super-structure of the cars. It is the highest quality steel in this respect in the world, regardless of price.
>
> (Ford & Crowther, 1922, p. 68)

While Ford did not define quality, it is obvious from his description that excellence was the determining factor of quality. Ford indicated that quality steel was the best steel available at any price.

Tuchman's (1980) definition described quality as excellence that:

> means investment of the best skill and effort possible to produce the finest and most admirable results possible . . . quality is achieving or reaching for the highest standard against being satisfied with the sloppy or fraudulent . . . it does not allow compromise with the second-rate.
>
> (Tuchman, 1980, cited in Reeves & Bednar, 1994, p. 420)

Quality as excellence means being distinguished as exceptional for a product or service.

Quality is value

Quality conceived as value implies that consumers of less-than-perfect products or services can still perceive them as quality if they are

152

positioned financially as providing value. In other words, if you "get what you pay for," then quality transactions involve providing value instead of absolute excellence.

Saad and Siha (2000) emphasized quality as more than just an end result; it is an ongoing "dynamic process of value creation" (p. 1152). An interpretation of this definition of quality was offered by corporate executive Dave Watkins (2006). He indicated, "Quality defines how well an enterprise satisfies the performance element in the value equation" (p. 23). He clarified the concept by indicating that the customer defines value (performance relative to cost). Both definitions acknowledge that quality is relative to the price consumers pay for the product or service. Those who pay more want more in return.

Quality is meeting and/or exceeding customers' expectations

Quality has been conceived as meeting and/or exceeding customers' expectations; we have all heard the motto "under-promise, over-deliver." In a manufacturing environment, if the expectation for a set of golf clubs is that it should last four or five seasons, each summer spent golfing with the same clubs beyond this duration may be seen as a bonus – exceeding expectations. However, when it comes to defining expectations for a service, varied opinions prevail.

Zeithaml, Parasuraman and Berry (1990) noted that "service quality, as perceived by customers, can be defined as the extent of discrepancy between customers' expectations or desires and their perceptions" (p. 19). This definition is of some use when considering the expectations of event attendees. It acknowledges that each patron is unique and may have unique needs or wants that they wish to fulfill by attending your event. It also notes that the onus is on the attendee to decide if their expectations were fulfilled.

Aesthetic quality

Aesthetic quality focuses on the "interactions between the consumer and the aesthetically pleasing characteristics of the service environment" (Yoshida & James, 2011, p. 21). This type of quality concentrates on the *atmosphere* generated at a sport, recreation or tourism event. This atmosphere encompasses conditions that elicit excitement, participation and/or an appreciation of the appearance. Aesthetic quality can be generated with high standards in seating and services; the inclusion of participatory activities, such as athlete signing sessions; consumer tours that allow groups of individuals to walk across a stage; or an event location that is of remarkable natural beauty. Aesthetic quality can be expressed in themes that are displayed in designs and decorations to enhance the atmosphere of an event. The crowd experience is an important and foundational characteristic of aesthetic quality.

Functional quality

This next type of quality is based on the "interactions between the customer and functional services" (Yoshida & James, 2011, p. 21). Functional quality, thus, is derived from products and services delivering what they are "supposed to deliver." For example, a bicycle with wheels that will not turn does not deliver functional quality. Similarly, from an event perspective, staff and volunteer *services*, including *attitudes* and *behaviours* are a part of the functional quality – an usher who will not direct attendees to their seats does not deliver functional quality. The staff and volunteer function must also be supported with elements such as easy access to the seats, the provision of excellent seating space, as well as crowd density that is conducive to easy movement.

Technical quality

Finally, technical quality is described by Yoshida and James (2011) as consisting of characteristics expressed by *the participants' behaviour* during the practice of their craft. In sport, recreation and tourism events, this includes the participants' individual practical behaviour and their group behaviour between participants and/or between opposing members. Behaviours are guided by rules established for each event and violations can influence the technical quality perceived by the consumers.

A LACK OF GUIDANCE FOR QUALITY IN EVENT MANAGEMENT

Current definitions of quality fall short when it comes to event management. Let's briefly re-examine the basic definitions of quality to explore

154

their shortcomings when they are applied to the role of an event manager. To begin, let's consider the definition of "quality as conformance to specifications" in the context of event management. This definition applies when there are, for example, predetermined specifications in a contract for a stage and lighting, or for equipment. However, there are no predetermined, agreed-upon specifications for services. Can you imagine getting everyone involved in an event to agree on what, specifically, constitutes an "entertaining" event? What about trying to agree how long concession lines should be if an event involves tens of thousands of people? Should service still be able to be provided within a minute or two as some may expect? The specifications for these types of services are not perceived in the same manner by all stakeholders, as they are not predetermined in writing. There is the opportunity for stakeholders to apply their personal idea of specifications. However, even if all of the stakeholders could agree on specifications for many service elements, including entertainment outcomes, the event manager does not have control over all the elements.

When "quality is defined as excellence," there are factors that hinder an event manager from meeting this standard. For instance, resources (financial, human, natural) may not be available to make every component of the event the best it can be. As a result, compromises must be made if, for example, the budget is restrictive. Does this mean that any event that is forced to compromise due to budgetary restrictions should not be staged as it will not be a quality event? If it is staged, with certain conciliations, can an event manager ever meet the standard of quality?

When "quality is defined as value," the notion is that the consumer incurred a financial cost for attending the event. In some cases, however, events are free to spectators. Does this mean that a non-paying customer cannot be disappointed? In such cases, can event managers deliver subpar services because "the event is free?" The answer clearly is no! Even if a spectator incurs no financial cost to watch an event, that person still invested their time and experienced opportunity costs by forgoing other opportunities. These consumers need to know that it is worth the time it takes to attend an event, and that quality will be delivered.

When quality is defined "as meeting and/or exceeding customers' expectations," not all customer expectations are realistic. The old adage "you can't please all of the people all of the time" is something that event managers should never forget. For instance, if an event manager facilitates easy parking and venue access, quality food provision, clean restrooms, excellent sight lines and exciting performers, but the consumer was hoping there would be free childcare, then the evaluation of the event as meeting expectations is based on different categories. Can a food and beverage service offer enough varied cuisine to meet the tastes of all stakeholders? Not every credit card will be accepted at the box office. If the expectations for an event are personally established, is it realistic to believe that an event manager can meet and/or exceed all of the expectations for every stakeholder group? It is our contention that some expectations may be unreasonably high. If an event manager used the definition of quality as meeting and/or exceeding expectations to guide their work, could they ever be successful? Would it not always be the case that some of the many stakeholders go away unhappy? Does this mean that the event manager did not produce a quality event?

When quality is defined based on the "aesthetic quality," an event manager must create conditions within the operational plan that elicit excitement, participation and/or an appreciation of the environment. This can be as simple as decorating a venue. However, generally, an event manager does not have control over this aspect of an event; in medium-size to large events, generally someone skilled in designing the artistry of the event is hired. The event manager does, however, ensure that the operational plans for instituting the event and other areas of aesthetic quality are well planned and executed. Some of these other areas include the need, for example, for high-quality seating, but event managers may not have control over ensuring a high level of these types of service at the facilities. The crowd experience, however, is the foundational characteristic of aesthetic quality.

Event managers do have influence in terms of "functional quality." This type of quality means that they must design training for staff and volunteers that includes service-level expectations. This can include expected staff and volunteer attitudes and behaviours of the highest level. Some aspects of functional quality, however, are beyond the manager's control. Seat access, seating space and crowd density can be dictated by the size, age and type of venue utilized for the event.

Event managers may be guided by a wish for "technical quality," but it is difficult to ensure this type of quality. Technical quality is based on the participants' behaviour displayed during the sport, recreation or tourism event. The event manager may attempt to influence this type of quality by offering briefing sessions with the participants; however, the individuals' practical behaviour and the group behaviour between participants is difficult to control. These behaviours are guided by the rules established for each event. Frequent violations can influence the technical quality as perceived by event attendees and other stakeholders.

While the definitions of quality in the literature offer good points, none are truly applicable to all types of event. This certainly does not mean that the quest for quality should be disregarded by the event manager. It simply means that every event manager needs to *create a unique quality statement that can guide their work.*

ISSUES IN CREATING QUALITY STATEMENTS AND DEFINING QUALITY IN EVENT MANAGEMENT

Creating a guiding quality statement for event management is a difficult task. There are many issues that arise as an event manager attempts to define quality specifically for their role and their tasks. One of the parameters pertaining to quality statements is to concentrate on the items the event manager can control. You cannot promise a level of excellence if management literally cannot deliver at that level due to circumstances beyond their control. What follows is a list of issues that can directly affect whether or not stakeholders can have their reasonable expectations met. As you will see, many of these issues involve circumstances over which the event manager has little control.

Conflicting stakeholder expectations influence quality perceptions

What happens when one stakeholder group has expectations that are in direct conflict with the expectations of another stakeholder group? Consider the potential tension between event performers and sponsors. The title sponsor may have a hospitality area near the action where they entertain existing or potential clients, or host employees who are being rewarded for achieving excellence in their field. As part of a great experience for their guests, the sponsor may wish performers to be available for autographs, photos, and chatting with the guests. The performers, on the other hand, might want to focus on their tasks and may consider time in the hospitality area to be a distraction. As such, they may wish to have no obligation to interact with sponsors or guests. Even when contracted to do so, they may provide only a minimal level of service. How is an event manager expected to facilitate a positive outcome from these two contradictory expectations? By promising the elements they can control and making it clear that they cannot deliver certain elements that are outside their control, an event manager can potentially modify a stakeholder's reasonable expectations and facilitate a satisfactory outcome for all parties.

Limited control over inputs influences quality

An event needs inputs. The event manager will need to order supplies from the venue and from outside suppliers. Depending on the nature of the event, you may have to order all of the items for a media conference to be held just prior to the event. For instance, the order may include a platform and tables, along with tablecloths, microphones, chairs for the media and so on. A technical check is held just prior to the media conference, and all is determined to be working well. However, during the media conference, one microphone develops technical problems. Does this constitute an event that does not provide quality, or does the manner in which one handles the issue determine if the event is of quality? If you have a technician on hand to manage the issue or have pre-planned the use of an extra microphone for such a case, will this contribute to making a quality event? The answer is obvious. As has been mentioned before, contingency planning is a paramount concern for an event manager.

Financial constraints influence quality

Most event managers must deal with some financial constraints. Here, event managers might not be able to afford the inputs necessary to meet the reasonable expectations of some stakeholders. For example, spectators may wish to purchase high-end items at your souvenir stand, such as embroidered sweatshirts. However, the cost of ordering these items is high, and given the time it takes for the garment supplier to fill a large custom order, you must place the order weeks in advance. It is prudent to give them a delivery date a few weeks before the actual event as insurance in case of delays. This might mean that you are paying for these sweatshirts before you have any cash flows that you expect to generate during the actual event (same-day ticket sales, sales at the concession stand, sales at the souvenir stand, etc). Ideally, the event manager would have sponsors pay part of their sponsorship fees well in advance, and would have a budget that takes these advance cash flows into account. This will help

158

ensure that there is sufficient cash flow long before the day the event opens in order to buy all the quality inputs required. If, however, in the weeks leading up to the event the actual revenue from sponsorship and advance ticket sales falls short of the projected numbers forecast in the budget, there may not be enough funds available to purchase items such as embroidered sweatshirts. As a result, the event manager may be forced to buy cheaper items (such as silk-screened T-shirts made of a cotton–polyester blend) to stock the souvenir stand. As a consequence, the lack of premium items could create negative associations with quality for this part of the event in the eyes of some consumers.

How can the event manager avoid this type of negative perception? There are no easy answers. Issues of finance and cash flow plague many businesses and organizations. If financial survival depends on selling sponsorships and tickets in advance of the event, then you, the event manager, must impress upon the sales staff that sales success in the months and weeks before the event is crucial. As for the bigger picture, all students interested in event management may wish to consider learning all they can about the sales process; the quality of your future event may depend on your ability to sell.

Contingency plans influence quality

No event manager needs to be told that things can go wrong. Managers need to plan ahead to identify potential bumps in the road; this planning is vital and necessitates the development of contingency plans. For example, an experienced event manager might anticipate that the food wholesaler may not deliver the exact product that was ordered. In such a case, a contingency plan may empower the director of concessions to call an alternative wholesaler to arrange the delivery of the necessary product. This is fairly straightforward and ensures a quality product. However, not all contingency plans can be implemented in such a straightforward manner. Consider an outdoor event that cannot be held in inclement weather, such as a fireworks show. A simple contingency plan for a fireworks show is to advertise both the specific date (weather permitting) on which the event will be held, and the rain date should the show be cancelled due to bad weather. The problem lies in the unpredictability of bad weather. Imagine that your fireworks show is slated to take place at 21:00 on a Saturday, with the following day listed as the rain date. Starting on the Wednesday prior to the event, the weather forecasts predict evening thunderstorms on the Saturday. You can be sure that the phone will start ringing that Wednesday and throughout the remainder of the week with worried potential attendees asking if the event will be postponed. Maybe the people who are calling live a few hours away and plan on leaving home mid-afternoon on Saturday to do some shopping and enjoy dinner before the fireworks. They do not want to spend many hours in the car and not see fireworks. While you understand their situation, you also know that even if the weather forecast is true, an evening thunderstorm might mean rain from 17:30 until 18:30, leaving plenty of time for things to dry out enough for the 21:00 show. Or, it could mean rain starting at 23:00, long after the event is over. You also know that for every attendee who could easily attend the event on the rain date, there is one who cannot. Maybe hundreds of tourists have planned a weekend getaway around your event and have hotels booked for Saturday night only, having to return to their home towns during the day on Sunday. If you postpone the fireworks a day or two in advance and it turns out that things are dry enough at 21:00 on Saturday for the show to have taken place, the out-of-town tourists will probably conclude that their reasonable expectations were not met. If you wait until the night of the show and decide to postpone, the people who drove in that day, who could just as easily have rescheduled their day trip until the following day, will probably conclude that their reasonable expectations were not met. As the event manager, what can you do?

Unfortunately, the nature of weather forecasting often means that the event manager must rely on both the data provided and their gut instincts regarding decisions on the event. If, in the hours leading up to the event, it still looks as if there is a reasonable chance that the event can go ahead as scheduled, the event manager may elect to proceed until the skies open just minutes before the start time. If, however, the noon weather forecast clearly shows a massive slow-moving weather system heading your way, which meteorologists state will bring six straight hours of heavy rain starting at 19:00, the event manager may announce the postponement of the event at 13:00. In most cases involving inclement weather, the telephones at the event headquarters may ring non-stop before, during and after the event with people wanting to know if the event is still proceeding, wanting to know when the decision to cancel (or not) will be made, wanting to know why the decision to postpone the event was not made sooner, wanting to complain that their weekend plans were ruined by the poor decisions of the event staff, etc. The best an event manager can do is to train the staff handling the phones about what to say to the callers

160

and how to say it. If all the staff are briefed on the reasons why decisions to proceed or to postpone are made, they have the opportunity to educate the callers. This education may actually enlighten the caller to the point where they conclude that their expectations for the event might not have been as reasonable as they thought. In such situations, the caller (who questioned the quality of the event when the phone call was first made) may not have that opinion by the time the phone call has concluded.

As noted above, although there are difficulties, an event manager is expected to be able to produce work that is of quality. Therefore, they must be able to define a quality statement to guide their work in the development and implementation of event operational plans.

GENERATE YOUR QUALITY STATEMENT IN EVENT MANAGEMENT

Every event manager who wishes to provide a quality product or service should address the issue by *generating their personal written statement on what quality is based upon* for each event. This quality statement should address the specific definition of quality, and how quality will be delivered and evaluated.

To be sure, there is no "one way" to create a quality statement. A quick internet search reveals a large number of organizations attempting to create quality statements. The quality statement can be as short as two sentences and as long as multiple pages. If a statement is too short, there is a chance that it will be so vague as to be meaningless. If it is too long, it might not be practical enough to serve as a useful guide.

At this time, think of an event that you see yourself managing soon or in the future. Take some time right now to create a quality statement for this event. Consider what the literature offers when defining quality and what elements you can utilize from this literature. Consider also that the event may currently have a mission statement, vision statement and a statement of values. Your quality statement should be congruent with these other event statements. The difference is that *the quality statement you are developing must guide your work as a facilitator* and needs to be available as a realistic platform from which to evaluate your work throughout and at the end of an event.

Your quality statement needs to seamlessly integrate the facilitation activities that you are personally responsible for as an event manager.

A SAMPLE QUALITY STATEMENT

Imagine a recreational three-on-three basketball tournament that is held annually in a small city. It is organized and managed by a local youth basketball organization, which has named it "Rally in the Valley." The tournament is meant to be both a celebration of the game of basketball and a fundraiser for the organization. Temporary outdoor courts are set up throughout a park located in a residential neighbourhood near the city's downtown area. Dozens of teams, grouped according to age, gender and skill level, will play games all weekend until winners in each division are determined late on Sunday afternoon. What could a quality statement for Rally in the Valley look like?

QUALITY STATEMENT FOR RALLY IN THE VALLEY

Rally in the Valley is committed to meeting or exceeding the reasonable expectations of all the event's stakeholders, including the players, spectators, sponsors, volunteers and city government. Rally in the Valley management will actively encourage the input of all stakeholder groups for the purpose of mutually determining what constitutes "reasonable expectations." This process will be ongoing, as "reasonable expectations" may change from year to year as the event evolves. A thorough training process to educate the volunteers will be implemented before the event that will empower them to handle routine stakeholder concerns during the event, so that reasonable expectations can be met in a timely manner. Rally in the Valley management will be in constant radio contact with the volunteers, should non-routine stakeholder concerns arise during the event. In such cases, management will meet with any concerned stakeholder as soon as possible to address the concern. After the event's completion, Rally in the Valley management will make themselves available to meet with concerned stakeholders to rectify any issues regarding meeting their reasonable expectations.

While it is debatable whether or not this quality statement has too much or too little detail, it seems to meet the basic requirements of a quality statement: to define quality and to indicate how quality will be delivered and measured.

162

To provide further input to guide you in developing a personal quality statement, here are some comments about quality from members in the event management industry. These observations illustrate some of the specific components that drive quality and, although they are not full quality statements, they offer ideas to consider when generating your personal quality statements for an event.

With only one chance at a first impression, it is crucial to carefully plan for all possible situations. Planning well thought-out contingencies for situations are oftentimes the difference between a successful event and an event that will no longer be continued.
(Andrew Pittam, Operations Manager, Event Properties International Management Group [IMG] Canada)

Whatever happens on the field or court will take care of itself. We want the visiting team to be impressed by the way we treat them; beginning from the moment they arrive until their departure from our campus. That is our philosophy that guides the quality in our game operations.
(Tom Calder, Director of Athletics and Recreation, Johns Hopkins University, winners of nine Division 1 Men's Lacrosse National Collegiate Athletic Association [NCAA] championships)

A well-managed event in a clean, modern facility with superior customer service and a product that exceeds expectations will create satisfied customers and ambassadors for your event. A poorly managed event, on the other hand, can negate the effects of all the money you've spent and work you've put into attracting patrons to your event. A poorly managed event that detracts from the fan experience will cost you patrons in the future and limit the ability of your event to grow and flourish.
(John Pesetski, Director of Advertising and Promotions, National Hot Rod Association)

Quality is critical in providing an outstanding experience for our 30,000 participants and enhancing our brand. Collectively we develop a plan which helps us stay focused and on track. Our ultimate goal is for participants to have a positive experience and return to our event year after year.
(Lindsay Crosby, Manager, Run for the Cure, Canadian Breast Cancer Foundation, Toronto, Ontario, Canada)

CHAPTER SUMMARY

No event manager wants to put in countless hours dedicating their time and energy to stage an event that lacks quality. All of the careful planning leading up to the event must be done with quality in mind. Because of the unique components of each event, managers must define quality in a way that makes sense for their particular situation. To ensure more effectively that their conceptualization of quality is met, they must also institute policies in a quality statement that are meaningful and easy to implement. Managers should also be mindful that other issues, such as conflicting stakeholder expectations, limited control over inputs, financial constraints and contingency planning, can create challenges for anyone wishing to facilitate a quality event. Event management is a complex and challenging field; a personally established statement of quality to guide the facilitation of an event is a key element in succeeding in this industry.

CHAPTER QUESTIONS

1 Describe the characteristics of the seven different definitions of quality (conformance to specifications; excellence; value; meeting and/or exceeding customers' expectations; aesthetic; functional; technical) and show how these definitions can guide event managers.
2 Discuss how stakeholder perceptions, limited control, financial constraints and contingency plans affect an event manager striving for quality.
3 Consider a specific sport, recreation or tourism event and generate a guiding quality statement for the event manager. Record the issues that arise as you attempt to create a definitive guiding quality statement.
4 Consider the same event as above (question 3) and list three or four items that you think would be expected by the four different stakeholder groups (participants or performers, spectators, sponsors, volunteers and staff) to consider the event to be of a high quality.
5 Discuss why quality can be an elusive concept in event management and how knowledge of quality can aid you in your work as an event manager.

164

CHAPTER 11

EVENT BIDDING

CHERYL MALLEN

In this chapter, the process of bidding to procure a sport, recreation or tourism event is presented. Five key elements within the bid process are defined: a feasibility study, a candidature document, a bid questionnaire, a bid dossier/submission and the bid tour. Importantly, this chapter emphasizes critical factors for successful bids that have been outlined in the research literature. This is followed by a presentation and discussion on the proposition that there is one key factor that is vital to successful event bidding.

WHAT IS A FEASIBILITY STUDY?

The first key document in a bid process is the feasibility study which includes an assessment and opinion on the capability of a group to stage or host the particular event. An ability to host involves a determination as to the availability of the necessary resources required to host the event sought. This document records the elements that have been considered and the determination of whether or not it is feasible to host the event. These elements can include, for example:

- event goals;
- objectives;
- intentions;
- activities;
- the event history;

- the cultural context (such as the population growth in the area, the consumer power and economic development);
- facility and equipment availability (such as parking, seating, accessibility and spatial requirements, including space and the capability for simultaneous activity use);
- resource availability (including competent and experienced human resources);
- venue service access (such as scheduling, ticketing, media, crowd management and security services, the union regulations, zoning regulations for noise, along with health and fire codes);
- technical resources;
- financial resource availability.

Overall, a feasibility study outlines the assessment of the availability of resources to meet the needs for hosting an event along with a determination as to whether pursuing the event bid is a practical and reasonable initiative. This means that a feasibility study outlines the plausibility of meeting the bid requirements with the resources available.

WHAT IS A CANDIDATURE DOCUMENT?

The second key document in a bid process is the candidature document. This document is provided by the organization that is accepting the event bids. The candidature document outlines the critical path of deadlines and processes that must be followed for a bid submission to be eligible for consideration. Each deadline must be adhered to by each bid group in order to complete the bid process.

WHAT IS A BID QUESTIONNAIRE?

The third key document in a bid process is a bid questionnaire. This questionnaire is often contained within the candidature document and outlines the list of questions that must be answered in the bid submission. The bid questionnaire provides the format and frames the context for a bid dossier and must be followed precisely. This framework allows for easy comparisons with other bids being considered by the governing body or organization that is awarding the rights to host the event.

166

WHAT IS A BID DOSSIER?

The fourth key document in event bidding is a bid dossier or submission. This document follows the framework outlined in the bid questionnaire. The dossier outlines the overall plan, the particular strategies, supporting resources and supplementary details of the bid. It will also contain testimonials of support and all of these items serve to set the bid submission apart from the other bidding competitors. Each question listed within the bid questionnaire must be answered within the bid dossier, in precisely the order requested, and be numbered to directly correspond to the number assigned in the bid questionnaire.

One of the best examples of a candidature document and bid questionnaire is provided by the International Olympic Committee (IOC) and is available for viewing on its website (https://stillmed.olympic.org). One document to access from this site is the *2024 Candidature Procedure and Questionnaire* (IOC, 2015). This 137-page document outlines the candidature procedures for the 2024 Olympic Games, including the deadline dates, signatures required, the schedule of payments, guarantees required, the bid questionnaire, presentation layout and requirements, along with an outline for the visit by the evaluation commission and the selection decision process. An Olympic bid questionnaire is subdivided into the 17 themes outlined in Figure 11.1. Each theme is further subdivided into a series of questions that must be answered in the bid dossier.

Theme	Sample bid questionnaire topic areas to be answered in a bid dossier
Theme 1: Olympic Games concept and legacy	The event vision, impact, legacy, motivation and plans for sustainable development
Theme 2: Political and economic climate and structure	Guarantees provided, government structure, stability, per capita income, inflation rate, referendum results and opinions concerning support
Theme 3: Legal aspects	Stipulation of authority, event exclusivity, trademark protection, official languages
Theme 4: Customs and immigration formalities	Visa regulations, guarantee of entrance for those with Games accreditation, health and vaccination requirements, restrictions on media broadcasts, regulations on imported print media, guide dogs and equipment

Theme	Sample bid questionnaire topic areas to be answered in a bid dossier
Theme 5: Environment and meteorology	Construction agreements and guarantees, protocols to protect the environment, geographical features, environmentally and culturally protected areas, collaborative efforts, plans and systems to manage the environment, the environmental impact, temperatures, humidity, precipitation, wind directions and strength
Theme 6: Finance	Budget template outlining the financial details, including capital investment, cash flow, sponsorship and contributions, ticket sales, licensing, lotteries, disposal of assets, subsidies and other hosting costs
Theme 7: Marketing	Guarantees of a marketing program, domestic sponsorship, ticketing, advertising and advertising controls
Theme 8: Sports and venues	Venue descriptions, competition schedules, technical manuals for meeting competition standards, venue responsibilities and the tendering process and agreements, reporting, monitoring and management plans, workforce and sport experience
Theme 9: Paralympic Games	Plans for financial, security, accommodations, transportation, sport venues, opening and closing ceremonies, finances, accessibility and so on for hosting the Paralympic Games
Theme 10: Olympic village	Concept, location, venue design and construction, financing, including guarantees for construction, types of accommodation, distance from competition venues, control of commercial rights, accessibility and post-event use
Theme 11: Medical services and doping control	Plans for meeting the world anti-doping code and the IOC anti-doping rules, guarantees of investment in anti-doping, medical service facilities, public health authorities, epidemiological issues in the region and systems for managing Games medical expenses, including serving visiting foreign nationals
Theme 12: Security	Safety and peaceful hosting guarantees, international, national, regional and local government security involvement, analysis of risks concerning fire, crime, traffic, terrorism and so on, security organizations and intelligence services to be involved and financial planning for security
Theme 13: Accommodation	Hotel room capacity, guarantees on room availability and room rate and other pricing controls, construction guarantees, work timelines and finances, binding contracts, accommodation tables with maps outlining sites and distances

Theme	Sample bid questionnaire topic areas to be answered in a bid dossier
Theme 14: Transportation	Traffic management guarantees, including public and private transport, control centres, distances, airport capability, parking and additional transport infrastructure, training and testing, timelines and authorities
Theme 15: Technology	Guarantees of competent bodies offering communication services, systems and broadcast capabilities for print, radio, television and internet, network support
Theme 16: Media operations	Provision of broadcast centres for print, radio, television, and internet outlets, construction, timelines, financing, media transport and accommodation
Theme 17: Olympism and culture	Protocols, plans for ceremonies including opening, closing and awards ceremonies, provision of intent, location, seating capacity, financing and facilities

Figure 11.1 Themes and topic areas requiring answers in the International Olympic Committee bid questionnaire

To advance your common knowledge on the process of bidding, it is suggested that you select at least three events that are of interest to you and review their event candidature documents and bid questionnaires. Many of these documents can be located on the internet (Figure 11.2). Specific examples include:

- The European Football Championship Final Tournament bid documents can be found at www.uefa.com. You will find a number of bid documents on this site, including the bid regulations and reports on bid dossiers submitted for hosting events.
- Information on how to bid for the Universiades organized by the Fédération Internationale du Sport Universitaire (FISU) or the International University Sports Federation can be found at www.fisu. net. Be sure to review the critical path of deadlines required for bids as they begin years prior to the event.

Another website you may want to visit to find bid documents is: www. gamesbids.com.

You may also want to approach festivals, conferences and conventions in your area to obtain their bid documents.

Federation	Bid document	Website
Fédération Equestre Internationale	FEI Nations Cup™ jumping finals 2017 and 2018: Bid application and questionnaire	www.fei.org
International Triathlon Union	Multisport festival bid document 2017	www.triathlon.org
International Convention on Science and Medicine in Sport (ICSEMIS)	ICSEMIS 2016, Brazil, candidate procedure and questionnaire	www.fims.org
International Floorball Federation (IFF)	IFF event organizer bidding questionnaire completed by the Singapore Floorball Association and/or by the Danish Floorball Federation	www.floorball.org
FISE World Series	Bid documents for FISE World Series, BMX, skateboard, roller, mountain bike slopestyle and wakeboard (amateur and professional)	www.bidfise.com
European Commission	European Capitals of Culture 2020–2033, Guide for cities preparing to bid	www.ec.europa.eu
International Olympic Committee (IOC)	IOC's candidature procedure and questionnaire: Olympic Games 2024	www.olympic.org
Special Olympics	Bid form to organize and conduct European or invitational single-sport competitions	www.media.specialolympics.org
Commonwealth Games Federation (CGF)	2022 Commonwealth Games candidature: Report of the CGF Evaluation Commission, July 2015	www.thecgf.com

Figure 11.2 Resource: online bid documents

170

WHAT IS A BID TOUR?

A bid tour involves hosting the members of a bid evaluation commission that will make the selection of the winning bid. The opportunity to stage a bid tour generally means that the bid submission has been placed on the shortlist of potential groups that are eligible to host the event. The tour offers an opportunity to present the information outlined in the bid dossier, to tour and highlight the planned ceremonies and facilities, to demonstrate local community and business support for the bid and to promote the reasons why your bid should win the competition to host the event.

A bid tour involves arranging for the needs of the bid evaluation commission members from the moment of their arrival until their departure. To meet this requirement, an event manager facilitates the adaptation of the event planning model phases to generate operational plans specifically for a bid tour.

To begin, a bid tour follows the phases of the event management planning model. First, the development phase of the planning model is instituted. This involves the facilitation of elements such as the organizational structure for governance of the tour, the policies and volunteer practices along with the determination of how corporate social responsibility can be incorporated within the tour. Next, the event operational planning phase involves the facilitation of the written logical, sequential and detailed operational plans for the bid tour, including the arrangements for components such as transportation, accommodation, entertainment, tours of the facilities and a presentation of the bid to the commission members. Contingency plans and a plan refining process should always be considered within the operational plans. Further, a bid tour involves the implementation, monitoring and management phase as the bid tour moves from the conceptual stage to reality. Finally, the evaluation phase must take into account the priorities of the bid commission members, as they will ultimately make the decision on the winning bid.

To understand the evaluation criteria used by bid evaluation committee members, a review of the literature has identified several factors that appear to be critical in winning the bid process. These critical factors are outlined below.

WHAT ARE THE CRITICAL FACTORS IN A SUCCESSFUL BID?

The literature outlines several factors for successful event bidding; however, different studies describe an assortment of elements that lead you in many directions. We will review the key factors for success offered by researchers such as Emery (2002), Westerbeek, Turner and Ingerson (2002), Persson (2000) and Hautbois, Parent and Séguin (2012). This text then puts forward the proposition that the natural environment is another key factor in bidding and that there is one further element that is vital to successful bidding.

To begin, Emery (2002, p. 323) suggested five essential factors for event bid success:

1 relevant professional credibility;
2 fully understanding the brief and formal/informal decision-making process;
3 not assuming that decision makers are experts, or that they use rational criteria for selection;
4 customizing professional (in)tangible products and services and exceeding expectations;
5 knowing your strengths and weaknesses relative to the competition.

Emery (2002) suggested that "credibility and capacity to deliver are fundamental to any application, but not normally the discriminating factor between success and failure" (p. 323). Emery emphasized the point that bid success was "dependent upon in-depth knowledge of networks, processes and people – in other words external political support at the very highest levels of government and the commercial sector" (p. 329). Therefore, the organizing team itself is actually an element that could make a difference in the pursuit of a winning bid. Emery suggested that an organizing team should be made up of members who have considerable experience with successful events.

Emery (2002) also stated that "the information process and protocol must never be underestimated" (p. 329). Some of the bid organizing team must have experience in the political aspects of bidding, as this area is an important element in the bid process. According to Emery, this means that a bid needs to be politically positioned for success. In addition, Emery suggested that an assumption concerning the use of rational and consistent criteria to select the winning bid may not be correct. An interpretation of

172

this view is that the key factors for winning a bid may actually change depending on the members in a bid commission who are evaluating a submission. Each member's personal perspective on the priorities for the bid must somehow be ascertained and then taken account of. Consequently, trying to anticipate the receptivity of a bid commission with several different members is a complex task that is underscored with uncertainty, but it is a necessary part of a successful bid process.

Another researcher, Persson (2000), suggested that a success factor for an Olympic Games bid involved "the fit between the bidder's and the IOC members' perceptions of the bid offers" (p. 27). This implies that the bid committee members must anticipate what the IOC will perceive as important in a bid. The IOC bid commission has several members, and the priorities of a bid are therefore subject to personal bias or agenda. Thus, both Persson and Emery assert that a key component to achieving success in a bid is gaining understandings of the priorities of the bid commission members, and meeting those priorities through political positioning of the bid.

Persson (2000) further offered the suggestion that infrastructure was important to the success of a bid. Infrastructure, according to Persson, involves the capacity for the provision of appropriate accommodation, transportation, venues, finances, telecommunications and technology as well as a top-notch media centre.

Ingerson and Westerbeek (2000) found that experience in event hosting was a key element for success along with the scope of knowledge of the members on the bid team. This was based on the contention that the more experience a member has, the greater the opportunity they have previously had to develop relationships that may drive the success of the current bid and ultimately the event itself. As Westerbeek et al. (2002) have stated, "The ability to organize an event is evidenced by having a solid track record in organizing similar events" (p. 318). Thus, another theme arising from the literature is that experience in hosting previous events is a key factor for future success in bidding.

There was a general consensus by Emery (2002) Persson (2000) and Ingerson and Westerbeek (2000) that the political aspects of a bid were vitally important to bid success. However, other researchers continued to promote additional success factors.

Westerbeek et al. (2002) promoted stability as a key factor for bid success. Stability was defined as involving politics, but from a different perspective than being politically positioned for advantage with the bid commission. The political reference in this instance meant the stability of the country and the municipal politics of the city, along with the stability of the financial support for an event.

Westerbeek et al. (2002) outlined eight factors that were important in the process of bidding. Although these researchers emphasized sport event bidding, these factors are also very applicable to recreation and tourism events. The eight factors outlined by Westerbeek et al. (2002) comprise:

1 *Ability to organize events.* This element involves multiple items such as the intra-organizational network established to manage an event, the technical expertise within the network, the equipment and the overall financial support for the bid.
2 *Political support.* This element involves support from the government for the event bid. This support is used to assist in gaining access to financial and human resources, as well as access to facilities.
3 *Infrastructure.* This element involves providing convincing proof of the availability of excellent facilities and an ability to meet event component requirements to deliver the transportation, accommodation and so on to produce an event.
4 *Existing facilities.* This element involves the current status of the major event facilities at the time of the bid submission.
5 *Communication and exposure.* This element involves the host city's reputation as a destination and the available support system to handle the technological communication system requirements for hosting and promoting the event.
6 *Accountability.* This element involves proof of the event's reputation, presence and support in the event market, previous success in hosting events and excellent venues.
7 *Bid team composition.* This element involves the talent mixture of the members involved in the development of the bid as important for increasing the favourable perception of the bid evaluators. The bid team members should be able to provide a high profile, build relationships, have the skill to manage the complexity of a bid and provide credibility concerning their expertise to host.
8 *Relationship marketing.* This element involves the ability to gain access to the members of a bid evaluation team and to influence these members to promote a bid through the development of "friendship."

174

These eight factors for success in bidding outlined by Westerbeek et al. (2002) were listed in order of priority. This suggested that the most important factor in bidding was proof of one's ability to organize the network of personnel and the finances for an event.

Management effectiveness as indicated by Kerzner (1995) was dependent upon an ability to balance a number of items such as time constraints, cost and performance with the pressures of the environment, including political pressures. While Kerzner discussed project management, the link between the fields of project management and event management is apparent and represents one of the focal points in this text.

Hautbois et al. (2012) found that the bid environment was very complex. They suggested that it was both the involvement of public officials and athletes that made the difference for a winning bid. These researchers concluded that from "a political, symbolic and strategic point of view, public officials . . . were central in the network of stakeholders" (p. 11). Yet it was deemed important to ensure that all groups or stakeholders involved were engaged in the bid process "as opposed to one single actor (i.e. mayor)" (p. 11). The participants were noted as being instrumental in ensuring that an event was designed for their needs.

A relatively new element gaining prominence in the literature, and promoted in this text as an important factor in event bid success, is environmental sustainability. Over the last 10 years, environmentalism has moved onto the agenda. The authoritative United Nations Environmental Programme (UNEP) Intergovernmental Panel on Climate Change (IPCC, 2007) has pulled together the world's leading researchers to study the issue that the world's natural resources –including forests, fisheries, water, soil and air – are at risk: this has created a social and environmental challenge. It has been noted that there is a need to shift to sustainable practices (Gadenne, Kennedy & McKeiver, 2009; Mitchell & Saren, 2008). This shift to sustainability has been used as one key factor in bid success. For example, the Fédération Internationale de Football Association (FIFA) released a legacy report on the environmental practices from the Germany World Cup (FIFA, 2006). This report illustrated the efforts made by event organizers to promote sustainable environmental practices. The International Federation of Motorcycling (IFM, 2006) produced a code for protecting the environment to be followed when producing events that is now instituted for all races. In addition, in 1999, the International Olympic Committee (IOC) established Agenda 21, a document designed to bring its members into a program that supports the environment (IOC, 2014). This Agenda was promoted on the IOC website as "putting sport at the service of humanity" (IOC, 2014, p. 1). In 2006, the IOC released an athlete code of conduct which stated that athletes were environmental role models (IOC, 2006). The IOC code of conduct presented six key principles: avoid wasting water; avoid wasting energy; travel as efficiently as possible; consume responsibly; dispose of waste properly; and support environmental conservation and education. The IOC expects event organizers and athletes to protect and promote the sustainability of the environment. Further, as major events can be a driver for tourism, the IOC code of conduct for environmental sustainability can also be extended to tourists and this element can also be outlined in bids.

There are, however, issues concerning bids that have stated safeguarding the natural environment in the initial bid phase of an event. The issue is that the bid plans have not always translated into reality during the implementation, monitoring and management phase of an event. These bids have positioned the natural environment as a priority in the up-front bid phase, but it has then moved to a non-priority in the hosting phase. Does this constitute lying in the bid process? Generally, no punishments have been enacted for events which have found themselves in this position; however, the negative media publicity that ensues is a type of punishment. Where do you stand on this issue? How would you resolve this issue during bidding and event implementation?

Overall, the research literature has suggested that there are a number of critical factors for bid evaluation success. The suggestions are multidirectional, which increases the complexity of the bid and the uncertainty of bidding success. The complexity stems from the need for multiple groups that must come together to create a cohesive event bid.

Multiple areas of emphasis contained within a bid have created a complexity that could strain the cohesiveness of any given committee and thereby compromise the potential for success. In addition, there is political complexity. This means that while the guiding documents outline the bid requirements, intangibles such as underlying political requirements are not explicitly stated in a bid questionnaire. These intangibles need to be anticipated as they may be important in the final decision making. This means that uncertainty is inherent in the bidding process. In the end, only one group is awarded the prize in a bid competition. Unfortunately, the rest have to bear the cost of competing in the process without receiving anything in the end.

176

To assist in working through the complexity and uncertainty of the bid process, the question is posed: is there one critical factor that can be used to enhance the opportunity for a successful bid? This text promotes the view that there is *one* critical factor in event bidding.

WHAT IS THE ONE CRITICAL FACTOR FOR BID SUCCESS?

This text presents the proposition that *communication* has been under-played in the literature and should be positioned as *the one critical factor* in event bidding. Greenberg (2002) defined communication as "the process through which people send information to others and receive information from them" (p. 217). An application of this definition means that a bidding process "constitutes a communication process between the actors involved" (Persson, 2000, p. 139). Thus, event bidding is conducted within a social context and this vital communication element is the key factor in the process of winning an event bid.

Communication in event bidding is discussed in the literature, although the support is not emphatic that communication is the single key factor in successful bidding. The literature does indicate that, "Event bidding is about communication to a degree, initially you have got to have communication, and you've got to be a really, really sharp communicator" (Hörte & Persson, 2000, p. 67). Westerbeek et al. (2002) included communication as one of the eight key factors in bidding; however, they indicated it was in a group of elements that were "more likely to be supporting rather than vital factors" (p. 317). Westerbeek et al. positioned communication as important in event bidding; however, they discussed communication from the perspective of providing contemporary technology for use in facilitating communication during the event.

This text, however, positions communication as the one key factor in suc-cessful bidding because the event context is teeming with opportunities to advance the success of a bid with the use of written, verbal and visual communication. An ability to communicate underlies every task in the bid process and it can therefore be a deciding factor in the success of a bid dossier, a bid tour and all other components in the bid process.

Communication is critical in a bid dossier. A dossier must clearly and succinctly express the intention to host and provide answers to a bid questionnaire. This document communicates the proposed plan for hosting an event. The level of planning detail (level 1, 2 or 3) communicated in the document can hinder or enhance the success of the articulated plans and can influence the interpretations concerning bid activities made by the bid commission members in their assessment. Depending on the event, a bid dossier may also require written communication in more than one language. An ability to clearly express the bid details and the subtle nuances of the bid in multiple languages is an opportunity to position the bid for success.

Communication is a critical factor in conducting a bid tour. A written operational plan for a bid tour outlines the activities to be conducted. In addition, verbal communication is used to aid the network members implementing the bid tour plans to clearly understand the tasks. Poor communication can impact the success of a bid tour, illustrating that communication is a critical factor.

Formal and informal verbal communication is a critical factor in a successful bid. Examples of formal verbal communication opportunities include structured meetings with the bid commission members to present the highlights of the bid; meetings with key stakeholders such as the sponsors or venue managers; and meetings used to build relationships with the grassroots supporters such as volunteers, small businesses and organizations. Examples of informal verbal communication include casual conversations with the bid commission members evaluating the bid or with the grassroots supporters of a bid. Each formal and informal communication opportunity can facilitate the transfer of knowledge concerning the bid or bid tour to all members in the bid network and to the bid commission members. Poor formal and informal communication can, from this viewpoint, profoundly impact the success of an event bid undertaking.

Visual communication is also a critical factor in bid success. The inclusion of visual elements in presentations, such as the use of diagrams in the bid dossier, video presentations or a fireworks display in the bid tour, can enhance either the understandings of the bid detail or the enthusiasm for a bid. Visually communicating the bidder's message can have a significant impact on the success of a bid.

Communications technology is also a critical factor in bid success. The use of the latest technology which allows for excellent verbal, written and visual communication can clearly demonstrate the host's ability to maximize the use of technology in the conduct of the event.

178

Communication is also an underlying critical factor in the majority of bid activities that go beyond the topics covered in this text. For example, the financial component of a bid relies on an ability to communicate facts and figures that will attest to the host's financial capacity to successfully host the event with no negative long-term impact on the community following the event. Marketing and sponsorship in event bidding rely heavily on the ability to convey enticingly the opportunity to be a partner in the event, as well as the marketing and sponsorship opportunities that might be secured. Written, verbal and visual communications along with the communications technology are all critical factors in the success of marketing and sponsorship proposals.

The bid process involves communicating to groups such as the network members, the potential sponsors and the bid commission members. Communication is the critical factor in event bidding and must be facilitated in a manner that enhances the overall bid effort. Your facilitation skills will be tested throughout the bid process. A focus on enhancing communication at all levels when facilitating an event bid is a critical factor for success.

CONCLUSION

Overall, this chapter defined a feasibility study, candidature document, bid questionnaire, bid dossier and bid tour. The viewing of a number of candidature documents, bid submissions and bid questionnaires was encouraged to develop your common knowledge about the requirements of bidding. You can follow a variety of bids on the internet at www.games bids.com. The research literature discussed indicated that there is a complex array of critical factors for successful bids. It was also indicated that environmental sustainability is a new key factor in bidding. Importantly, this text proposes that communication is the most critical factor for success in event bidding. Without a clear consensus, and bearing in mind the fact that each bid is unique, it is important for you to weigh the key factors to win a bid, to analyze the requirements and then to apply the factors based on your own conclusions.

CHAPTER QUESTIONS

1 Describe a feasibility study, a candidature document, a bid question-naire, a bid dossier and a bid tour.
2 List at least five key elements of successful bidding that were outlined in the literature.
3 Do you feel that concern for the natural environment should be part of the bid process? If so, how should the natural environment be safeguarded at events?
4 Do you agree with the author's assertion that communication is the one key factor in successful event bidding? If not, why? If yes, explain how you see communication being utilized in the process of facilitating an event bid.

CHAPTER 12

POLITICS IN EVENT BIDDING AND HOSTING

TRISH CHANT-SEHL

This chapter focuses on the underlying political aspects of event bidding and hosting. Managing and mitigating the political aspects of events is a key skill for an event manager. It would be ideal to be able to tell you how to manage each type of political situation. Due to the complexity of places, people and scenarios, however, this is not possible. To become a skilled political manager of events, you must develop knowledge and experience concerning where to expect political maneuvers, how they could come into play, and then devise personalized management strategies based on your own knowledge and experience. To aid in the foundational knowledge necessary for this skill, this chapter defines "politics"; applies this definition to bidding and event hosting experiences; explains the role that politics play through the event continuum in three distinct phases – including bidding, transition and review, and event hosting; examines scenarios; and offers some insightful ways in which the political effect can be mitigated. A case study in event bidding is included to guide the reader to develop personal insights regarding politics and a series of questions is posed to encourage the reader to contemplate how they might choose to navigate the complex world of politics in event bidding and hosting.

WHAT IS MEANT BY THE "POLITICS OF EVENTS?"

One does not have to look far to discover numerous definitions for "politics." Many definitions include a connection to government and/or government policy. The Merriam-Webster dictionary (www.merriam-webster.com) defines politics as "3a: political affairs or business; especially:

competition between competing interest groups or individuals for power and leadership"; and "5a: the total complex of relations between people living in society." In addition, Trevor Taylor defines politics as that which "involves matters of power, of control and of influence over people's behaviour" (quoted in Allison, 1986, p. 30). These definitions guide the discussion within this chapter. Therefore, "politics" is understood as encompassing the competing relationships and interests between individuals and groups, as well as the political environment, as it relates to the event organization and/or government's interest.

POLITICS IN THE DECISION TO BID OR NOT TO BID

The world of event bidding is fraught with political agendas from the very beginning of the process. This is not surprising given that bids are human initiatives. It is almost impossible to discern a time throughout the bid process when politics are not involved. From the moment that the idea to bid for a specific event is conceived, politics play a role.

As the world of international event bidding becomes more sophisticated, and costly, it is incumbent upon interested bidders to spend time and energy on assessing the "winnability" of a bid (the likelihood of their bid being successful) prior to formally launching a bid for a specific event. There are a number of items to consider when assessing a bid's winnability, many of which are political in nature. For example:

- Is there a competitor who is already being seen as the likely next host?
- Has your area or region recently hosted the same event, or an event of similar size and scale?
- Do you have the full support of the necessary levels of government or organizational bodies?
- Is there a regional rotation at play for the event?
- Have other interested cities previously bid for the same event and feel that it is their turn to host?
- Is there an influential champion for your bid, and more importantly, for a competitor's bid?
- Who can influence the decision-making process?

These questions are important ones to ask and answer before making a final determination on whether or not to proceed with launching a formal bid. It is worth noting, however, that despite doing the due diligence on winnability, the outcome of a bid process is never certain and political influences play a part in this uncertainty.

If the bidders' assessment of the winnability of their initiative is favourable, then it is time to proceed with completing the necessary bid requirements, as well as preparing for the inevitable politics that will arise. It is imperative that the bidders accept the role that politics play throughout the entire process and enter into the bid environment knowing that they must understand, navigate and mitigate or utilize the political aspects of bidding and hosting events. Consider strategies you could adopt to improve your knowledge and ability to manage politics in event management.

POLITICS IN THE EVENT BID PHASE: THE COMMITTEE

Before delving into the politics involved within the bidding process, it is important to identify the governance structure for an event, whether it is an international, national or small-scale local event. The larger-scale events have formalized bid processes; however, smaller-scale events can have many governance structure options which range from no formal bid protocols to fairly well-established processes that mirror some international bid procedures. For example, for some national events, there is a regional rotation whereby it is known each year which region will host, but not which specific community or city. At the local and regional level, there may not be a formal bid process, but rather expressions of interest by different leagues or communities. In these situations, the decision may be made by a staff representative, a committee or perhaps a board of directors.

For the purpose of this chapter, we are assuming that a national governing authority has endorsed a competitive bid process for an international event. Perhaps the easiest place to start when discussing the role of politics in this scenario is with the bid committee itself.

If you recall, the earlier definition of politics was "competition between competing interest groups or individuals" which situates politics within a bid committee. The determination of both who and what is represented on a bid committee is not an easy decision – and is open to political maneuvering from those interested in serving on this committee. Large events are seen as exciting to be a part of, as well as being thought of as potential "once in a lifetime opportunities." For these reasons, and several others, there are many people and organizations who want to be represented on a bid committee to serve and/or to ensure that their opinions and interests are given due consideration. Very often, the specific event program is not pre-determined and organizations therefore see the bid phase as a significant opportunity to influence the inclusion of their focus within the program. Being represented on a bid committee is then considered an excellent means by which to achieve this objective. What criteria would you use to make selections?

In Senn's (1999) book entitled *Power, Politics and the Olympic Games*, an excellent example of the politics involved in committee membership is presented. This example is focused on the International Olympic Committee (IOC) and not a particular bid committee, but it is applicable. Senn indicated that:

> With the inclusion of the [former] Soviet Union and the newly emerging countries of the Third World, the Committee came to tolerate a much more active role on the part of governments. It has also recognized that its members work basically in states, rather than regions. Although it still refuses to give a seat to every state, it makes an effort to represent the various parts of the world. It rejects the thought that any country has the "right" to be represented or even the right to name its own representative; but it has often accepted official nominees. The Old Guard in the IOC long insisted that they were freely electing their colleagues, but in 1951, for example, when the Soviet Union demanded a seat and nominated its own candidate, the IOC simply yielded. In dealing with the United States, in contrast, it has shown considerably more independence in choosing its membership.
>
> (Senn, 1999, p. 7)

This example indicates that bid committee membership has been rife with political scenarios over the decades. Overall, when establishing a bid committee, it is important to remember that the goal of bidding is to win the right to host the event. This may seem like a simple point, but it is one that is often overlooked when community and event leaders and/or government representatives try to influence the committee membership. Pulling together a bid is a major undertaking and one that is usually done within a tight timeframe. In short, there is a significant amount of work to be done. It is important that each bid committee member be able to deliver value to the bid process.

This value includes the criteria of being able to provide guidance and oversight as well as completing the work requirements. To mitigate some of the politics of membership on a bid committee, another criterion is to meet the necessary options for strategically placing individuals and groups to be engaged with the bid process without being named to the formal bid committee. The volume of work to be completed for a bid necessitates the development of sub-committees associated with a bid. Of key importance, however, is to weigh the placement of members who can complete the tasks and ensure the cooperation of sub-committees above the political appointments.

POLITICS IN THE EVENT BID PHASE: THE PROPOSAL

Despite the prescriptive nature of a national or international bid dossier, there are still many important decisions that a bid committee needs to make and which are open to political maneuvering. One particular item is the venue or facility requirements. International events are often seen as a way in which a community can benefit from new facilities, including sport, recreational and tourism venues. The construction of new facilities requires that many questions be answered. For instance:

- Where should the new facility be built?
- Who should own and operate the facility?
- Who will pay for ongoing facility maintenance?
- Who will have access to the facility?
- What type of amenities should be included in the new facility?
- Can locating facilities in a specific area of the city help further a political or community interest?

It is easy to see how politics can come into play when attempting to answer the questions posed. A recent example to illustrate this point is the 2012 Olympic Games in London. It was noted during the bid process that

> the BOA [British Olympic Association] refused to give up and had already won the support of the Mayor of London, Ken Livingstone, provided the bid fulfilled his vision for transforming the desperately deprived East End and increased investment in the capital.
>
> (Lee, 2006, p. 7)

The bid committee was therefore open to political maneuvering regarding social issues and not just concerned with the best construction of facilities for the staging of the event.

If facilities do not need to be constructed, the use of existing venues still poses some opportunities for political maneuvering. For example, when existing facilities are utilized, decisions need to be made concerning a number of elements, such as:

- Which facilities will receive upgrades and/or renovations as part of their participation in the event?
- What level of service is the facility owner expected to provide for the event?
- Will a facility be compensated accordingly for the services?

These questions are important ones to consider during the bid phase to ensure that political issues are mitigated and that facility owners and operators have reasonable expectations of their participation within a bid, and ultimately as an event host.

Facility decisions are not the only ones where politics come into play during the proposal phase. Decisions around delegate accommodations require careful consideration and political savvy. For instance:

- Which hotel should be named as the "host hotel"?
- Who has priority access to the limited rooms available at the premier hotel?

In instances where an event has a cultural or festival component, there are many additional questions to answer, such as:

- Which cultural communities will be involved in the event?
- Who will speak at the opening ceremonies and/or formal dinners?

In the case of large and/or international sport or tourism events that attract significant sponsorship dollars and television audiences, the politics involved are even more demanding. In this case, questions include:

- Who can be an event sponsor?
- Which broadcast entity should be a partner?

Political maneuvering in determining the answers to these questions requires careful attention.

POLITICS IN THE EVENT BID PHASE: THE DECISION MAKERS

In event bidding, perhaps the most likely example of politics stems from the decision-making process whereby people are responsible for making final decisions concerning the event. The Salt Lake City scandal surrounding the selection process for the 2002 Winter Olympic Games shone light on the political games of corruption and bribery inherent in the IOC bid process at the time. Significant reform has taken place within the IOC, and the bidding process is now more structured and transparent; however, the final decision still rests with individual IOC members. That is to say, the human element cannot be overlooked when it comes to decision making within a bid process. The IOC is not the only international governing body to utilize membership voting as the means by which it chooses the successful bid. The Commonwealth Games Federation (CGF) and the Pan American Sports Organization (PASO) are two other examples of organizations that have their membership vote to determine a winning bid.

The IOC, as well as the CGF and PASO, have documented bid guidelines and protocols that must be adhered to by all bid candidates. There are, however, many opportunities for politics to come into play with both the voting delegates and bid committee members. In some instances, the politicking will fall outside the scope of the rules, and could be subject to disciplinary action by the governing body. In other scenarios, the politics at play are more subtle. A region or group of nations may plan to bid for the subsequent event and thus have a vested interest in where the current bid will be situated. Their votes may then have little to do with the quality of the bids, and more to do with geography and planning for their own future.

Another example of the politics within bidding is with the bid decision process itself – which is typically secretive in nature. Whether a bid is local or international in scope, if individuals are required to vote for one bid over another, then politics will come into play. Enthusiastic and hard-working bid teams will do their best to develop and present an excellent bid package to the voting delegates. Each bid committee will do its best to convince the voters to choose their bid over their competitors. In the secret ballot voting scenario, there is no negative consequence to the voting delegate who pledges their support to all candidates as it is never known who votes for which bid. This makes the bidding environment vulnerable to politically motivated activities such as voting delegates asking for special favours, or bid committee representatives promising more than they can deliver.

In John Furlong's (2011) book *Patriot Hearts: Inside the Olympics that Changed a Country*, the former CEO of the 2010 Vancouver Olympic and Paralympic Winter Games shared personal stories of his time with the Vancouver bid team and the host organizing committee. He supported the concept of potential politics in the voting strategy when he indicated his thoughts concerning his city's win for the right to host. The fact that he mentioned this scenario means that it was a political point of potential importance. His statement was as follows:

> I was surprised at how close the final vote was. Three votes. We were behind after round one but grabbed all of Austria's 16 votes to sneak by the Koreans 56–53. Scary close. Only a couple of other decisions in IOC history had been closer than ours – both those determined by one vote. There would be a lot of talk about the role geopolitics played in our victory. How European countries wanted the 2012 Summer Games, so were not going to vote for a European city to win the 2010 Games. I never put much stock in that theory.
>
> (Furlong, 2011, p. 75)

It does not need to be a large event for this type of politics to come into play. Small and medium-sized events also have to maneuver through the politics from some of the decision makers.

POLITICS IN THE EVENT BID TRANSITION AND REVIEW PHASE

Eventually, decision day will arrive and one bid will be selected as the next host location for the event. After months, and sometimes years, of hard work, the bid process is complete. Now what? Depending on the outcome of the specific bid, the next steps are very different. Next steps for unsuccessful bids include financial reconciliation, closing down the bid office, file storage and documentation, filing of any necessary legal paperwork, holding a bid committee post-mortem and writing a final

188

report. Given the time, money and resources put into bidding for events, it is not surprising to see politics at play even after a bid has been lost. There can be a tendency for blame and second-guessing of decisions that were made during the bid process. How would you manage these types of political situations? It is important that the bid team takes time to evaluate the bid process and document areas in need of improvement and general thoughts on why the bid was not successful. This type of analysis and documentation will be an asset for future bid committees. This falls within the transfer of knowledge concept and should be common practice for all bid processes – win or lose.

For those bid committees fortunate enough to win the bid competition and be named as the next host location, the next steps and the politicking can be daunting. Making the transition from a bid committee to a host organizing committee can be very stressful, given that few people have had an opportunity to be involved in such a complex undertaking. For larger, international events, the bid committee is usually well structured with full-time staff, office space, formalized policies and procedures as well as financial and legal accountabilities. Small and medium-size events, though, are not generally exempt from having to deal with bid transition politics.

The bid committee is now no longer needed and a host organizing committee is required to take its place. While the bid committee is winding down, and the transition team is planning for the future host committee, there is an expectation that work continues with planning for the event. This is a key challenge as there is no shortage of politics at play concerning who is leading the process. Interested candidates may campaign strongly, and publicly, for their preferred position within the new host organizing committee structure. Individuals who may have been colleagues on the bid committee may now be adversaries in the competition for a specific position on the organizing committee. Leaders within key stakeholder groups, including governments, who have significant interests in the success of an event, may try to wield their influence over the decision-making process.

The composition of the new organizing committee is not the only forum where politics play a role in the transition and planning phase of an event. Perhaps one of the most politically charged tasks within any event planning process is the final determination of the venue. Although bid dossiers are required to include full details on all venues, once a bid is won, the host committee has an opportunity to revisit the original plans.

Despite best efforts at planning during the bid phase, there will inevitably be changes once a bid has been won. These changes happen for many reasons, such as a change in government officials or priorities, revisited cost estimates, a change in the program and issues with land acquisition, pressure from the public or other special interest groups.

Changes in government will happen and neither bid committees nor host committees can control this change. The change could have a positive effect on the event in the form of available office space or personnel secondments. Or it could have a negative effect, such as a demand to change the location of a venue. For example, a new ward councillor may not support a bid plan for the construction of a new building in their ward and may publicly campaign for a move to a different site within a city. This type of discussion opens the door for political jockeying as other ward councillors, land owners, neighbourhood associations and businesses begin to lobby the organizing committee for their preferred site. Further, there are compounding effects on the event plans as delays in site selection can result in increased construction costs due to shortened timelines, and later-than-anticipated opening of the venue, resulting in less time for testing the venue and its systems for the event.

What additional political scenarios can you envision for the event transition phase for an event in which you may be involved?

Host organizing committees will be faced with significant change throughout the planning process, some of which will be political in nature. The key issue for any committee is how its members choose to deal with the politics. This will be discussed again later in this chapter.

POLITICS IN THE EVENT HOSTING PHASE

This chapter has discussed the politics evident throughout the bid phase and the transition phase of planning an event. Given the amount of time spent on these activities, it is not surprising that politics play a more significant role in the lead up to hosting an event than during the actual event hosting period. Events can last for one day or more; for instance, tourism events can last for months; regardless, the hosting timeframe is dramatically shorter than the time taken to bid and to plan. As a result, there are fewer opportunities for politics to come into play. The event production time period, however, is not exempt from political maneuvering.

190

One area where politics may emerge is with the very important persons (VIPs) attending the event. These VIPs could be government officials, sponsors, media or other organizational representatives. Some events will have established protocols for VIP management, while others will not. Regardless, VIPs may have unrealistic expectations of the event organizers and can use their influence and strong connections to the event to try to get what they want. The event management team needs to pay careful attention to how they handle this group of individuals: VIPs may engage in politics by trying to use their influence to obtain free tickets to the event, or merchandise, or to participate in ceremonies. Ensuring a sense of fairness for all VIPs is an important task for the event management team.

In addition to recognized VIPs, there may be individuals who believe they should be recognized as VIPs, and should be entitled to special treatment. These types of requests may seem like minor headaches; however, how an organizer deals with them can have an impact on the success of an event as their sharing of negative perceptions with the public and others can have a significant impact. It is, thus, important for event organizers to anticipate these types of scenarios during the planning process, and to have planned messaging in place prior to being confronted with the reality.

Another example of how politics can come into play at events involves the performers. Organizations and advocates may use the performers as a vehicle to lobby for additional funding. For instance, if a performer gains a high level of success, government funders may utilize the publicity as a demonstration of their government's commitment and support of the program or a group may use it to promote their next bid and hosting initiative.

OVERCOMING POLITICS IN EVENT BIDDING

This chapter has examined how politics play a role in bidding and hosting of events. A range of examples has been provided within the three distinct phases: bidding, transition and planning, and event hosting. Understanding the role that politics can play in bidding and hosting is important and learning how to be successful in spite of the politics is critical. It is naïve to believe that event bidding and hosting can occur without politics coming into play, given the working definition we have been using, with politics as "the total complex of relations between people living in society," according to the Merriam-Webster definition.

It is proposed, then, that eliminating politics from the bidding and hosting process is impossible. It is important, therefore, to have the skills to be able to deal with the politics.

A key factor in managing event politics: consistent communication messaging

Consistent communication is the first tenet for successfully dealing with the politics involved in the bidding and hosting experience. One of the reasons people and organizations engage in politics is because this type of activity can yield their desired result, even if it is not in the original bid or event plans. Very often, this success is due to a lack of consistency within the messaging, or in understanding what the committee or organization is trying to achieve. This provides opportunities for political maneuvering by outside groups or individuals to exploit the inconsistency in communication.

Bid committee and event hosts need to spend time developing their vision for the event, and the strategy by which they plan to fulfill the vision. They must spend time as a team ensuring that all members of their respective organizations understand what they are trying to achieve, and how they plan to get there. This requires consistent communication within the entire bid team, as well as the external stakeholders. Communication needs to not only be consistent over time, but also must be honest, open and transparent and two-way to allow for feedback and questioning.

A key factor in managing event politics: establishing core values

The second tenet for successfully dealing with the politics of bidding and hosting is the establishment of core values. One of the first steps that a small or large event bid or host committee should undertake is to identify what their core values are, and commit to having their values guide their decision making and their actions. Examples of these values are:

- promoting and encouraging diverse participation;
- a commitment to develop competencies, leadership and personal development;
- contributing positively to the tourism, sport and recreation industries;
- developing and advancing mutually beneficial partnerships;
- behaving ethically and with integrity.

192

It is often difficult, however, to abide by these values when it is close to bid decision day and when a political maneuver or the promise of a vote in return for a favour is presented.

The leadership of an event bid must clearly articulate the importance of their organization's values and ensure that they will lead by example in demonstrating the values in each and every decision. The values must be more than a poster on the wall in the lunch room, and all team members must ensure that their behaviours are reflective of the values in their everyday work. A good question to ask when in a difficult situation is: Would you be comfortable if this decision or action was on the front page of the newspaper? This is an effective way to remind yourself of the importance of being true to the values that are important to you and your team. It is much easier to deal with the politics involved in the bidding and hosting process when you have a strong set of values to help you navigate your way through the murky waters of political maneuvering.

The only way to develop management skills for politics in event bidding and hosting is to develop understandings of the types of political maneuvers that can arise, and to practise potential responses to these. Figure 12.1 offers a case study for you to read in small groups, to consider different

---

Read the scenario below and consider the questions posed at the end.

ABC Bid Committee had been working on their bid proposal for the 74th International Multisport Games for 19 months and was ready to do the final review before sending it to print. The bid dossier was over 250 pages long and covered all of the required components for bidding. The Bid Committee had worked tirelessly to put together a sport and venue plan which would appeal to the voting delegates, yet still provide a meaningful legacy for the community. The jewel of their bid was a world-class basketball and volleyball facility with an adjacent indoor football pitch that was to be built in an economically depressed area of the city. The Bid Committee had the support of both the local and regional elected officials to construct the arena complex on the desired site. As a courtesy, the Bid CEO had agreed to share the bid dossier with the local, regional and national sport organizations for basketball, volleyball and football before sending the final version to print. The day after sending the final version of the bid dossier to these officials for review, the Bid CEO received a call from one of the national offices demanding that the seating for the facility be expanded by 5,000 seats in order to accommodate plans for a future professional league. During the call, the representative from this national office noted that their president was an influential member of the executive committee of the Multisport Games organization. The addition of 5,000 seats to the facility had significant financial implications, as well as a major impact on the amount of land needed, and the relationship with the proposed adjoining indoor football pitch.

Figure 12.1 Case study in event bid politics

potential responses and to determine the impact of each response on a bid and, ultimately, on the hosting of the event.

CHAPTER SUMMARY

This chapter examined the role of politics in both event bidding and hosting. The notion of politics has been defined and broken into three phases for discussion. First, the bidding phase was explored and included the initial assessment on whether or not to bid for a specific event, the bid committee competition, development of the bid proposal and the decision makers involved in determining the successful bid. Second, the transition and planning phase between bidding and hosting was discussed, followed by the event hosting period. Finally, two key tenets were presented for dealing with the politics of bidding and hosting. The first factor, consistent communication, supports the work of Mallen and Adams (2008) which also promoted communication as a key element in successful bidding. The second factor was the establishment of core values. Overall, the discussion in this chapter emphasizes that it is crucial for event managers to develop their understandings and abilities to become skillful at anticipating and handling issues in event bidding and hosting.

CHAPTER QUESTIONS

(based on Figure 12.1)

1 Describe the politics at play in this scenario.
2 If you were the Bid Committee CEO, what would you do in response to the official's telephone call to increase the seating capacity by 5,000 seats?
3 Identify the actions that could have been taken to prevent the official from making such a demand of the bid committee?
4 Based on the information outlined in this chapter, do you feel that politics in event bidding and hosting can have a positive impact on the process?

T. Chant-Sehl

CHAPTER 13

ETHICAL DECISION MAKING IN EVENT MANAGEMENT

CHERYL MALLEN

As event managers, we are obligated to act in an ethical manner. What you do and how you choose to act can determine reputation, success or failure or future employment opportunities in the event industry. This chapter encourages you to examine ethically-based decisions for a number of event issues/problems that have been selected from a wide array of possible issues. Five event issues/problems are presented, and you are asked to propose ethically-based decisions for moving forward on each respective event issue. To help you make decisions, we present the following: an eight-point framework for event issue/problem decision making for your review. Second, the utilitarian ethical approach, which involves reflecting upon the consequences of any decision in event management, is outlined. Third, an adaptation of the International Association of Facilitators' (www. iaf-world.org) Statement of Values and Code of Ethics is offered to aid in reflecting on your proposed options. Fourth, five ethical issues/ problems in event management are presented. Fifth, you are encouraged to think through each issue/problem as an individual and determine how you would manage each one as the event manager. Finally, I encourage you to participate in small group discussions and reach a consensus on how to manage each issue for a selected event. You should discuss how each member of the group determined how the issue/problem should be managed. You then should work to achieve consensus on how to move forward with the event issue/problem. Overall, these types of discussions can further your understanding of options, standards and/or best practices in ethical issue management.

Ethical reasoning or decision making in event management means you are making decisions concerning issues/problems using "reflective practice"

(Ciulla, 2004, p. 27). During this reflective process, as a facilitator of an event, you apply selected features that will guide your decisions concerning the subsequent actions or behaviours for the issue/problem within event management practice. Ethical decisions, and the associated actions or behaviours, are generally based on what you accept as the "moral rules, principles, obligations, agreements, and values and norms" (McNamee & Fleming, 2007, p. 426).

At the outset, it is important to note that ethics differ from the practice of law (Mansurov & Mallen, 2014). The law involves mandatory behaviour or an imposed penalty that is applied for not following the prescribed legal requirements. These legal requirements are not consistent around the world as they are based on one's society or culture. Decisions based on ethical reasoning, however, are not mandated or imposed and are based on individual and/or group perspectives concerning rules, principles, obligations, agreements, values and norms. While sport, recreation and tourism events must still follow local laws, ethical reasoning can differ from event to event based on the selected features that underscore decisions. What one event manager allows, may not be acceptable for another event manager. In addition, facilitating consensus concerning ethical decisions for each event can be a difficult task for an event manager.

FRAMEWORK FOR ETHICAL EVENT ISSUE/PROBLEM DECISION MAKING

The following decision-making framework is provided to help you determine how to manage event issues/problems. Review the issue/problem outlined below and then follow the eight steps in the framework during the process of reflecting and making the decision on how to move forward. The steps are as follows:

1 *Individually, establish the context concerning the event issue.* Select an event and review the issue and establish the context by recording any historical facts that could potentially be obtained; consider how you would decipher any legal, medical and/or contractual facts; consider how the issue applies to current event policies, procedures and established strategies; and, importantly, establish a statement of expectations for event staff and volunteer behaviour and actions.
2 *Consult on the issue.* Consider which stakeholders should be consulted and how their wishes and/or interests based on the event issue could be integrated into the decision-making process.

196

3   *Determine the guiding elements that will underscore your decision on how to manage the event issue.* In this chapter, the guiding elements will include utilizing (i) the utilitarian ethical approach that is outlined below and which encourages you to determine the consequences of each option for managing the issue/problem; and (ii) the International Association of Facilitators' Statement of Values and Code of Ethics that is also outlined below.
4   *Establish your issue management options.* List the options that you conceive to manage the event issue/problem. Be sure to list the consequences for each option, as well as the option impacts based on the International Association of Facilitators' Statement of Values and Code of Ethics.
5   *Select your personally preferred option for managing the event issue.* Select the one option that you have decided is the best option for managing the event issue/ problem. Remember that this one option can involve a combination of items considered, and that in many cases, it can be a combination of items within different options that can be correct for a situation.
6   *Determine the activities needed to implement the decision.* Establish a list of the steps that need to be completed to enact your decision. For example, how will the decision be communicated, and do policies and procedures need to be adapted?
7   *In small groups, evaluate your decisions through debate.* This means that in small groups (between four and six people), each member presents their option for ethically managing the event issue/problem. Each option is to be debated based on its application to the utilitarian ethical approach concerning the event consequences, as well as the International Association of Facilitators' Statement of Values and Code of Ethics. Importantly, each small group should also debate the individual statements concerning expectations for event staff and volunteers' behaviour and actions.
8   *Come to a consensus.* Work to come to a consensus in your small debate group on how to manage the event situation. What compromises are needed to establish a consensus?

THE UTILITARIAN ETHICAL APPROACH

There are multiple approaches that can be used in ethical decision making. Each approach can contribute to a reflective process to assess and guide event decisions. The approach offered in this chapter is the *utilitarian ethical approach which involves reflecting upon the consequences of any decision in event management.* The various event stakeholders, along with the options for managing each event issue/problem, can determine event consequences. For instance, how does a particular decision impact the event participants, staff and volunteers and sponsors? Further, there can be consequences based on situational factors for a particular event site, or constraints based on a particular situation. Consequences can also be based on individual factors or choices influenced by a set of constraints. Each event manager must determine what the acceptable or appropriate and unacceptable or inappropriate consequences are for a particular event. The best course of action is determined by which consequences contribute the most to the event, in conjunction with what decision poses the least harm to the event – the greatest good for the greatest number. This includes an assessment of the consequences based on their impact on event practices such as policies, procedures, participants, sponsors, etc. Further, you are also encouraged to reflect on the elements in the International Association of Facilitators' Statement of Values and Code of Ethics, adapted for event management, outlined below.

AN ADAPTATION OF THE INTERNATIONAL ASSOCIATION OF FACILITATORS' STATEMENT OF VALUES AND CODE OF ETHICS FOR EVENT MANAGEMENT

To aid in ethical reflective practice, an adaption of the International Association of Facilitators' Statement of Values and Code of Ethics as applied to event management is presented. This code is based on five elements and you are encouraged to reflect on these elements for each of your decision options. The elements comprise:

1   That an event facilitator ensures the decision makers *understand the event expectations and desired event outcomes.* This feature involves *valuing the group as an entity that is guided to work together toward the common goal(s).* Consequently, an event manager needs to value and facilitate a process to establish clear communications and consensus concerning event expectations and outcomes.
2   That an event facilitator ensures a process that promotes *open, honest communications* and, importantly, seeks to minimize *conflicts of interest.* An event manager, therefore, is responsible for the process utilized for event communication.

198

3   That an event facilitator promotes *excellent group autonomy* – this includes *respect for the event processes and people* (including the boards of directors, staff, volunteers, participants, media, sponsors, etc.). This respect involves areas such as *safety, equity, trust, collegiality and confidentiality*. Further, the author of this chapter proposes that this feature also includes the concepts of integrity and inter-dependence, as well as transparency in disclosures.
4   That an event facilitator ensures that *all event processes, methods and tools are designed to directly meet the event goals.*
5   That an event facilitator *supports processes that develop the knowledge of those involved in the event, as well as stewarding the process to develop further event knowledge.* This includes ensuring the opportunity for professional development through event management participation.

A COMPENDIUM OF ETHICAL ISSUES/PROBLEMS IN EVENT MANAGEMENT

I have selected five ethical issues/problems that you may encounter as an event manager. These issues will allow you to utilize the frameworks provided to arrive at a considered and, it is hoped, a workable and ethical solution.

Ethical issue/problem 1: ensuring that event staff and volunteers' behaviour meets the standard of conduct

During the implementation, monitoring and management phase of an event, you, as the event manager, are responsible for ensuring that all staff and volunteers maintain a high standard of conduct. In this scenario, you find that the pressure of hosting the event is impacting some of the staff and volunteers and they are yelling at others, swearing, and utilizing body language that is not conducive to a productive working environment. Utilizing the eight points in the framework outlined above, reflect on your options for managing this situation; in particular, reflect on the consequences of each option. The objective is for you to formulate your opinions as to how to manage the issue; then to debate the management options in a small group; and then to reach a group consensus on the strategy for managing the issue. For example, based on the elements provided by the framework, you should consider the following questions. How can potential consequences impact decision makers and their *understandings of the event expectations and desired event outcomes*? How can the process used for decision making regarding the issue/problem offer *open, honest communications* and minimize *conflicts of interest*? How could the event manager facilitate *excellent group autonomy* – this includes *respect for the event processes and people*, including areas such as *safety, equity, trust, collegiality and confidentiality*? How does the decision fit within *event processes, methods and tools that are designed to directly meet the event goals*? How do the decisions and actions *develop the knowledge of those involved in the event, as well as enabling you to steward the process to develop further event knowledge*. Following the *utilitarian ethical approach, what are the consequences of the options for managing the issue/problem*? Additionally, what is your *expected level of conduct*, especially for staff and volunteers who are under conditions of stress or pressure when implementing their event tasks?

Ethical issue/problem 2: inclusiveness in event management operational planning networks

In this second scenario, you – the event manager – have received a complaint that the operational planning network has not been inclusive with respect to gender balance, disability inclusion, has an age-related bias and lacks cultural inclusiveness. Inclusion within society is the responsibility of our institutions. Is an event an institution that should do its part concerning this responsibility? If so, what level of responsibility should be shouldered by the event manager, and what does this mean for the event management team that is already under stress to ensure that the hosting of the multiple event components is implemented successfully? If not, how would you resolve the complaint? In the process of determining how to manage this situation, complete the eight points in the framework outlined above. Further, consider the following in your decision-making process:

■ If an event manager is the architect of the event working group, then who should be involved in the make-up of this group? Consider the gender balance between men and women; the inclusion of those who are challenged – including mentally, physically, emotionally or age-challenged such as youth and seniors; and what cultures should be represented.

200

- What are the associated tolerance expectations surrounding the inclusion of members of those groups within an event?
- What do you need to do to ensure that the event is inclusive? Consider the event processes and support strategies that are needed to implement your decision.

Ethical issue/problem 3: transparency in event management

It is typical for an event management team to receive requests for free tickets to an event. In this scenario, the request comes from an event volunteer directly to the event manager. The request is for 50 tickets to supply disadvantaged or underprivileged children with the opportunity to attend the event. Tickets are in high demand and short supply. In addition, there are other special interest groups that have expressed an interest in attending the event. How would you respond to this request? Is it ethical to refuse this individual and disappoint these children? When making your decision, consider the following:

- What is a fair and equitable process for providing free tickets for the event? Will all organizations asking for free tickets be given the same consideration? Is it ethical to distribute the free tickets in a haphazard manner? Under what conditions will you provide the tickets?
- What supervision requirements do you have for organizations obtaining free tickets for children?
- What ethical requirements do you have to ensure the safety of any underage child utilizing the free tickets? For instance, how are you ensuring that the tickets are not being used to lure the children to an event so unscrupulous people have unsupervised access to them?

Follow the framework above.

Ethical issue/problem 4: safety of the participants in niche events

Niche events are being developed that push the boundaries of safety for the participants and support workers. For instance, Red Bull (an energy drink company) sponsored a niche event that involved a free-fall from space. This event had an individual go approximately 39 kilometres (24 miles) into the air and then free-dive back to earth in a special space suit (see YouTube videos on Felix Baumgartner's Red Bull Stratos full space jump for further information on this event). When it comes to event management, there are participants who are willing to take risks; however, what is the ethically appropriate and acceptable, and inappropriate and unacceptable, level of safety that an event manager should consider allowing? Is there a difference in the safety requirements when an event is broadcast on live television, or is streamed live, as a participant can be seen heading to their death? If events continue to extend the boundaries of safety, when should you ethically determine that the limits of reasonable risk have been exceeded?

Ethical issue/problem 5: balancing television and sponsor needs with the event participants' needs

A final event scenario is when the television management and sponsors push for activities that can impact the participants' needs. For instance, television can dictate the timing of event activities. This timing can impact the best-case timing for the participants, such as the time they need to stretch their muscles, or to warm up their musical instruments, or how much time they must stand around and wait after they have warmed up. Further, within an event's opening ceremonies, you may expect that participants be in attendance. However, when the ceremony is elaborate and protracted and perhaps, held late at night, is it reasonable to expect participants to attend when they have to perform early the next day? Determine the ethical balance between meeting television and sponsor requests and the best-case timing for participants for an event that you have selected.

CHAPTER CONCLUSIONS

Facilitators of events are faced with a multitude of challenging issues and problems to handle on a regular basis. You must learn to navigate the options for ethically-based decision making. It is important, therefore, to understand a framework for making ethical decisions as well as the elements for arriving at a decision. This chapter has provided a framework and the elements of ethical decision making for a number of selected issues/problems. The list of issues provided is not comprehensive, but is designed to provide you with the opportunity to practise moving from being confronted with an issue to a workable and appropriate ethical solution.

202

1   After exploring options and making a decision concerning the issues/ problems presented above, how would you adapt the decision-making framework offered above for your future use?

2   What does using the utilitarian ethical approach mean to you as an event manager?

3   How could you adapt or add to the elements offered above as a basis for making your ethical decisions?

CHAPTER 14

CONCLUSIONS

LORNE J. ADAMS

Event management – it sounds finite. It sounds like a discrete point in time. Indeed, it has a beginning and an end point, but event management is certainly not static. It is best to view events as dynamic, complex and ever-changing entities. No two events are the same; what worked in one situation may not necessarily work in a similar but different situation. That is why this text does not provide you with a series of prescribed checklists that you can simply mark off as you go along. While checklists are helpful, they are static and do not, cannot, take into account the contingency that you will have to deal with. We have spent some time introducing you to some theories that support the notions of change, contingency and complexity. We suggest that you do further reading in that area. A sound theoretical framework will provide you with an anticipatory mindset that will help you deal with deviation and the inevitable unforeseen issues. In fact, a message that we have delivered is the need for anticipation in the short term and anticipation in the long term. As a critical element in the dynamic system of event management, you should now understand that anything you do has the potential to affect many other things. Some of those outcomes will be positive, others will create unforeseen outcomes.

We have also stressed the importance of setting goals and writing them with clarity. Goals need to be communicated clearly to everyone involved. The less clarity, the greater the chance for misinterpretation, and we want everyone to be on the same page and heading in the same direction. You will note throughout the text how often the need for clear goals is expressed both directly and indirectly.

204

We also have spent a good deal of time talking about planning and committing that planning to paper. We have pointed out the need to plan using the three horizons. You should also be aware that planning exists on a continuum with overplanning and underplanning as polar opposites. The more uncertain we are, the greater the tendency to overplan. The concrete act of planning can become a trap; it can become an end in itself. Immersing yourself in the process feels good, it feels like you are actively involved in problem solving and it produces a highly detailed, visible product – the plan of the event. The more certain we are about an event, perhaps through having done it a number of times, the greater the tendency to underplan. You know what to do because you've been there before, or "this is the way it has always been done." Unfortunately, this approach leads to many assumptions about, for instance, who is responsible for what, or what needs to be done. Because the plan is unstated, the chance for oversight or misinterpretation increases dramatically.

Somewhere between these polar extremes is the amount of planning that is right, not only for the event but also for the people involved. Where is that magic place that is not too much and not too little? Unfortunately, there is no way of prescribing where that might be. It is, as we have already mentioned, in those indeterminate zones (Schön, 1983) that go beyond simply what you have been taught. Experience will help you find that place. As an emerging professional, take the opportunity to volunteer at different events and to do as many different jobs as you can. As you begin to see events from different perspectives, you will see how written plans affect your particular function. You will then be developing "event sense" in the same way experiences in the lived world help you develop common sense. You will learn that there are very few absolutes either in life or in event management. There are lots of "sometimes," "in many cases," "in general," "based on my experience." While the running of an event could be seen as the most exciting piece of the process, we have pointed out that this phase too is not without its issues and problems. In Chapter 7, Greco pointed to some of the issues that can arise, but has also provided a number of best practices from experts in the field. These experiences and insights can help you form your own ways of resolving problems unique to your own situation.

We have also pointed out the need to analyze events. It is essential to analyze errors, where they might have come from, what processes were in place that set the stage for their occurrence, and so forth. At some point in time, you will accept your own fallibility – that sometimes errors are a direct result of our own action or inaction, that we tend to court disaster in our own unique ways through prior experience, bias or ability. Error, however, is only a small part of the overarching need for evaluation. Once again, though, evaluation needs to be placed in context. For what purpose, to what end is evaluation being conducted? What is or should be evaluated? These questions have been posed in previous pages, and we have tried to give you a reasonable starting point to answer them.

We live in a dynamic, changing world and we now recognize that what we do in the name of event management can have long-lasting and permanent effects on our most valuable resource – the environment we live in. It is essential that we consider carefully what these impacts might be and how they might be mitigated. As Dingle indicated in Chapter 9, our resilience and ability to adapt to a changing environment will be an essential skill as an event manager. While it might seem that this is just one more thing to consider, concern for the environment is now a central focus for event organizers, hosts and the communities that are potentially impacted. The section on environmental sustainability should provide you with a sense of the reach that events can have, and also how you might manage some of the responsibilities that ensue.

Event management is a human initiative with many interested stakeholders, both within and outside the event management team. Not everyone has the same agenda and indeed, there may even be some opposition to what you are trying to accomplish. Trying to navigate your way through and around some of these political issues will challenge you as an event manager. While some of the "politics" can be anticipated readily, some other political concerns can be far less obvious and require an anticipatory mindset or that you "read" the situation properly. It is a skill set that will be developed over time as you increase your base of knowledge and experience.

As an event manager, you will be confronted with many challenges and choices that need to be made to ensure a quality event and a quality experience for all parties involved. You are therefore expected to act in an ethical manner – not a small task. We have provided some frameworks to help you develop this advanced skill. Once again, careful thought and a sense of the "big picture" will help you navigate your way through a sometimes difficult process.

Finally, you will note that many of the examples we have used pertain to big events, such as the Olympic Games or other major attractions. These examples clearly provide information about the multi-level detail and advanced preparation required to successfully host these spectacles. It would be a mistake, however, to conclude that events on a much smaller scale require little thought and would not benefit from the processes described in this text. From a charity dance to a banquet or a small golf tournament, the process is the same – only the scale differs. We are confident that what you have been provided with will equip you to be a successful event manager.

Many different authors have tried to bring to bear their experience and to condense a vast amount of knowledge into manageable and useful sketches that will help you develop the tools to be a successful event manager. None of the chapters in this text is intended to be conclusive. We have recommended throughout the text that you continue to read in the various areas – to develop common knowledge that will help you develop advanced knowledge. Some of the chapters will seem like they are speaking directly to you, they will resonate with your experience, skills and present abilities. Some of the chapters you will struggle with. They will take you outside the comfort zone of your present skills and abilities. This is the place you want to be. It is where the greatest development will take place. Spend time with them until you are comfortable, and then seek out the next place of discomfort. We have mentioned in several places that events will grow and evolve – so will you. If the previous pages have been or can be an agent in that evolution, we have done our job.

APPENDICES

APPENDIX A: EXAMPLES OF EVENT GOALS AND ASSOCIATED OBJECTIVES, POLICY AND CONTRACT TOPICS

Examples of event goals and objectives

(by Brenden McVicar)

Goal: to host the most memorable event

Associated objectives for the event
- to uphold the event standards, while maintaining the leadership position in the energy drinks industry;
- to deliver superior customer service in a highly profitable and efficient manner.

(by Landon Fletcher)

Goal: to host the most memorable event in its time; for this event to be used as a reference for many years to come

Associated objectives for the event
- that all event component staff have effective communication (including policies, procedures and technology);
- that all staff are treated fairly and with respect;
- to create proper contracts, ensuring all angles of liability are covered.

(by Paul Grimaldi)

Goal: to ensure a safe, but very entertaining event

Associated objectives for the event
- to provide fans with the ultimate sport experience through the TV.

(by David McDonald)

Goal: to bring top athletes from every sport together to participate in a Frisbee golf tournament designed to create an entertaining atmosphere for fans and athletes alike, while raising money for charities to assist children in sport

Associated objectives for the event
- to raise no less than $10 million for the charities involved.

(by Jonathan Hanley)

Goal: to create a world-class accommodation experience for event guests and participants staying at the ___ Hotel. This includes providing a fast and easy check-in and check-out service, having a safe and secure hotel environment, being friendly and helpful to every event guest and ensuring that no guest is confused with any part of the accommodation facility

Associated objectives for the event
- to have a satisfaction rating of four stars out of five or higher from every event guest staying at ____ Hotel for the event;
- to have a check-in and check-out service time of 15 minutes or less;
- to have a maximum of three complaints from event guests about hotel accommodations for the event.

(by Brenden McVicar)

Further associated objectives for this event:
- to ensure that each guest receives prompt, professional, friendly and courteous service;
- to maintain clean, comfortable and well-maintained premises for our guests and staff;
- to provide at a fair price nutritional, well-prepared meals, using only quality ingredients;
- to ensure that all guests and staff are treated with the respect and dignity they deserve;
- to thank each guest for the opportunity to serve them.

212

Examples of event policy and contracts topics

Suggestions by Landon Fletcher:

- event health and injury policy;
- scheduling policy;
- alcohol and drug policy;
- ineligible participant's policy;
- violence policy;
- policy concerning types of transportation to be available – for people with disabilities, VIPs, participants;
- how will drivers know who can be transported (proper accreditation)?;
- routes and scheduling policy;
- parking services contract;
- tow truck company contract;
- limo and bus companies contract.

Suggestions by Jonathan Hanley:

- smoking policy;
- volunteer and employee policy;
- media policy;
- spectator policy;
- information privacy and confidentiality policy.

Suggestions by David McDonald:

- food and beverage policy;
- accessibility policy;
- translation services contract;
- security consultant services contract;
- catering contract;
- tent and furniture rental contract;
- vehicle contract;
- cell phone service contract;
- portable restroom/washroom contract .

Suggestions by Brenden McVicar:

- music and noise policy;
- security policy;
- clean-up and maintenance policy;

- damages policy;
- parking services policy;
- advertising contract;
- requirements for approvals (i.e. ability to sign contracts).

Suggestions by Paul Grimaldi:

- sponsorship policy;
- insurance contract;
- clothing contract;
- broadcasting contract;
- emergency policy: fire, police, ambulance;
- food and beverage policy and contract.

APPENDIX B: SEGMENTS OF EVENT VOLUNTEER MANAGEMENT OPERATIONAL PLAN

(by Iain Sime)

Timeframe	Activity	Person responsible
Six months prior to event	**Volunteer recruiting** *Volunteer orientation session timeframe:* • Establish volunteer orientation session date, time at event site *Develop and post volunteer recruitment information on event website and send to local team websites for posting:* – Website posting to include: • event name • event dates • how to apply to volunteer • request volunteer name, address, email, telephone number, cell phone number, previous volunteer or work experience • a checklist of volunteer opportunities and an overview of tasks • minimum age requirements • deadline date for applications • shirt size (men's/women's – small, medium, large or extra large) • mandatory volunteer orientation session date/ time information • volunteer shirts as uniform to be provided – shirts to be provided at volunteer session; volunteers to wear black pants and comfortable shoes • complimentary ticket policy for volunteers • contact site for further information on the event and volunteer roles *Word-of-mouth volunteer recruitment activities:* • Develop a business-card-style information sheet indicating volunteers needed for event • Include on card: event name, dates and website for further information • Distribute business cards at league basketball games to potential volunteers	Volunteer Coordinator and Volunteer Committee members

Timeframe	Activity	Person responsible
	Twitter and Facebook – call for volunteers (and other sites your group utilizes) • Direct all potential volunteers to the website *Develop newspaper volunteer recruitment posting:* • Develop local newspaper ad(s) to attract volunteers (include event name, dates, and how to apply via the website)	
Five months prior to event	**Volunteer orientation session preparation** *Work with the Venue Coordinator to put all details into place for the volunteer orientation session, including:* • Date and time confirmed • Venue room finalized; space based on number of people to be in attendance • Venue entrance gate to be used by volunteers finalized • Plan venue tour • Generate a volunteer placement list with the name of the volunteer assigned to each role; have a copy at the volunteer orientation session as a sign-in process; manage any volunteers not in attendance • Arrange for volunteer parking for orientation session • Work with the Accreditation/Credentials Committee to arrange for accreditation passes to be developed and distributed at the orientation session • Ensure Volunteer Room has a whiteboard (and markers) along with a bulletin board (and tacks) • Design training session to review each volunteer position • Order wireless microphone • Order volunteer golf shirts (gain pre-approval from Event Committee for colour and logo prior to order) • Volunteer Media Manager and volunteers to develop media package for distribution at event (hard copy and online copy) • Entertainment volunteers to obtain prizes for tossing into the crowd and for entertainment prizes	Venue Manager, Volunteer Coordinator and two Volunteer Committee members assigned to orientation session plus Accreditation Coordinator

216

Timeframe	Activity	Person responsible
	• Arrange for parking passes to distribute to volunteers at the orientation session (determine number of passes required and the distribution process) • Prepare to discuss the emergency protocols and generate written overview sheets for distribution • Arrange for the volunteer communication system (a number of cell phones) and be prepared to explain how a volunteer signs one out and returns it to the system; prepare a list of all cell phone numbers and the name/title of each person in possession of one of the event phones	
Four and a half months prior to event	**Order for Volunteer Room** • Room to be set up by 8 am on date: ____ • Coat racks (× 3: to hold 20 coats per rack) • Eight tables (10' round; white table cloths) positioned in two rows of four in room for volunteers • 10 chairs at each table for a total of 80 chairs • Arrange for two security staff to be stationed just outside the Volunteer Room doorway for the orientation session and the event date(s) • Arrange for food and beverages for volunteer orientation session (to be available 45 minutes prior to start of orientation session for 60 people; to include coffee/tea/orange juice/apple juice; four kinds of muffins and bread sticks; fruit tray and vegetable tray) • Arrange for tables for food and beverages: three 3' × 8' tables, white table cloths, basketball centrepiece (× 3), tables placed on north wall • Generate a diagram showing where tables, coat racks, food, etc. are to be positioned within the Volunteer Room	Volunteer Coordinator and Venue Manager
Three months prior to event	**Volunteer selection and confirmation** • Review volunteer applications and selection pool of volunteers • Select six "rover" volunteers who will learn all roles and be able to fill in whenever necessary	Volunteer Coordinator and all Volunteer Committee members

Timeframe	Activity	Person responsible

	• Subdivide list between Event Committee members and ensure all volunteers are called
	• Establish an overall checklist to confirm each volunteer's participation/confirmation and their attendance at the mandatory volunteer orientation session
	• Send all volunteers an email confirming their role, agreement to participate and the details concerning the mandatory volunteer orientation session (date, time, site, specific room, parking arrangements, that coffee, tea, etc. will be provided and event contact name/contact information)
	• Prepare for a number of volunteer selection issues, such as:
	  i. If more than enough interested volunteers are available, how you will respond to those not getting a role at the event
	  ii. Keeping a reserve group of volunteers in case they are needed as replacements	

Three weeks prior to event	**Volunteer orientation session** Date: Time: Venue: Room: Attendance required from ____ to ____pm Attendees: *Set-up:* • Room to be set up two to three hours prior to orientation session (see set-up requirements in preparations above) • Place at each seat an information card welcoming all volunteers to the upcoming volunteer appreciation night; card to include the date, time and site; agenda for the orientation session • Place emergency protocols sheet at each seat • Ensure that the Accreditation Committee is set up to begin taking headshots and adding required information for the printed and laminated accreditation passes one hour prior to the orientation session; lanyards to be available; distribution process pre-established	Volunteer Coordinator, Venue Manager, Event Accreditation Coordinator and volunteers

218

Timeframe	Activity	Person responsible

- Ensure security staff in place 45 minutes prior to orientation session
- Meet and greet all volunteers as they arrive

Orientation agenda:
1 Welcome and introductions (ask all volunteers to sign in next to their name on the volunteer sheet)
2 Review of volunteer roles (see list below)
3 Volunteer communication system explained
4 Emergency protocols discussed (provided in writing)
5 Review process for volunteer breaks during event
6 Facility tour
7 Dress code and distribution of volunteer golf shirts
8 Accreditation distribution
9 Parking pass distribution
10 Discuss volunteer complimentary tickets; how to order and pick up their tickets
11 Discuss the volunteer appreciation night

Examples of volunteer roles to be reviewed:

Anthem singer – informed of timing, confirm introduction for public address (PA), where they are to walk/stand, direction to face, bilingual version anthem required, where they go after anthem, pre-event technical check time and site on event day

Team hosts – one per team; to ensure teams know their assigned warm-up and game schedules, etc.

Statistics Managers – to gather pre-event team statistics, to distribute statistics to media and PA announcer at pre-assigned intervals throughout the event

Game Sheet Manager – to manage the completion of the official game sheet for each team within a predetermined timeframe; information distributed to Media Manager

Media Manager and volunteers – to meet and greet media in attendance, to develop and distribute a media package, to develop event

Timeframe	Activity	Person responsible
	statistics and distribute in a timely fashion to media at pre-assigned intervals throughout the event in print form and via the website; to aid media in their arrangements to interview coaches and players *Volunteer security* – to ensure only those with the correct accreditation have access to the Volunteer Room, the team rooms, the Media Room, etc. *Entertainment volunteers* – to secure prizes and to design and conduct fan entertainment during team timeouts/between quarters and during halftime; to work directly with the public address (PA) announcer to ensure promotions are announced *Communication Managers* – if two-way radios are available, then the volunteers should be shown how to use them. If there are not enough radios for each volunteer, then just assign the radios to the volunteers whom you determine need them the most. i. Make sure volunteers stay in constant contact with one another as well as yourself ii. If any problems occur, make sure they are communicated to one another right away	
	Process for volunteer orientation for those missing the preparation session: • Place a copy of the volunteer orientation information on the website • Confirm attendance of volunteers who did not attend the volunteer orientation session and then direct them to the website orientation information site • Answer any questions the volunteers have accordingly	Volunteer Coordinator
Two weeks prior to event	**Volunteer management contingency plan development** *Generate "What if scenarios" and the response for each situation:* • What if a volunteer doesn't show up? – Train three "floater volunteers" who are prepared to do any of a list of multiple volunteer jobs	Volunteer Coordinator

Timeframe	Activity	Person responsible

	• What if a volunteer unexpectedly brings their young child with them?
	  – If you can do the event without their help, then you could inform them that their child cannot attend
	  – If you have a spot where the child could stay supervised, then they can leave their child supervised while the event is going on
	• What if they lose their accreditation or volunteer golf shirt?
	  – Make sure to keep extra shirts and accreditations on hand in case they are forgotten
	  – If there is more than one type of accreditation, then make sure you have some extra of each type	

Eight days prior to event	**Volunteer reminder notices** • Send out an email reminding all volunteers about the event, including the date, time and their role; and the fact that the orientation information has been posted on the website for their review/reminders • Update them on any new information regarding the event	Volunteer Coordinator
Five days prior to event	**Volunteer Room final preparations** • Prepare to post on Volunteer Room bulletin board an overview of each volunteer position (reference material) – state name of volunteer to complete each task • Double-check on the order for tables, chairs, food and beverages, and communication equipment	Volunteer Coordinator
Four to six hours prior to event	**Volunteer Room set-up** • Post all job assignment overviews with name of volunteer to complete each job on the bulletin board • Set up food and drink in the locker room for volunteers • Volunteer Room security staff to be stationed at the entrance of the room	Volunteer Coordinator

221

Timeframe	Activity	Person responsible
Two hours prior to event	**Final volunteer meeting** *(subdivided into their volunteer groups).* • Checklist utilized to know if all volunteers have arrived • If a volunteer has not arrived, replace with a "floater volunteer" • Distribution of volunteer communication system (sign-out list utilized) • Coordinator available in Volunteer Room for any questions and to manage issues • Answer arising questions	Volunteer Coordinator
Event time	**During the event** *Distribution of volunteer communication system of cell phones:* • list of all contacts and their cell phone numbers provided with phones • utilize checklist of volunteers to ensure that all are in attendance and in position; manage volunteer absentees • Monitor volunteer activities; manage arising issues *Volunteer breaks:* – Make sure volunteers get at least one break during the event – Stagger breaks so not all volunteers are on break at once – Limit breaks to 15 minutes – Make sure volunteers keep their radios with them during break in case of an emergency	Volunteer Coordinator
At the end of the event	**After the event** *Volunteer communication system collection* **Say thanks and encourage attendance at Volunteer Appreciation Night**	Volunteer Coordinator
One week post-event	**Obtain confirmation of attendance for Volunteer Appreciation Night** • Confirm attendance • Establish agenda • Order awards • Establish a Master of Ceremonies for the night • Complete preparations for food and beverages	Volunteer Coordinator

Timeframe	Activity	Person responsible
Four weeks post-event	**Volunteer Appreciation Night** *Room set-up:* • Set up tables and chairs • Put out drinks and food on a "snack table" • Coat racks available • Music predetermined; have music and speakers ready to go *Master of Ceremonies briefing:* • Written overview of event details (order of speakers) and their timing, along with specific announcements to be made to be provided to Master of Ceremonies; reviewed/discussed verbally *Awards:* • Hand out awards to each of the volunteers	Volunteer Coordinator

APPENDIX C: SEGMENTS OF VIP MANAGEMENT OPERATIONAL PLAN

(by David McDonald)

Date/Time	Task	Responsibility
Two months prior to event	• **VIP security** Purchase cell phones for off-site communication between all drivers, security staff, and event management, as well as two additional batteries per phone as back-up and an additional 10 batteries as a back-up bank – all on unlimited ___ network plans from ___ Co. using event credit card. • Manually program all cell phones with phone numbers for VIP Manager, Intern, Security Consultant, catering company staff, drivers and security staff • Purchase secure wireless headsets plus two additional batteries per unit plus an additional 10 batteries as a back-up bank for on-site communication (for VIP Manager, Intern, Security Consultant, catering company staff, drivers and security staff) from local retail ____ Store, using event credit card • Program headsets with appropriate channels for each relevant party	Intern

One week prior to event	• Meeting at venue with Security Consultant
	  o May 29, 2019
	  o AGENDA
	    ▪ Field test all headsets and cell phones
	    ▪ Identify any potential dead zones in the venue
		VIP Manager

Two days prior to event	• Meeting at venue with all security, transportation, catering and event management staff
	  o June 1, 2019
	  o AGENDA
	    ▪ Provide each individual with one cell phone, one wireless headset, and two additional batteries for each unit
	    ▪ Conduct training on how each device operates
		VIP Manager and Intern

224

Date/Time	Task	Responsibility

Two days after event	• Wrap-up meeting with all drivers and security staff
	  o June 6, 2019: 9 am
	  o AGENDA
	    ▪ Review any security incidents that took place
	    ▪ Retrieve all cell phones and headsets from all equipped drivers and security staff
		VIP Manager

Within 60 days	• Receive and pay invoice from ____ for cell phone coverage services	VIP Manager

Two months prior to event	**VIP flight arrangements**
	
	• Meet with Project Manager at ____ Charter Services Inc. company headquarters
	  o April 2, 2019: 8:30 am
	  o AGENDA
	    ▪ Draft contract for charter flights for VIPs (put copy into appendix) Intern
	    ▪ Obtain contract signatures
	• Confirm travel documentation requirements (i.e. travel visas) by contacting required embassies by telephone, and communicating documentation needs to VIPs via email
		VIP Manager

Seven weeks prior to event	• Meet with Project Manager (name) at ____ Charter Services Inc. company headquarters
	  o April 10, 2019
	  o AGENDA
	    ▪ Plan all charter flights for VIPs to arrive two days prior to event start
	    ▪ Arrange all luxury amenities on flights
	    ▪ Request background checks on all pilots
		VIP Manager

One month prior to event	• Host GoTo Meeting with Project Manager (name and email address) at ____ Charter Services Inc.
	  o May 3, 2019: 11 am
	  o AGENDA
	    ▪ Confirm all charter flights are still on schedule to ensure no gaps in VIP arrivals
		VIP Manager

Date/Time	Task	Responsibility
	• Receive all paper background checks via secure courier (____ Courier, contact information) from Project Manager (name and email address) at ____ Charter Services no later than May 5, 2019)	Intern

	• Meeting with Security Consultant (name)
	  o May 6, 2019: 10 am
	  o AGENDA
	    ■ Review background checks of all pilots sent by ____ Charter Services
		VIP Manager and Intern

	• Scan all background checks, and store them on secure online event server for event's own records	Intern
	• Contact all VIPs via telephone (see Appendix I for list of phone numbers) to ensure they all have required travel documentation (i.e. travel visas) to come to the event.	

One week prior to event	• GoTo Meeting with Project Manager
	  o May 29: 3 pm
	  o AGENDA
	    ■ Final confirmation that all charter flights are on schedule for both departures and arrivals
		VIP Manager

Within 60 days	• Receive and pay invoice from ____ Charter Services	VIP Manager
Four months prior to event	**VIP tent/furniture** • Determine parameters and post Request for Proposal (RFP) for VIP tent and furniture for tent on ____ website o Selected ____ Tent Rental Co.	VIP Manager

Three months prior to event	• Meet with Project Manager (name) at Tent Rental Co. headquarters
	  o March 3, 2019: 10 am
	  o AGENDA
	    ■ Discuss needs for rented equipment:
	      • 150' × 150' outdoor tent
	      • Bicycle rack barricade to surround VIP Area
	      • Furniture for tent :
	        o Nine couches (seating three each)
	        o 10 tables (round), seating six with chairs
	        o All red tablecloths/white seat covers
	        o Two Additional pieces of all as back-up
		VIP Manager

Date/Time	Task	Responsibility
	• Delivery and set-up crew at venue four days prior to event (tent) and two days prior to event (furniture), complete by 12 pm on day of delivery • Develop furniture layout plan • Same-day on-site support • Teardown crew and removal one day after event (furniture) and three days after event (tent) • Removal of trucks from site during duration of event ▪ Draft contract ▪ Sign contract	

Two months prior to event	• Meeting with event Security Consultant
	  o April 2, 2019: 10 am
	  o AGENDA
	    ▪ Discuss layout of tent and furniture in the VIP Area, as well as VIP Smoking Area
	    ▪ Establish secure routes from:
	      • VIP entrance to VIP Area
	      • Field of play to VIP Area
	      • Clubhouse to VIP Area for catering staff
	      • VIP tent to VIP Smoking Area
	      • (See Appendix for site map)
		VIP Manager and Intern

One month prior to event	• Contact Foreman at ____ Electrical Services (name and contact information) via telephone to make appointment for pre-event VIP Area electrical inspection on May 30, 2019 at 8:30 am • Contact Chief Engineer at ____ Structual Services (name and contact information) via telephone to make appointment for pre-event tent inspection four days prior to event on May 30, 2019 at 12 pm	Intern

Five days prior to event	• Meeting with venue management personnel at venue site
	  o May 29, 2019: 5 pm
	  o AGENDA
	    ▪ Arrange special main gate access for both VIP Hospitality Manager and Intern for set-up access
		VIP Manager, Intern and Venue Manager

Date/Time	Task	Responsibility

Four days prior to event	• Venue site meeting with Project Manager (name and contact information)
	  ○ May 30, 2019: 6 am
	  ○ AGENDA
	    ▪ Access to venue to allow tent set-up
		Intern

	• Venue site meeting with Foreman at ____ Electrical Services (name and contact information)
	  ○ May 30, 2019: 8:30 am
	  ○ AGENDA
	    ▪ Site inspection and electrical set-up for VIP Area electrical services
		Intern

	• Venue site meeting with site Chief Engineer (name and contact information)
	  ○ May 30, 2019: 12 pm
	  ○ AGENDA
	    ▪ Tent inspection for structural integrity to ensure safety for all parties involved
		VIP Manager

Two days prior to event	• Meeting with Project Manager at venue site
	  ○ June 1, 2019: 7 am
	  ○ AGENDA
	    ▪ Provide site access for furniture set-up inside VIP tent
		Intern

One day after event	• Meeting with Project Manager at venue site
	  ○ June 5, 2019: 8 am
	  ○ AGENDA
	    ▪ Provide access for removal of all furniture from site
		Intern

Three days after event	• Meeting with Project Manager (name and contact information) from ____ Tent Rental Co. at venue site
	  ○ June 7, 2019: 8 am
	  ○ AGENDA
	    ▪ Provide access for teardown and removal of VIP tent from site
		Intern

Within 60 days	• Receive and pay invoice for tent rental, electrical services and structural services	VIP Manager

APPENDIX D: SEGMENTS OF OPERATIONAL PLAN FOR EVENT GUEST INFORMATION BOOKLETS

(by Jonathan Hanley)

Date/Time	Task	Responsibility

Four and a half months prior to event	**Research information booklets**
	
	• Call ___ Printing and speak with Manager (name and contact information)
	• Inquire about:
	  o Ordering information booklet for event guests
	  o Size of information booklet
	  o Shape of booklet
	  o Type of paper used
	  o Colour of ink in booklet
	  o Information included in each booklet:
	    ▪ Details of each hotel room type
	      • Type of beds
	      • Washroom details
	      • Living area details
	    ▪ Hotel details, i.e. spa area, pool area, gym location
	    ▪ Food and services available
	    ▪ Amenities of hotel
	    ▪ Transportation information
	    ▪ Medical information in hotel
	    ▪ Tourist information
	  o How many information booklets to be printed
	  o Budget and total costs of booklets
		Accommodation Manager

Four months prior to event	**Order information booklets**
	
	• Call ___ Printing and speak with Manager
	• Order information booklets:
	  o Size of information booklet (11 × 8 inches)
	  o Shape of booklet (rectangular)
	  o Type of paper used (recyclable)
	  o Colour of ink (blue, red, black)
	  o Information included in booklet
	    ▪ Details of each hotel room type
	      • Type of beds
	      • Washroom details
	      • Living area details
	    ▪ Hotel details, i.e. spa area, pool area, gym location
		Accommodation Manager

Date/Time	Task	Responsibility
	■ Food and services available ■ Amenities of hotel ■ Transportation information ■ Medical information in hotel ■ Tourist information o How many information booklets (500) o Total cost of booklets ($3,000) o Pay with event credit card	

Five months prior to event	**Research information booth**
	• Call ____ Hotel and speak with Hotel Manager (name and contact information)
	• Inquire about:
	o Information booth in hotel lobby
	  ■ Booth will provide hotel and tourism information
	o Hotel employee working at information booth
	o Booth open from 7 am to 9 pm
	o Details of set-up for information booth
	  ■ Table size
	  ■ Table shape
	  ■ Number of chairs
	  ■ Type of chairs
		Accommodation Manager

Four and a half months prior to event	**Information booth**
	• Call ____ Hotel and speak with Hotel Manager
	• Confirm use of information booth
	o Information booth in hotel lobby
	  ■ Booth will provide hotel and tourism information
	o Hotel employee working at information booth
	o Booth open from 7 am to 9 pm
	o Request the following:
	  ■ Table size (5 × 2.5′)
	  ■ Table shape (rectangular)
	  ■ Number of chairs (three)
	  ■ Type of chairs (fold-up)
		Accommodation Manager

230

Date/Time	Task	Responsibility

Two weeks prior to event	**Receive delivery of information booklets**
	
	• Call ____ Hotel and speak with Hotel Manager
	• Inform Hotel Manager that information booklets have arrived
	• Check to confirm information booklets are as ordered
	  o Size of information booklet (11 × 8 inches)
	  o Shape of booklet (rectangular)
	  o Type of paper used (recyclable)
	  o Colour of ink (blue, red, black)
	  o Information included in booklet
	    ▪ Details of each hotel room type
	      • Type of beds
	      • Washroom details
	      • Living area details
	    ▪ Hotel details, i.e. spa area, pool area, gym location
	    ▪ Food and services available
	    ▪ Amenities of hotel
	    ▪ Transportation information
	    ▪ Medical information in hotel
	    ▪ Tourist information
	• Store information booklets in storage room A by hotel elevators
		Accommodation Manager

Three days prior to event	**Set up information booth**
	
	• Call ____Hotel and speak with Hotel Manager
	• Ask for information booth components
	  o Table (5 × 2.5', rectangular)
	  o Three fold-up chairs
	• Set up information booth in hotel lobby
		Accommodation Manager

One day prior to event	**Disperse information booklets**
	
	• Get information booklets from storage room A by hotel elevators
	• Disperse information booklets to various areas of hotel:
	  o Hotel lobby desk
	  o Concierge desk
	  o Information booth
		Accommodation Manager

Date/Time	Task	Responsibility
Event days June 2–4, 2019: 7 am	**Hotel booth check** • Ensure one hotel employee is at hotel information booth in hotel lobby at 7 am • Ensure that one employee will be at information booth in hotel lobby until 9 pm	Accommodation Manager
Event day, June 5, 2019: 7 am 3:30 pm	**Hotel booth check: check-out day** • Ensure a hotel employee is at hotel information booth in hotel lobby at 7 am • Inform hotel employee they can leave information booth at 3:30 pm after check-out of event guests **Volunteer information booth teardown** • Inform volunteers to go to information booth in hotel lobby • Teardown of information booth • Bring table and three fold-up chairs to storage room B by hotel elevators	Accommodation Manager

One day post-event	**Recycle extra information booklets**
	• Pick up unused information booklets from
	  o Hotel lobby desk
	  o Concierge desk
	  o Information booth
	• Put unused information booklets in hotel recycling dispenser by exit 6 of ____ Hotel
		Accommodation Manager

APPENDIX E: SEGMENTS OF OPERATIONAL PLAN FOR EVENT SUPPORT FOR TELEVISION PRODUCTION

(by Paul Grimaldi)

Date/Time	Operational activity	Responsibility
Seven months prior to event	**Meet with TV production management** Date: August 9, 2019 Time: 12 pm Site: TV offices ***Negotiate television contract*** – What will ____TV Co. be responsible for? – ____TV Co. will provide you with two hosts who specialize in the event – ____TV Co. will also be responsible for providing and setting up the equipment to run the broadcast	TV Production Manager
Six months prior to event	**Meeting with accreditation** Date: September 1, 2019 Site: ____ Co. headquarters Time: 2:00 pm Agenda: – Determine how many volunteer badges will be needed – Determine what colour the media pass will be – Determine where employees from ____ Network receive media passes – Determine where volunteers sign in/where they go to pick up media badge – Determine where announcers go to receive media badge – Discuss hours of operation and contact information for any other questions – Discuss the appropriate times for ____ Network, volunteers and announcers to arrive/depart from event – Discuss where media crew should set up – Discuss the designated areas for parking and unloading/loading media trucks	TV Production Manager

Date/Time	Operational activity	Responsibility
	Meeting with volunteer management Date: September 20, 2019 Site: ____ Co. headquarters Time: 10 am Agenda: – Determine how many volunteers will be needed for TV production (five volunteers will be needed) – Discuss where volunteers are to meet for instructions on what they will be helping with – Determine where event will be getting volunteers from – Discuss how volunteers will be helping ____ Network production team – Discuss the importance of volunteers already having experience working with TV production – Discuss hours of operation and contact information for any other questions	TV Production Manager
Five months prior to event	**Venue production meeting** Date: October 25, 2019 Site: ____ Co. headquarters Time: 4 pm Agenda: – Determine how many rooms will be needed for production – Discuss how the rooms will be set up with equipment *Broadcast dressing room* – Where will they get ready? – Determine if every sports broadcaster should have their own dressing room – Determine if ____ Network will provide make-up artist or whether the event needs to provide its own *Set up broadcasting room* – Determine what room will be the broadcasting room – Discuss how the room will be set up – Discuss when the room will become available for ____ Network to come and set up for production – Discuss where the production trucks should be set up	TV Production Manager

234

Date/Time	Operational activity	Responsibility

Set up cameras
- Discuss where would be the best locations to set up cameras for the event
- Discuss where the TV production trucks should be located in order to ensure production runs smoothly

TV production trucks
- Where will they be located?
- How many does the event need?
- How far can they be from the course?
- Discuss hours of operation and contact information for any other questions

Commercials
- Discuss what type of commercials will be run during the event
- Discuss how much will they pay to have their commercial run
- Discuss how much each time slot costs
- Determine what types of company the event will do commercials with (e.g. it doesn't want to do ads with cigarette companies, as it looks bad on a sporting event to be associated with cigarettes)

Interviews
- Will ____ Network be the ones conducting the interviews?
- Discuss when the interviews will take place (before or after the race)
- Discuss where the interviews will be conducted (on the course, on the side after the race)
- Determine which athletes will be interviewed (1st, 2nd, 3rd or 4th)
- Discuss if the interviews will take place after every race
- Discuss whether there will be background stories for television to get the fans at home more involved and intrigued in the event
- Determine which athletes will receive background stories
- Determine how to get these stories about the athletes (e.g. from coaches, parents, managers)
- Discuss which athletes' stories will be used during the broadcast.
- Discuss if there will be press conferences after the race
- Determine who will have access to these press conferences after the race

Date/Time	Operational activity	Responsibility
	– Discuss how much time each press conference can last – Discuss hours of operation and contact information for any other questions	
Four months prior to event	**Meeting concerning awards/closing ceremony** Date: November 10, 2019 Site: ____ Co. headquarters Time: 2 pm Agenda: *Location* – Determine where the closing ceremony show takes place *Cameras* – Discuss where each camera will be set up for the closing ceremony – Determine how many cameras will be needed – Discuss the different types of camera shots during the event *Time of broadcast (i)* – Determine when the closing ceremony will take place – Discuss how long the closing ceremony will run for *Award ceremonies* – Discuss when award ceremonies will take place – Discuss when awards will be handed out to the athletes – Discuss how much time is needed to hand out each award *Shots of trophy* – Discuss taking shots of the trophy before the event begins – Determine where the shots should be taken on the track *Time of broadcast (ii)* – Determine when the half-time show will take place – Discuss how long the half-time show will run for – Discuss when the opening ceremony will take place – Discuss how long the opening ceremony will run for	TV Production Manager

236

Date/Time	Operational activity	Responsibility
Four months prior to event	**Media management**	TV Production Manager

Media management

Commercials
- Have a set list of commercials to be played during the event
- Determine which commercials are to be played at what times
- Determine how many times each commercial is to played
- Determine which are the appropriate times to cut to a commercial break

Interviews
- Have commentators ready to do post-race interviews after each race
- The winner of each race will have an interview on the ice, and head back to do a press conference as well
- Ensure that there is a camera at the bottom of the race to tape the interview so it can be aired on TV
- Contact the Media Manager to ensure s/he has provided the background stories for each athlete
- Determine which background stories will be used during the event
- Determine when to play these background stories (normally, before or after the race)
- Determine if the press conference will even air on television (only if it will engage the fans' excitement)
- Ensure with the Media Manager that all the cameras are ready to be set up for the press conferences
- Ensure that the Media Manager has set up microphones for conducting the interview
- Determine what highlights will be used during the event

Accreditation
- Contact the Accreditation Manager to confirm that all the media passes will be ready for the volunteers, production team and announcers
- Confirm where the volunteers are supposed to meet to sign in/pick up volunteer badges and shirts (if any changes have been made, email volunteers immediately to inform them)
- Confirm when it is okay for volunteers to show up (6 am)
- Confirm where the designated areas for parking are, and where unloading/ loading will take place

APPENDIX F: SEGMENTS OF OPERATIONAL PLAN FOR EVENT TRANSPORTATION OPERATIONAL

(by Landon Fletcher)

Date/Time	Operational activity	Responsibility
11 months prior to event	**Begin the development of transportation policies for the event** Date: Jan 5, 2019 Time: 11 am Location: ____ Lounge, ____ University Agenda: Policies for: • Routes and schedules • Specific detours (road closures) • Types of transportation • Disabled transportation • VIP transportation • Athlete transportation • How will drivers know who can be transported (proper accreditation) • Transportation communication system • Event parking	Transportation Manager and staff
Seven months prior to event	**Initial meeting with staff to discuss general questions regarding transportation and parking** Date: April 1, 2019 Time: 12 pm Location: ____ Lounge, ____ University Invitees: Transportation staff Confirmed attendance: By email Agenda: Discuss team goals, organization goals, policies, procedures and processes leading up to the event Questions that will be asked include: • Due to the fact the event is three days in duration, who from the transportation staff will be available for which day? What hours can they work during those requested days? • What type of transportation method is best? (School bus, coach bus, public transit bus, limo, taxi) • How many vehicles will be needed each and every day? • Who will be in charge of directing traffic on the day of the event?	Event transportation staff led by Transportation Manager

238

Date/Time	Operational activity	Responsibility
	• Where will the vehicles be stored overnight? And where does everyone suggest the best place to store the vehicles will be? • Security on vehicles? • Routes, schedules and parking for fans, participants, special guests and alumni as well as media • Communication distribution of transportation information	
Five months prior to event	**Meeting: with event Security Manager** Date: June 1, 2019 Time: 12 pm Location: ____ Lounge, ____ University Invitees: Security Manager Confirmed: By email Agenda: Discuss the role of security needed for transportation and parking • Hiring security guards (12) • Negotiate pre-made contract • Security will be assigned in groups of two in case one of them needs to use the washroom • Two security guards at the participants' hotel for transportation boarding area security • Two security guards will be located at venue Lot B • Two will be located at the rented parking lot across from the venue • Two will be located at the bus terminal located at the loop in the middle of the venue route • Two security guards available to ensure participants have safe access to their transportation areas at all times • Two security guards will be placed overnight to watch the vehicles • Contract to cover fees and payment process	
Three months prior to event	**Meeting with hire bus and limo companies** Date: July 31, 2019 Time: 4 pm Location: Over the phone Invitees: Limo service, bus service Confirmed: By phone Agenda: Inquire and commit to the days of the event	Transportation Manager to assign task

Date/Time	Operational activity	Responsibility

	This meeting will ensure that:
	• The negotiated contract is finalized; then signed and submitted
	
	Bus:
	  o Discuss bus routes and times
	  o Discuss bus fares/passes
	  o Discuss detour routes
	  o Discuss accreditation
	  o Discuss bus maximum capacity
	  o Negotiate contract (payments, people with disabilities, liabilities, length of contract)
	
	Limo:
	  o Discuss routes and times
	  o Discuss fares
	  o Discuss accreditation
	  o Negotiate a contract (payment, length, VIP transportation, dress code, special event shirts)	

Six weeks prior to event	**Meeting to re-connect with security staff** Date: September 20, 2019 Time: 2 pm Location: Over the phone (conference call) Invitees: Manager of Security Services and any of their staff Confirmed: Over the phone Agenda: • 12 security guards needed for November 6, 7 and 8 • There is no requirement for these security guards as long as they are identifiable, with bright shirts outlining that they are security guards • Each guard will work in pairs and make $20 per hour; they will be needed every day of the event from 7 am until 10 pm (or until the event finishes) • Their responsibility will be as follows: o Two security guards will be placed at the hotel where the athletes are staying, as there may be problems after the games between the players when emotions may be high	Transportation Manager to assign task

240

Date/Time	Operational activity	Responsibility
	o Two security guards will be located at Lot B, directing traffic and ensuring that no problems occur. o Two will be located at the rented parking lot across from ____ Complex ensuring that everyone who enters has a proper parking pass. o Two will be located at the bus terminal located at the loop in the middle of ____ University. These security guards will ensure that fans and students who have been drinking or having fun respect the drivers of the bus. o There will be two security guards placed between the team dressing rooms; this ensures that the players will get safely to and from their bus before and after the games. o Last, two security guards will be placed overnight to watch the vehicles, so as to avoid these being damaged or vandalized in any way possible	
Six weeks prior to event	**Meeting in connection with opening and closing ceremonies** *Opening ceremonies* Date: September, 21, 2019 Time: 12 pm) Location: __ Lounge, ____University Invitees: Ceremonies Manager Confirmed: By email Agenda: Discuss potential transportation opportunities This meeting will focus on: • Where the ceremonies are going to be held; date; participant transportation needs *Closing ceremonies* Date: September 21, 2019 Time: 2 pm Location: ___ Lounge, ____ University Invitees: Closing ceremonies staff Confirmed: Over the phone Agenda: • Where the ceremonies are going to be held (most likely ____ University alumni field)	Transportation Manager to assign task

Date/Time	Operational activity	Responsibility
	• Discuss which day the ceremonies are happening: last event day (November 8) or the following day (November 9) • Once the date is set in stone, consider timing so there is sufficient time to arrange proper transportation of VIP guest or celebrities • Discuss what time VIP guest needs to be brought to field • Where VIP closing ceremony individuals need to be dropped off	
Five weeks prior to event	**Meeting with transportation staff** Date: September 30, 2019 Time: 12 pm Location: ____Lounge, ____ University Invitees: Entire transportation staff Confirmed: By email Agenda: Discuss operations • Ensure everyone is aware of the contingency plans and how to operate them • Discuss everyone's role on the event days • Ensure all drivers are fully licensed, this ensures liability purposes • Have everyone sign a contract and do a health and safety test • Inform staff where to pick up their accreditation (day before event, at ____ University ___ Lounge between 12 pm and 8 pm); staff need to be in full uniform and have proper accreditation; it is vital they go to the ___ Lounge on November 5 between the hours mentioned	Transportation Manager to assign task
Five to six weeks prior to event	**Have transportation signs made** • Signs will have a blue background and be in a rectangular form, these signs will be bright so people driving into the venue cannot miss them	Transportation Manager to assign task

242

Date/Time	Operational activity	Responsibility
Four weeks prior to event	**Meeting: Tow truck company** Date: October 10, 2019 Time: 12 pm Location: _____ Lounge, ___University Invitees: _____Towing Confirmation: By phone Agenda: • Discuss having them as our client for the full three days; this will ensure that if any of the event buses, limos or cars break down, they can safely be towed back • Flat-rate contract $700 for the three days • Explain to them all the bus routes and car routes. This will ensure that if one of the event vehicles breaks down, their company will know where to go make the tow • Explain emergency routes in case of an accident, meaning they need to get there in a hurry • 2 trucks needed on site at all times; this works as a contingency plan just in case something goes wrong	Transportation Manager to assign task
One day prior to event	**Delivery of transportation signs to _____ Lounge, _____ University**	Transportation Manager to assign task

APPENDIX G: SECTIONS OF EVENT OPERATIONAL PLAN FOR EVENT FOOD AND BEVERAGE

(by Brenden McVicar)

Date	Task	Responsibility
Six months prior to event	**Budget planning** • Obtain and create budgetary parameters for event • Develop a budget overview chart to personally keep track of event food and beverage spending • Continuously develop the budget details to have a realistic picture of the budget at all times	Food and Beverage Manager
	Meeting: Event Venue Manager Date: September 30, 2019 Site: MC203 Time: 10 am Agenda: • Number of spectators to be at the event • Location/size of food and beverage tents • Set-up time • Location for licensed drinking area • Parking for contractor/service vehicle • Services (electrical, internet, phone, storage area, security)	Food and Beverage Manager

	Develop and distribute food vendor information package
	
	• Email to confirmed restaurants/wineries/breweries the information package, including:
	  o Dates and site details
	  o Parking
	  o Assigned set-up location
	  o Time allotted for set-up/teardown
	  o Event activity details
	  o Financial details
	  o Services provided
	  o Contact details for further information
		Intern and Food and Beverage Manager

Date	Task	Responsibility
Five months prior to event	**Meeting: Media Management food and beverage requirements** Date: October 30, 2019 Site: MC203 Time: 2 pm Agenda: • Confirm media centre food and beverage requirements • Tables/table cloth and site of food/beverage distribution area • Plan for: 1,000 water bottles (16 ounce), plus an additional 1,000 drinks (sports drinks, cans of cola, lemonade, orangeade and three types of fruit juice) • Confirm cooler fridge in media centre available; check size • Arrange for continuous refill of coffee, hot water (with tea refills); milk/cream/sugar/ sugar substitute • Snacks: 2,000 granola bars and 2,000 protein bars, along with fresh fruit trays to be refilled throughout the day	Food and Beverage Manager
Five months prior to event	**Place order to ____ Store for Media Centre items** • Phone _____ Store (contact details) • Place order to deliver to ____ one week prior to event • Request: o 1,000 water bottles o 1,000 cans and sports drinks o 2,000 assorted granola bars ▪ Must have 1,000 nut-free o 23 fruit trays (24 inches in diameter, 5 fruit assorted) o 20 milk cartons (2L, 1%) o 20 cream cartons (2L) o 20 containers of coffee (31.5 ounces: 10 pre-ground house blend; 10 dark roast) o Assorted tea pack of 24 (5) o 2,000 assorted protein bars ▪ 1,000 being nut-free • Finalize payment on event charge card	Intern

Date	Task	Responsibility
Five months prior to event	**Acquire storage locker key** Date: October 30, 2019 Time: 11 am Place: MC203 Agenda: • Meet with Accreditation Manager and Merchandise Manager to acquire one storage locker key	Food and Beverage Manager

APPENDIX H: SECTIONS OF OPERATIONAL PLAN FOR THE NATIONAL COLLEGIATE ATHLETIC ASSOCIATION (NCAA) MEN'S BASKETBALL CHAMPIONSHIP, ROUND 2, SAN JOSE, CALIFORNIA: THE HOSPITALITY COMPONENT

(by Lauren Thompson)

Timeframe	Task	Responsibility
Three months prior to event	*Budget development:* Obtain budget for the hospitality committee from host university • Develop budget overview chart to personally keep track of your hospitality spending • Continuously develop budget details to have a realistic picture of the budget at all times	Facilitated by the Event Hospitality Coordinator
	Hospitality preparation: Create overview of all of the hospitality areas to be set up in the competition venue, the potential capacity, constituents to cater to, food/beverage requirements for patrons and volunteers and equipment requirements • Include: staff/media buffet, locker rooms, officials' rooms, official evaluators' room, basketball committee room, black room/press conference area, media refreshment area and breakfast/evening hospitality room at the host hotel • Include: constituents to cater to – athletes, coaches, officials, official evaluators, media, host university staff, volunteers and basketball committee	Event Hospitality Coordinator
	Competition venue Facility Manager meeting: Meet the host venue's Facility Manager and event coordinators with host university staff • Go on a site visit and become familiar with the venue • Determine: the hospitality food and beverage areas, all set-up details, storage areas available, including size and access process • Obtain diagrams of the facility and create a specific	Event Hospitality Coordinator and competition venue Facility Manager

Timeframe	Task	Responsibility
	• Site-map of all event hospitality areas • Develop a written timeline and list of hospitality preparation or set-up details	
	Confirmations: Confirm set-up areas with the host university staff by: • Communicating with the Facility Manager the site-map timeline and details	Event Hospitality Coordinator
	Competition venue food services meeting: Arrange meeting with the facility's Food Services Manager • Prepare for meeting by creating an outline for discussion of the different areas for hospitality services, the number of people to cater to and the type of food/beverages to be served • Obtain the already existent sponsorship contacts and the list of products that will be provided that apply to the hospitality component of the event • Attend meeting and discuss the catering options based on the event budget and the type and number of people for catering service • Also discuss event beverage sponsors who will provide certain products to be served • Determine the appropriate area and time for product drop-off • Develop potential catering contracts (determine approval process for approving and signing contracts) • Confirm catering contracts at venue with the host university staff • Communicate with the facility's Food Services Manager the final food/beverage requirements for the venue catering contracts. Notify them that the delivery times will be communicated at a later date, once game and practice times are established	Event Hospitality Coordinator and competition venue Food Services Manager

248

Timeframe	Task	Responsibility
	Host hotel meeting: Arrange meeting with host hotel to discuss hotel hospitality area and menu options/contracts for the daily media breakfast and evening drinks and snacks • Attend meeting with the host hotel and determine the area for media hospitality, the hours of operation and establish the food and beverage contracts. Food and drinks should be served in a buffet-style format. During the evening hospitality time, a server will be required to serve alcoholic beverages. All of the details should be agreed upon based on the hospitality committee's budget • Confirm hotel catering contracts with the host university staff • Communicate with the host hotel the final food/beverage requirements for the catering contracts	Event Hospitality Coordinator and host hotel Food Services Representative
	Coordinate sponsor hospitality details: • Work with the Sponsor Committee to communicate to event sponsors the details for hospitality product time and drop-off at the venue and host hotel	Event Hospitality Coordinator and the Sponsor Committee
Two months prior to event	*Hospitality volunteer development:* Obtain the tentative schedule for event game and practice times from the host university • Determine the hospitality areas where volunteer staff will be needed • Determine the number of volunteer staff required to fulfill the duties of the hospitality areas • Determine the potential shift times for the volunteer positions based on the tentative schedule for game and practice times. • Communicate the staffing requirements to the Staffing Coordinator. Make sure to include extra bodies to help cover positions in case of drop-outs or no shows. The Staffing Coordinator will be responsible for volunteer recruitment and assignment	Hospitality Coordinator and Staffing Coordinator

Timeframe	Task	Responsibility
	Hospitality signage: Determine all signage needs for the hospitality areas • Provide diagram of all signage placement in the venue and host hotel • Communicate to the host university the signage required and its placement (including date and time requirements)	Hospitality Coordinator and Signage Committee
One month prior to event	*Volunteer assignment:* Obtain list of contacts who will be volunteering for the hospitality component from the Staffing Coordinator • Determine appropriate hospitality volunteer shifts for each of the four days of the tournament • Assign volunteers in the contact list to daily hospitality shifts • Prepare daily schedule of events, individual schedules, and list of responsibilities and duties to be included in the volunteer training packages for the Hospitality Committee to distribute at volunteer training. Also include the venue site-map of the hospitality areas • Submit the Hospitality Committee documents for the volunteer training packages to the Staffing Coordinator and determine the volunteer training dates. The Staffing Coordinator will make all of the training packages and call each volunteer to inform them of their training times • Create volunteer training agenda for the volunteer training night. Following the main presentation, volunteers will be broken up into committees for 30 minutes for specialized training and a venue walk-through	Hospitality Coordinator and Staffing Coordinator
Two weeks prior to event	*Volunteer hospitality training:* • Attend volunteer training sessions • Conduct specific training session to communicate all of the Hospitality Committee details to the assigned volunteers	Hospitality Coordinator and Staffing Coordinator

250

Timeframe	Task	Responsibility
	• Conduct walk-through of the venue and point out where all of the hospitality areas are as well as the beverage storage area to be used if beverages are running low before new delivery times • Show volunteers where the proper entrances and exits are and where radios (if necessary) and credentials can be picked up • Ensure time is allocated for a question-and-answer period • For those hospitality volunteers unable to attend the training, ensure arrangements are made for them to pick up their training package and uniform and communicate any essential information from the training session	
	Credentials or accreditation: • Arrange for the creation of credentials or accreditation for the Hospitality Coordinator and all of the hospitality volunteers for the competition venue and host hotel. The credentials indicate the name and access areas the person is allowed to enter • Arrange for the distribution of credentials for the Hospitality Coordinator and hospitality volunteers • Distribute information to all volunteers concerning their access, entrance areas for the competition venue and host hotel and their credential access allowance • Understand the system for replacing credentials should anyone lose or forget their credentials	Hospitality Coordinator and Credentialling Coordinator
	Confirmations: • Confirm game and practice times with the host university • Confirm and adjust the catering and staffing details, if needed • Contact Sponsor Committee and ensure food/beverage event sponsors' product and delivery times are confirmed, and exact delivery site and contact names are	Hospitality Coordinator

Timeframe	Task	Responsibility
	provided. Ensure all deliveries will take place the day before the event begins. Keep an overview of contact names and numbers to call should deliveries be delayed • Confirm with Facility Manager the set-up areas and where signage is to be hung (and how it is to be fastened) • Confirm signage has arrived at facility from the Signage Committee to the venue and has been delivered to the Facility Manager • Confirm with the Food Services Manager at host hotel: the catering contracts, all menu items, including breakfast and evening catering requirements, delivery times, clean-up times, sponsor product use and placement, the signage to be placed at the hotel directing patrons to the hospitality area and the signage in the hospitality area to be hung by the event volunteers • Receive a copy of all finalized contracts from the venue and host hotel and review details again	
	Event daily review meetings: • Arrange meeting time and location with the host university venue and host hotel facility managers for each morning of the event to ensure all hospitality details are reviewed and are correct	Hospitality Coordinator, competition venue Facility Manager, and host hotel Facility Manager
Day prior to event	*Final preparations:* • Arrive at venue and conduct a venue walk-through to oversee that all hospitality areas are in the proper spots, are set up correctly and that all of the necessary signage is present • Ensure all sponsor product has been delivered and is stored at the proper location • Check into the hotel • Conduct a walk-through of the host hotel hospitality areas and ensure all are correctly set and signage is up	Hospitality Coordinator

Timeframe	Task	Responsibility
Day 1: practice day	*Event day activities*	
6:30 am	• Arrive at host hotel hospitality area, be sure to have credentials on hand • Ensure all breakfast set-ups are complete and that the proper food is out for the buffet, signage is out properly • Speak with the hotel representative in charge and retrieve an extension number to call if any food/beverage is running low	Hospitality Coordinator and Volunteer A
7:00 am– 10:00 am	• Welcome media guests into the breakfast room • Check for proper credentials upon each person's entry	Volunteer A
8:00 am	• Go to the competition venue, be sure to have credentials on hand • Conduct walk-through of the competition venue hospitality areas to ensure all areas are set up correctly • Conduct a final volunteer briefing session	Hospitality Coordinator
8:30 am	• Meet with the competition venue Food Services Manager to confirm all daily catering details	Hospitality Coordinator and competition venue Food Services Manager
8:45 am	• Report to media refreshment area and go through your checklist to ensure that all food, beverages and supplies (cups, napkins, bowls, tablecloths, cloths to wipe up spills and so on) have been delivered to the media refreshment area • Ensure tables are set: one table for beverage distribution and the other for snacks to be distributed	Volunteers B,C, D and Hospitality Coordinator
8:30 am– 5:00 pm	• Main duty is to be a floater and conduct regular checks on every hospitality area to ensure its smooth functioning as well as to fulfill any special requests and manage volunteers	Hospitality Coordinator

253

Timeframe	Task	Responsibility
9:00 am	• Work areas and courtside areas open to the media	Competition venue Facility Manager
9:00 am–5:00 pm	• Work in the media refreshment area; drinks should be poured for the media by the volunteers in order to save product • Ensure that the area is kept tidy at all times • The food services staff will be doing regular deliveries; however, if product is running low, communicate to either the Coordinator or one of the food service staff. If necessary, use stock from the storage area • The janitorial staff will complete regular clean-ups as scheduled; however, if their services are required at other times, communicate to either the Coordinator or one of the janitorial staff directly • Volunteers at the media refreshment area will take turns eating lunch and take breaks as scheduled, ensuring the area is never unattended	Volunteers B, C, D
10:00 am	• Arrive at venue, be sure credentials are on hand • Gather beverages from storage areas and fill two coolers in each locker room with drinks and ice (one with water, and one with a sponsored replenishment drink). Ensure different flavours of the replenishment drink are present. The coolers and buckets of ice will already be placed in the locker rooms by the food services staff	Volunteer E
10:00 am–4:30 pm	• Conduct regularly scheduled check of the locker rooms to ensure coolers remain stocked with fresh ice throughout the duration of the day. Note: do not enter the locker rooms if they are occupied by the teams	Volunteer E
10:30 am	• Team entrance opens	Competition venue Facility Manager

Timeframe	Task	Responsibility
10:30 am	• Ensure that the Basketball Committee room is set up and that their meals, beverages and snacks are all in place	Volunteer F
11:00 am–2:00 pm	• Ensure that the Basketball Committee room stays tidy and meal food stays hot and fresh • The food services staff will be doing regular deliveries; however, if product is running low, communicate to either the Coordinator or one of the food service staff	Volunteer F
11:00 am–4:30 pm	• Ensure that the Basketball Committee room stays tidy and snacks and beverages stay stocked • The food services staff will be doing regular deliveries; however, if product is running low, communicate to either the Coordinator or one of the food service staff. If necessary, use stock from the storage area	Volunteer F
11:00 am	• Facility opens to the public	
11:00 am	• Arrive at venue and obtain credentials • Ensure that the media/staff buffet area is set up and that the correct food, beverages and supplies are in place according to the catering contracts • Put up the "Staff Only" buffet sign in the staff/media buffet area	Volunteer G
11:30 am–12:30 pm	• Check the buffet area to ensure it is ready and then communicate over the radio that the staff buffet is ready and for all coordinators to send their volunteers when they are able to get away for their meal • Staff buffet takes place • Ensure the area remains tidy and stocked and that no bottles leave the area. All drinks must be poured into cups • The food services staff will be doing regular deliveries; however, if product is running low, communicate to either the Coordinator or one of the food service staff • The janitorial staff will be doing regular clean-ups; however, if their services are required, communicate to either the Coordinator or one of the janitorial staff	Hospitality Coordinator and Volunteer G

Timeframe	Task	Responsibility
12:00 pm–12:50 pm	Team #1 practises.	
12:30 pm–2:00 pm	• Ensure the "Media Buffet" sign is up in the staff/media buffet area • Welcome the media personnel into the buffet area • Check for proper credentials at the door • Watch for and keep any person without proper media credentials out of the area • Ensure the area remains tidy and stocked and that no bottles leave the area. All drinks must be poured into cups	Volunteer G
12:30 pm	• Ensure the delivery and proper set-up of Team #1's box lunches into their locker room is made on time	Volunteer E
12:30 pm	• Ensure that the area for the press conferences is set up and the beverages and supplies are stocked	Volunteer F

256

REFERENCES

1 TRADITIONAL AND NICHE EVENTS IN SPORT, RECREATION AND TOURISM

Bell, D. (1973). *The coming of post-industrial society: A venture in social forecasting.* New York: Basic Books.

Choo, C. W., & Bontis, N. (Eds.). (2002). *The strategic management of intellectual capital and organizational knowledge.* New York: Oxford University Press.

Cobb, P., Confrey, J., diSess, A., Lehrer, R., & Schauble, L. (2003). Design experiments in educational research. *Educational Researcher, 32*(1), 9–13.

Gallagher, W. (2012). *New: Understanding our need for novelty and change.* New York: Penguin Press.

Hirschhorn, L. (1984). *Beyond mechanization: Work and technology in a postindustrial age.* Cambridge, MA: The MIT Press.

Homer-Dixon, T. (2001). *The ingenuity gap: Can we solve the problems of the future?* Toronto, ON: Vintage Canada.

Jensen, R. (1999). *The dream society: How the coming shift from information to imagination will transform your business.* New York: McGraw-Hill.

Limerick, D., Cunnington, B., & Crowther, F. (1998). *Managing the new organization: Collaboration and sustainability in the post-corporate world* (2nd ed.). Sydney: Business and Professional Publishing.

Sproull, L., & Kiesler, S. (1991). *Connections: New ways of working the networked organization.* Cambridge, MA: The MIT Press.

Zuboff, S. (1988). *In the age of the smart machine: The future of work and power.* New York: Basic Books.

2 THE CONCEPT OF KNOWLEDGE IN EVENT MANAGEMENT

Bell, D. (1973). *The coming of post-industrial society: A venture in social forecasting.* New York: Basic Books.

Blackler, F. (1995). Knowledge, knowledge work and organizations: An overview and interpretation. *Organization Studies, 16*(6), 1021–1046.

Boisot, M. (2002). The creation and sharing of knowledge. In C. W. Choo & N. Bontis (Eds.), *The strategic management of intellectual capital and organizational knowledge* (pp. 65–77). New York: Oxford University Press.

Carney, M. (2001). The development of a model to manage change: Reflection on a critical incident in a focus group setting – an innovative approach. *Journal of Nursing Management, 8*(5), 3–9.

Castells, M. (2000). Toward a sociology of the network society. *American Sociological Association, 29*(5), 693–699.

Choo, C. W., & Bontis, N. (Eds.). (2002). *The strategic management of intellectual capital and organizational knowledge.* New York: Oxford University Press.

Collins, H. (1993). The structure of knowledge. *Social Research, 60*(1), 95–116.

Conner, K., & Prahalad, C. K. (2002). A resource-based theory of the firm: Knowledge versus opportunism. In C. W Choo & N. Bontis (Eds.), *The strategic management of intellectual capital and organizational knowledge* (pp. 103–131). New York: Oxford University Press.

Crane, L., & Bontis, N. (2014). Trouble with tacit: Developing a new perspective and approach. *Journal of Knowledge Management, 18*(6), 1127–1140.

Drucker, P. (1994). The age of social transformation. *Atlantic Monthly, 275*(5), 53–80.

Edvinsson, L., & Malone, T. (1997). *Intellectual capital.* New York: HarperBusiness.

English M., & Baker, W. (2006). *Winning the knowledge transfer race.* New York: McGraw-Hill.

Grant, R. (1996). Prospering in dynamically competitive environments: Organizational capability as knowledge integration. *Organization Science, 7*(4), 375–387.

Gupta, A., & MacDaniel, J. (2002). Creating competitive advantage by effectively managing knowledge: A framework for knowledge management. *Journal of Knowledge Management Practice, 3*(2), 40–49.

Hall, H. (2001). Input-friendliness: Motivating knowledge sharing across intranets. *Journal of Information Science, 27*(3), 139–146.

Harris, L., Coles, A., & Dickson, K. (2000). Building innovation networks: Issues of strategy and expertise. *Technology Analysis and Strategic Management, 12*(2), 229–241.

Kogut, B., & Zander, U. (1992). Knowledge of the firm, combinative capabilities, and the replication of technology. *Organization Science, 3*(3), 383–397.

Leonard, D., & Sensiper, S. (2002). The role of tacit knowledge in group innovation. In C. W. Choo & N. Bontis (Eds.), *The strategic management of intellectual capital and organizational knowledge* (pp. 485–499). New York: Oxford University Press.

Nelson, R., & Winter, S. (1982). *An evolutionary theory of economic change.* Cambridge, MA: Belknap.

Nonaka, I., & Takeuchi, H. (1995). *The knowledge-creating company: How Japanese companies create the dynamics of innovation.* New York: Oxford University Press.

258

Nonaka, I., Toyama, R., & Konno, N. (2000). SECI, *Ba* and leadership: A unified model of dynamic knowledge creation. *Long Range Planning, 33*(1), 5–35.

Schorr, L. (1997). *Common purpose: Strengthening families and neighborhoods to rebuild America.* New York: Doubleday/Anchor Books.

Shaw, G. B. (1930). *The apple cart: A political extravaganza.* London: Constable.

Spender, J. (1996). Making knowledge the basis of a dynamic theory of the firm. *Strategic Management Journal, 17*(S2), 445–462.

Spender, J. (2002). Knowledge management, uncertainty, and the emergent theory of the firm. In C. W. Choo & N. Bontis (Eds.), *The strategic management of intellectual capital and organizational knowledge* (pp. 149–162). New York: Oxford University Press.

von Krogh, G., & Grand, S. (2002). From economic theory toward a knowledge-based theory of the firm. In C. W. Choo & N. Bontis (Eds.), *The strategic management of intellectual capital and organizational knowledge* (pp. 163–184). New York: Oxford University Press.

Winter, S. (1987). Knowledge and competence as strategic assets. In D. Teece (Ed.), *The competitive challenge: Strategies of industrial innovations and renewal* (pp. 159–184). Cambridge, MA: Ballin.

Zack, M. (1999). Developing a knowledge strategy. *California Management Review, 41*(3), 125–145.

3 THE ROLE OF AN EVENT MANAGER: TO BE A FACILITATOR

Bens, I. (2000). *Facilitating with ease! A step-by-step guidebook.* San Francisco: Jossey-Bass.

Drucker, P. (1946). *Concept of the corporation.* New York: John Day.

Greenberg, J. (2002). *Managing behavior in organizations.* Upper Saddle River, NJ: Prentice Hall.

Kilmann, R., Pondy. L., & Slevin, D. (Eds.). (1976). *The management of organization design: Strategies and implementation*, Vol. I. New York: North-Holland.

Laird, D. (1985). *Approaches to training and development.* Reading, MA: Addison-Wesley.

Lambert, V., & Glacken, M. (2005). Clinical education facilitators: A literature review. *Journal of Clinical Nursing, 14*(6), 664–673.

Peel, D. (2000). The teacher and town planner as facilitator. *Innovations in Education and Training International, 37*(4), 372–380.

Rio 2016 (2013, March). Sustainability management plan: Rio 2016™ Olympic and Paralympic Games – Mission. Retrieved from www.paralympic.org/rio-2016/about-us

Rogers, C., & Freiberg, H. J. (1994). *Freedom to learn* (3rd ed.). New York: Merrill, Macmillan College Publishing.

Sawyer, K. R. (2006). Group creativity: Musical performance and collaboration. *Psychology of Music, 34*(2), 148–165.

Scribd.com (2012). The Olympics in London 2012. Retrieved from www.scribd.com/doc/16208292/The-Olympics-in-London-2012

Slack, T., & Parent, M. (2006). *Understanding sport organizations: The application of organization theory* (2nd ed.). Champaign, IL: Human Kinetics.

Thomas, G. (2004). A typology of approaches to facilitator education. *Journal of Experiential Education, 27*(2), 123–140.

Vancouver 2010 (2007). Organizing committee. Retrieved May 25, 2007 from www.vancouver2010.com/en/OrganizingCommittee

Vidal, R. (2004). The vision conference: Facilitating creative processes. *Systemic Practice and Action Research, 17*(5), 385–405.

4 THE EVENT PLANNING MODEL: THE DEVELOPMENT PHASE

Ellis, S. (2010). Differentiating between volunteering and working for pay. Retrieved October 26, 2016 from www.energizeinc.com/hot-topics/2010/january

Ghobadian, A., Viney, H., & Holt, D. (2001). Seeking congruence in implementing corporate environmental strategy. *International Journal of Environmental Technology and Management, 1*(4), 384–401.

Graff, L. (1997). Excerpted from *By definition: Policies for volunteer management.* Graff & Associates.

Hager, M. A, & Brudney, J. L. (2004a). *Balancing act: The challenges and benefits of volunteers.* Washington, DC: The Urban Institute.

Hager, M. A., & Brudney, J. L. (2004b). *Volunteer management practices and retention of volunteers.* The Urban Institute. Retrieved from www.national service.gov/pdf/Management_Brief.pdf

James, P., Ghobadian, A., Viney, H., & Liu, J. (1999). Addressing the divergence between environmental strategy formulation and implementation. *Management Decision, 37*(4), 338–347.

Penner, L. (2002). Dispositional and organizational influences on sustained volunteerism: An interactionist perspective. *Journal of Social Issues, 58*(3), 447–467.

Quirk, M. (2009). *Fourteen steps to developing a top-notch volunteer program.* CharityVillage.com. Retrieved from www.charityvillage.com [Under Topics/Volunteer Engagement/Volunteer Management]

Sarma, A., Herbsleb, J., & van der Hoek, A. (2008). Challenges in measuring, understanding, and achieving social–technical congruence. Workshop on Social–Technical Congruence, Leipzig, Germany. Available as Technical Report CMU-ISR-08-105, Carnegie Mellon University, Institute for Software Research International, Pittsburgh, PA.

Volunteer Canada. (2006a). About volunteerism. Retrieved from http://volunteer.ca/about-volunteerism

Volunteer Canada. (2006b). *The Canadian code for volunteer involvement: An audit tool.* Retrieved August 29, 2016 from https://volunteer.ca

Webster's new collegiate dictionary. (1985). Markham, ON: Thomas Allen.

260

5 THE EVENT PLANNING MODEL: THE EVENT OPERATIONAL PLANNING PHASE

Bowen, H., (2006). *The Salt Lake organizing committee: 2002 Olympics*. Boston, MA: Harvard Business School Publishing.

Doherty, N., & Delener, N. (2001). Chaos theory: Marketing and management implications. *Journal of Marketing Theory and Practice, 9*(4), 66–75.

Eisenhardt, M. K. (1989). Agency theory: An assessment and review. *The Academy of Management Review, 14*(1), 57–74.

Keirsey, D. (n. d.). The dilemma of science. In D. Keirsey, *Existence itself: Towards the phenomenology of massive dissipative/replicative structures* (Chapter 2). Retrieved August 28, 2016 from http://edgeoforder.org/pofdisstruct. html

Matusik, S. F. (2002). An empirical investigation of firm public and private knowledge. *Strategic Management Journal, 23*(5), 457.

Owen, R. G. (2001). *Organizational behavior in education*. Boston, MA: Allyn and Bacon.

Stacey, R. D. (1996). *Complexity and creativity in organizations*. San Francisco: Berrett-Koehler.

Wijngaard, J., deVries, J., & Nauta, A. (2006). Performers and performance: How to investigate the contribution of the operational network to operational performance. *International Journal of Operations & Production Management, 26*(4), 394–411.

6 THE EVENT PLANNING MODEL: THE EVENT IMPLEMENTATION, MONITORING AND MANAGEMENT PHASE

Buchanan, L., & O'Connell, A. (2006). A brief history of decision making. *Harvard Business Review*, January issue, 1–7.

Dörner, D. (1996). *The logic of failure: Recognizing and avoiding error in complex situations*, R. Kimber and R. Kimber, Trans. Cambridge, MA: Perseus Books.

Garvin, D., & Roberto, M. (2001). What you don't know about making decisions. *Harvard Business Review,* September issue, 1–8.

HBS Press & Harvard Business School Press (2005). *Keeping on track: Monitoring control.*

Konijnendijk, P. (1994). Coordinating marketing and manufacturing in ETO companies. *International Journal of Production Economics, 37*(1), 19–26.

Mallen, C. (2006). Rethinking pedagogy for the times: A change infusion pedagogy. Unpublished EdD dissertation, University of Southern Queensland, Toowoomba, Australia.

Mintzberg, H., Raisinghani, D., & Théorêt, A. (1976). The structure of "unstructured" decision processes. *Administrative Science Quarterly, 21*(2), 246–275.

Schön, D. (1983). *The reflective practitioner: How professionals think in action*. London: Temple Smith.

Various authors (2006). *How to stay on course: Sensing and responding to deviations from plan*. Boston, MA: Harvard Business Publishing.

Wijngaard, J., deVries, J., & Nauta, A. (2006). Performers and performance: How to investigate the contribution of the operational network to operational performance. *International Journal of Operations & Production Management, 26*(4), 394–411.

7 EVENT OPERATION PLANNING ISSUES AND STRATEGIES

Cashman, R. (2006). *The bitter-sweet awakening: The legacy of the Sydney 2000 Olympic Games.* Petersham, NSW: Walla Walla Press.

Costa, C. A. (2005). The status and future of sport management: A Delphi study. *Journal of Sport Management, 19*(2), 117–142.

Crowston, K. (1997). A coordination theory approach to organizational process design. *Organization Science, 8*(2), 157–175.

Cua, K., McKone, K., & Schroeder, R. (2001). Relationships between implementation of TQM, JIT, and TPM and manufacturing performance. *Journal of Operations Management, 19*(6), 675–694.

Dalkey, N., Brown, B., & Cochran, S. (1970). Use of self-ratings to improve group estimates: Experimental evaluation of Delphi procedures. *Technological Forecasting, 1*, 283–291.

Day, J., & Bobeva, M. (2005). A generic toolkit for the successful management of Delphi studies. *The Electronic Journal of Business Research Methodology, 3*(2), 103–116.

Dembowski, F. L. (2013). The roles of benchmarking, best practices & innovation in organizational effectiveness. *International Journal of Organizational Innovation, 5*(3), 6–20.

Dietz, T. (1987). Methods for analyzing data from Delphi panels: Some evidence from a forecasting study. *Technological Forecasting and Social Change, 31*(1), 79–85.

Fullerton, R., McWatters, C., & Fawson, C. (2003). An examination of the relationships between JIT and financial performance. *Journal of Operations Management, 21*(4), 383–404.

Greco, N. (2016). Major sport event operational planning issues and strategies: A multi-case Delphi study. Unpublished MA thesis, Faculty of Applied Health Sciences, Department of Sport Management, Brock University, Canada. Retrieved from https://dr.library.brocku.ca

Heugens, P. (2003). *Strategic issues management and organizational outcomes.* Tjalling C. Koopmans Research Institute Discussion Paper Series, 03–11, Utrecht School of Economics. Retrieved August 28, 2016 from www.academia.eu

Horne, J. (2010). Material and representational legacies of sports mega-events: The case of the UEFA EURO™ football championships from 1996 to 2008. *Soccer and Society, 11*(6), 854–866.

Jayaram, J., & Droge, C. (1999). The impact of human resource management practices on manufacturing performance. *Journal of Operations Management, 18*(1), 1–20.

Johnson, J. J. (1983). Issues management: What are the issues? An introduction to issues management. *Business Quarterly, 48*(3), 22–31.

262

Lawal, F. M., Elizabeth, O. O., & Oludayo, O. (2012). Effect of strategic issue management on organisational performance. *Transnational Journal of Science and Technology, 2*(10), 17–29.

Mallen, C., Adams, L., Stevens, J., & Thompson, L. (2010). Environmental sustainability in sport facility management: A Delphi study. *European Sport Management Quarterly, 10*(3), 367–389.

Malone, T. W. (1988). What is coordination theory? Paper presented at the National Science Foundation Coordination Theory Workshop, Massachusetts Institute of Technology, Cambridge, MA, 19 February. Retrieved from https://dspace.mit.edu/bitstream/handle/1721.1/2208/SWP-2051-27084940-CISR-182.pdf?sequence=1

Malone, T. W., & Crowston, K. (1990). What is coordination theory and how can it help design cooperative work systems? In *Proceedings of the 1990 ACM Conference on Computer-Supported Cooperative Work* (pp. 357–370). Retrieved from http://dl.acm.org/citation.cfm?id=99367

Martino, J. P. (1983). *Technological forecasting for decision making* (2nd ed.). New York: North-Holland.

Nigh, D. D., & Cochran, P. L. (1987). Issues management and the multinational enterprise. *Management International Review, 27*(1), 4–12.

Parent, M. M., Rouillard, C., & Leopkey, B. (2011). Issues and strategies pertaining to the Canadian Government's coordination efforts in relation to the 2010 Olympic Games. *European Sport Management Quarterly, 11*(4), 337–369.

Powell, C. (2003). The Delphi technique: Myths and realities. *Journal of Advanced Nursing, 41*(4), 376–382.

Preuss, H. (2007). The conceptualisation and measurement of mega sport event legacies. *Journal of Sport & Tourism, 12*(3/4), 207–228.

Tracy, S. J. (2013). *Qualitative research methods: Collecting evidence, crafting analysis, communicating impact.* Chichester, UK: Wiley-Blackwell.

Voss, C. A. (2005). Alternative paradigms for manufacturing strategy. *International Journal of Operations & Production Management, 25*(12), 1211–1222.

Wartick, S. L., & Heugens, P. R. (2003). Future directions for issues management. *Corporate Reputation Review, 6*(1), 7–18.

8 THE EVENT PLANNING MODEL: THE EVENT EVALUATION AND RENEWAL PHASE

Chelimsky, E. (1997). The coming transformations in evaluation. In E. Chelimsky & W. R. Shadish (Eds.), *Evaluation for the 21st century: A handbook* (pp.1–26). Thousand Oaks, CA: Sage.

Fetterman, D. M., Kaftarian, S. J., & Wandersman, A. (Eds.) (1996). *Empowerment evaluation: Knowledge and tools for self-assessment and accountability.* Thousand Oaks, CA: Sage.

Getz, D. (1997). *Event management and event tourism.* Elmsford, NY: Cognizant Communication Corporation.

Henderson, K. A., & Bialeschki, M. D. (2002). *Evaluating leisure services: Making enlightened decisions.* State College, PA: Venture Publishing.

Isaac, S., & Michael, W. (1981). *Handbook in research and evaluation.* San Diego, CA: Edits.

Jones, G., George, J., & Langton, N. (2005). *Essentials of contemporary management* (1st Canadian ed.). Toronto, ON: McGraw-Hill.

McDavid, J. C., & Hawthorn, L. (2006). *Program evaluation and performance measurement: An introduction to practice.* Thousand Oaks, CA: Sage.

McKinsey & Company. (2009). Enduring ideas: The three horizons of growth. *McKinsey Quarterly,* December issue. Retrieved from www.mckinsey.com/business-functions/strategy-and-corporate-finance/our-insights/enduring-ideas-the-three-horizons-of-growth

Rossi, P., Freeman, H., & Lipsey, M. (1999). *Evaluation: A systematic approach* (6th ed.). Thousand Oaks, CA: Sage.

Rossman, J., & Schlatter, B. (2003). *Recreation programming: Designing leisure experiences* (4th ed.). Champaign, IL: Sagamore.

Scriven, M. (1972). Pros and cons about goal-free evaluation. *Evaluation Comment, 3*(4), 1–7.

Stake, R. E. (1975). *Evaluating the arts in education: A responsive approach.* Columbus, OH: Merrill.

Stufflebeam, D. L. (1971). The relevance of the CIPP evaluation model for educational accountability. *Journal of Research and Development in Education, 5*(1), 19–25.

Worthen, B. R., Sanders, J. R., & Fitzpatrick, J. L. (1997). *Program evaluation: Alternative approaches and practical guidelines* (2nd ed.). White Plains, NY: Longman.

9 SAFEGUARDING THE NATURAL ENVIRONMENT IN EVENT MANAGEMENT

Adger, W. N. (2006). Vulnerability. *Global Environmental Change, 16*(3), 268–281.

Alexander, J. (2007). Environmental sustainability versus profit maximization: Overcoming systemic constraints on implementing normatively preferable alternatives. *Journal of Business Ethics, 76*(2), 155–162.

Amelung, B., & Moreno, A. (2012). Costing the impact of climate change on tourism in Europe: Results of the PESETA project. *Climatic Change, 112*(1), 83–100.

Barrett, J., & Scott, A. (2001). The ecological footprint: A metric for corporate sustainability. *Corporate Environmental Strategy, 8*(4), 316–325.

Cantelon, H., & Letters, M. (2000). The making of the IOC environmental policy as the third dimension of the Olympic movement. *International Review for the Sociology of Sport, 35*(3), 294–308.

Collins, A., Flynn, A., Munday, M., & Roberts, A. (2007). Assessing the environmental consequences of major sporting events: The 2003/04 FA Cup Final. *Urban Studies, 44*(3), 457–476. doi:10.1080/00420980601131878

Collins, A., Jones, C., & Munday, M. (2009). Assessing the environmental impacts of mega sporting events: Two options? *Tourism Management, 30*(6), 828–837. doi:10.1016/j.tourman.2008.12.006

FIFA (Fédération Internationale de Football Association). (2006). *Green goal – Environmental goals for the 2006 FIFA World Cup.* Öko-Institut e.V., Institute

264

for Applied Ecology, Berlin. Retrieved from www.oeko.de/oekodoc/169/2003-044-en.pdf

Finnveden, G., Hauschild, M. Z., Ekvall, T., Guinée, J., Heijungs, R., Hellweg, S. . . . Sangwon, S. (2009). Recent developments in Life Cycle Assessment. *Journal of Environmental Management, 91*(1), 1–21. doi:10.1016/j.jenvman.2009.06.018

Folke, C. (2006). Resilience: The emergence of a perspective for social–ecological systems analyses. *Global Environmental Change, 16*(3), 253–267.

Füssel, H-M. (2007a). Adaptation planning for climate change: Concepts, assessment approaches and key lessons. *Sustainability Science, 2*(2), 265–275.

Füssel, H-M. (2007b). Vulnerability: A generally applicable conceptual framework for climate change research. *Global Environmental Change, 17*(2), 155–167.

Gallopín, G. C. (2006). Linkages between vulnerability, resilience, and adaptive capacity. *Global Environmental Change, 16*(3), 293–303.

Government of Canada. (2010). *Fifth National Communication on Climate Change*. Retrieved August 21, 2016 from http://unfccc.int/resource/docs/natc/can_nc5.pdf

Hollender, J., & Breen, B. (2010). *The responsibility revolution: How the next generation of businesses will win*. San Francisco: Jossey-Bass.

Hums, M. A. (2010). The conscience and commerce of sport management: One teacher's perspective. *Journal of Sport Management, 24*(1), 1–9.

Ingebrigtsen, S., & Jakobsen, O. (2006). Environment and profitability in the reprocessing of paper in Norway: Contradictory research reports in the context of circulation economics. *Business Strategy and the Environment, 15*(6), 389–401.

IPCC (Intergovernmental Panel on Climate Change). (2007). *IPCC Fourth Assessment Synthesis Report: Climate Change 2007*. Cambridge: Cambridge University Press.

ISO (International Organization for Standardization). (2006). *ISO 14044:2006 Environmental management – Life cycle assessment – Requirements and guidelines* (1st ed.). Geneva, Switzerland: ISO. Retrieved from www.iso.org/iso/catalogue_detail?csnumber=38498

Jackson, T. (2009). *Prosperity without growth: Economies for a finite planet*. London: Earthscan.

Janssen, M. A., & Ostrom, E. (2006). Resilience, vulnerability, and adaptation: A cross-cutting theme of the International Human Dimensions Programme on Global Environmental Change. *Global Environmental Change, 16*(3), 237–239.

Jolliet, O., Margni, M., Charles, R., Humbert, S., Payet, J., Rebitzer, G., & Rosenbaum, R. (2003). IMPACT 2002+: A new life cycle impact assessment methodology. *The International Journal of Life Cycle Assessment, 8*(6), 324–330. doi:10.1007/BF02978505

Jones, C. (2008). Assessing the impact of a major sporting event: The role of environmental accounting. *Tourism Economics, 14*(2), 343–360. doi:10.5367/000000008784460382

Jones, M. (2011, Spring). Sustainable event management, ISO 20121. *The Business of International Events*. Retrieved from http://isuu.com/ifea_world/docs/ie_volume_22_issue_1

Kellison, T. B. (2015). Building sport's green houses. In J. Casper & M. Pfahl (Eds.), *Sport management and the natural environment: Theory and practice* (pp. 218–237). London and New York: Routledge.

Linnenluecke, M. K., & Griffiths, A. (2015). *The climate resilient organization: Adaptation and resilience to climate change and weather extremes.* Cheltenham, UK: Edward Elgar Publishing.

Linnenluecke, M. K., Griffiths, A., & Winn, M. I. (2013). Firm and industry adaptation to climate change: A review of climate adaptation studies in the business and management field. *Wiley Interdisciplinary Reviews: Climate Change, 4*(5), 397–496.

Lothe, S., Myrtveit, I., & Trapani, T. (1999). Compensation systems for improving environmental performance. *Business Strategy and the Environment, 8*(6), 313–321.

McDonough, W., & Braungart, M. (2002). Design for the Triple Bottom Line: New tools for sustainable commerce. *Corporate Environmental Strategy, 9*(3), 251–258.

Mallen, C., & Chard, C. (2011). A framework for debating the future of environmental sustainability in the Sport Academy. *Sport Management Review, 14*(4), 424–433.

Mallen, C., & Chard, C. (2012). "What could be" in Canadian sport facility environmental sustainability. *Sport Management Review, 15*(2), 230–243.

Mallen, C., Stevens, J., Adams, L., & McRoberts, S. (2010). The assessment of the environmental performance of an international multi-sport event. *European Sport Management Quarterly, 10*(1), 97–122.

Moscardo, G., Lamberton, G., Wells, G., Fallon, W., Lawn, P., Rowe, A., & Kershaw, W. (Eds.). (2013). *Sustainability in Australian Business: Principles and Practice.* Milton, Qld: Wiley.

Mulgan, R. (2000). Accountability: An ever expanding concept? *Public Administration, 78*(3), 555–573.

Ness, B., Urbel-Piirsalu, E., Anderberg, S., & Olsson, L. (2007). Categorising tools for sustainability assessment. *Ecological Economics, 60*(3), 498–508. doi:10.1016/j.ecolecon.2006.07.023

Nguyen, S. N., Trendafilova, S., & Pfahl, M. E. (2014). The natural-resource-based view of the firm (NRBV): Constraints and opportunities for a green team in professional sport. *International Journal of Sport Management, 15*(4), 485–517.

Packard, K. O., & Reinhardt, F. (2000). What every executive needs to know about global warming. *Harvard Business Review, 78*(128).

Parkin, S. (2000). Sustainable development: The concept and the practical challenge. *Civil Engineering, 136*(6), 3–8.

Perelman, M. (2003). Myths of the market: Economics and the environment. *Organization and Environment, 16*(2), 168–226.

Randjelovic, J., O'Rourke, A., & Orsato, R. (2003). The emergence of green venture capital. *Business Strategy and the Environment, 12*(4), 240–253.

Robinson, J. (2004). Squaring the circle? Some thoughts on the idea of sustainable development. *Ecological Economics, 48*(4), 369–384. doi:10.1016/j.ecolecon.2003.10.017

Rockström, J., Steffen, W., Noone, K., Persson, Å. III, Chapin, F. S., Lambin, E., & Foley, J. (2009). Planetary boundaries: Exploring the safe operating space for humanity. *Ecology and Society, 14*(2), article 32.

Scharwath, K. (2012, February 3). The super green bowl. Environmental News Network. Retrieved from www.enn.com/lifestyle/article/43947

Scott, D., Gössling, S., & Hall, C. M. (2012). International tourism and climate change. *Wiley Interdisciplinary Reviews: Climate Change, 3*(3), 213–232.

Smit, B., & Wandel, J. (2006). Adaptation, adaptive capacity and vulnerability. *Global Environmental Change, 16*(3), 282–292.

Sobhana, K. (2009, September 7). Games committee ropes in players to counter carbon footprint in 2010. Retrieved September 3, 2016 from www.archive. indianexpress.com

Steffen, W., Richardson, K., Rockström, J., Cornell, S. E., Fetzer, I., Bennett, E. M. . . . Sörlin, S. (2015). Planetary boundaries: Guiding human development on a changing planet. *Science, 347*(6223). doi: 10.1126/science.1259855

Tian, Q., & Brimblecombe, P. (2008). Managing air in Olympic cities. *American Journal of Environmental Sciences, 4*(5), 439–444.

UN (United Nations). (1987). 96th plenary meeting, United Nations General Assembly, *Report of the World Commission on Environment and Development: Our common future.* Brundtland Report. Retrieved September 4, 2016 from www.un-documents.net/our-common-future.pdf

UN (United Nations). (2010). United Nations Environment Programme: Sport and environment. Retrieved March 21, 2012 from www.unep.org/sport_env/

UNEP (United Nations Environment Programme). (2005). *Overview of the Millennium Ecosystem Assessment.* Retrieved October 3, 2014 from www. unep.org/maweb/en/About.aspx#14

UNEP (United Nations Environment Programme). (2007). *Global environment outlook GEO-4: Summary for decision makers.* Valletta, Malta: Progress Press.

UNEP (United Nations Environment Programme). (2011). *Towards a green economy: Pathways to sustainable development and poverty eradication: A synthesis for policy makers.* St-Martin-Bellevue, France: UNEP. Retrieved September 3, 2016 from: www.unep.org/greeneconomy

UNEP (United Nations Environment Programme). (2012a). *Keeping track of our changing environment: From Rio to Rio+20 (1992–2012).* Nairobi, Kenya: Division of Early Warning and Assessment (DEWA), UNEP.'

UNEP (United Nations Environment Programme). (2012b). UNEP evaluation of 2010 World Cup's green performance shows South Africa successes and the way forward for Brazil. Retrieved 6 September, 2016 from www.unep.org/ NEWSCENTRE/default.aspx?DocumentId=2697&ArticleId=9297

Wackernagel, M., & Rees, W. E. (1996). *Our ecological footprint: Reducing human impact on the earth.* Philadelphia, PA: New Society Publishers.

Weidema, B. P., Thrane, M., Christensen, P., Schmidt, J., & Løkke, S. (2008). Carbon footprint. *Journal of Industrial Ecology, 12*(1), 3–6. doi:10.1111/j.1530-9290. 2008.00005.x

Winn, M. I., Kirchgeorg, M., Griffiths, A., Linnenluecke, M. K., & Gunther, E. (2011). Impacts from climate change on organizations: A conceptual foundation. *Business Strategy and the Environment, 20*(3), 157–173.

Wright, L. A., Kemp, S., & Williams, I. (2011). "Carbon footprinting": Towards a universally accepted definition. *Carbon Management, 2*(1), 61–72. doi:10.4155/ cmt.10.39

WWF (World Wide Fund for Nature). (2014). *Living planet report 2014: Species and spaces, people and places.* Gland, Switzerland: WWF International.

10 FACILITATING QUALITY IN EVENT MANAGEMENT

Crosby, P. B. (1979). *Quality is free: The art of making quality certain*. New York: McGraw-Hill.

Ford, H., & Crowther, S. (1922). *My life and work*. New York: Doubleday Page.

Garvin, D. A. (1988). *Managing quality: The strategic and competitive edge*. New York: The Free Press.

Reeves, C. A., & Bednar, D. A. (1994). Defining quality: Alternatives and implications. *Academy of Management Review, 19*(3), 419–445.

Saad, G. H., & Siha, S. (2000). Managing quality: Critical links and a contingency model. *International Journal of Operations & Production Management, 20*(10), 1146–1163.

Watkins, D. (2006). Reflections on the future of quality. *Quality Progress, 39*(1), 23–28.

Yoshida, M., & James, J. (2011). Service quality at sporting events: Is aesthetic quality a missing dimension? *Sport Management Review, 14*(1), 13–24.

Zeithaml, V. A., Parasuraman, A., & Berry, L. L. (1990). *Delivering quality service: Balancing customer perceptions and expectations*. New York: The Free Press.

11 EVENT BIDDING

Emery, P. (2002). Bidding to host a major sports event: The local organizing committee perspective. *The International Journal of Public Sector Management, 15*(4), 316–335.

FIFA (Fédération Internationale de Football Association). (2006). *Green goal: The environmental concept for the 2006 FIFA World Cup*. Frankfurt am Main: Organizing Committee, 2006 FIFA World Cup.

Gadenne, D. L., Kennedy, J., & McKeiver, C. (2009). An empirical study of environmental awareness and practices in SMEs. *Journal of Business Ethics, 84*(1), 45–63.

Greenberg, J. (2002). *Managing behavior in organizations*. Upper Saddle River, NJ: Prentice Hall.

Hautbois, C., Parent, M., & Séguin, B. (2012). How to win a bid for major sport events? A stakeholder analysis of the 2018 Olympic Winter games French bid. *Sport Management Review, 15*(3), 263–275.

Hörte, S. Å., & Persson, C. (2000). How Salt Lake City and its rival bidders campaigned for the 2002 Olympic Winter Games. *Event Management, 6*(2), 65–83.

IFM (International Federation of Motorcycling). (2006). *Environmental code*. Mies, Switzerland: IFM.

Ingerson, L., & Westerbeek, H. (2000). Determining key success criteria for attracting hallmark sporting events. *Pacific Tourism Review, 3*(4), 239–253.

IOC (International Olympic Committee). (2006). *IOC guide on sport, environment and sustainable development*. Lausanne, Switzerland: IOC.

IOC (International Olympic Committee). (2014). Factsheet: The environmental and sustainable development update – January 2014. Lausanne, Switzerland: IOC. Retrieved September 2, 2016 from https://stillmed.olympic.org

268

IOC (International Olympic Committee). (2015, September 16). Candidature questionnaire Olympic Games 2024. Retrieved September 4, 2016 from https://stillmed.olympic.org/Documents/Host_city_elections/Candidature_ Questionnaire_Olympic_Games_2024.pdf

IPCC (Intergovernmental Panel on Climate Change). (2007). *Global environment outlook 4: Summary for decision makers*. Retrieved from www.unep.org/geo/ geo4/media/GEO4%20SDM_launch.pdf

Kerzner, H. (1995). *Project management: A systems approach to planning, scheduling, and controlling* (5th ed.). Princeton, NJ: Van Nostrand Reinhold.

Mitchell, I. K., & Saren, M. (2008). The living product: Using the creative nature of metaphors for sustainable marketing. *Business Strategy and the Environment, 17*(6), 398–410.

Persson, C. (2000). The International Olympic Committee and site decisions: The case of the 2002 Winter Olympics. *Event Management, 6*(3), 135–153.

Westerbeek, H., Turner, P., & Ingerson, L. (2002). Key success factors in bidding for hallmark sporting events. *International Marketing Review, 19*(3), 303–322.

12 POLITICS IN EVENT BIDDING AND HOSTING

Allison, L. (Ed.). (1986). *The politics of sport*. Manchester: Manchester University Press.

Furlong, J. (2011). *Patriot hearts: Inside the Olympics that changed a country*. Vancouver, BC: Douglas & McIntyre.

Lee, M. (2006). *The race for the 2012 Olympics: The inside story of how London won the bid*. London: Virgin Books.

Mallen, C., & Adams, L. J. (2008). *Sport, recreation and tourism event management* (1st ed.). Oxford: Butterworth-Heinemann.

Senn, A. (1999). *Power, politics and the Olympic Games: A history of the power brokers, events, and controversies that shaped the Games*. Champaign, IL: Human Kinetics.

13 ETHICAL DECISION MAKING IN EVENT MANAGEMENT

Ciulla J. (2004). *Ethics, the heart of leadership*. Westport, CT: Greenwood.

McNamee, M., & Fleming, S. (2007). Ethics audits and corporate governance: The case of public sector sport organizations. *Journal of Business Ethics, 73*(4), 425–437.

Mansurov, A., & Mallen, C. (2014). Sport ethics: Frameworks to guide sport managers navigating 21st century issues. Retrieved from www.eyqew.com

14 CONCLUSIONS

Schön, D. (1983). *The reflective practitioner: How professionals think in action*. New York: Basic Books.

INDEX

270

271